★ ★ ★

A THOUSAND SISTERS:

THE HEROIC AIRWOMEN OF THE
SOVIET UNION IN WORLD WAR II

BALZER + BRAY

An Imprint of HarperCollins*Publishers*

ELIZABETH WEIN

A THOUSAND

SISTERS

THE HEROIC AIRWOMEN OF
THE SOVIET UNION IN WORLD WAR II

Photograph credits: Pages 12, 83, 92, 103, 110, 118, 163, 210, 255, 287, 306: from the collection of Anatoly Plyac; pages 23, 94, 159, 194: Sputnik / Alamy Stock Photo; page 37: ITAR-TASS News Agency / Alamy Stock Photo; pages 49 and 213: TASS / Getty Images; page 60: Everett Collection Inc / Alamy Stock Photo; pages 72 and 209: Komsomol section of the Russian State Archive of Socio-Political History, refs. 7/2/1050/88 and 7/1/511/69; page 86: ©Topfoto / SCRSS / The Image Works; pages 87, 105, 126, 150, 191, 200: ©Sputnik / The Image Works; page 89: Elizabeth Gatland, Central Air Force Museum, Monino; page 104: ©World History Archive / TopFoto / The Image Works; page 134: ©SZ Photo / Scherl / The Image Works; page 138: ©Royal Aeronautical Society / Mary Evans / The Image Works; pages 161 and 245: Krasnogorsk; page 234: © Mary Evans / Meledin Collection / The Image Works; page 268: Pictorial Press Ltd / Alamy Stock Photo.

Balzer + Bray is an imprint of HarperCollins Publishers.

A Thousand Sisters: The Heroic Airwomen of the Soviet Union in World War II

www.epicreads.com

ISBN 978-0-06-245303-7 (pbk.)

Typography by Sara Corbett and Jessie Gang

19 20 21 22 23   PC/LSCH   10 9 8 7 6 5 4 3 2 1

❖

First paperback edition, 2020

FOR MY AGENT,
GINGER CLARK,
WHO DESERVES IT

"Life is life, and war is war."
—GALINA TENUYEVA, PILOT, 125TH GUARDS

★ ★ ★

"War is war, and life is life."
—ANTONINA BONDAREVA, PILOT, 125TH GUARDS

★ ★ ★

"If the women of the world united,
war would never happen!"
—ALEXANDRA AKIMOVA, NAVIGATOR, 46TH GUARDS

THE WESTERN USSR
AT THE TIME OF
OPERATION BARBAROSSA,
JUNE 1941

CONTENTS

PART IV

THE GREAT PATRIOTIC WAR
THE THIRD AND FOURTH YEARS: 1943–1945

PART V

AFTER THE WAR

BATTLE CRY

A PROLOGUE

Imagine a blockbuster movie about a world united in battle against Nazi oppression. In this sweeping international epic, black and white American soldiers protect each other under enemy fire in the African desert. A Chinese grandmother leads an army of thirty thousand guerrilla warriors against Japanese invaders. A beautiful French spy escapes murderous Gestapo agents in Paris; in the North Sea, British navy sailors brave a suicide mission against enemy submarines. A starving Greek community defies Nazi soldiers by hanging out thousands of forbidden national flags. And in the fiery skies above Russia, women drop bombs and fly fighter planes in aerial combat against German pilots.

This is the outline for *Battle Cry*, a movie optioned for Hollywood by director Howard Hawks in the middle of World War II.

In July 1943, Hollywood was fighting World War II along with the rest of the world. The streets of Los Angeles were full of uniformed men and women—not just American, but also British, Canadian, and French. Soldiers, sailors, pilots, and nurses were on their way to war in the Pacific. New bomber planes roared overhead in flight tests.

And moviemakers did their part by creating inspiring war films, designed to help raise people's spirits and support the troops—even though film sets struggled to hang on to staff, because so many young men were leaving to join the army. Director Howard Hawks's new movie, *Battle Cry*, would be Hollywood's most sweeping war film of them all.

For six weeks in Los Angeles during that turbulent summer, the American writer William Faulkner worked frantically to turn *Battle Cry* into a screenplay. Several writers had provided stories for the ambitious outline, and William Faulkner had the tough job of smoothing out its clunky transitions and pulling the whole thing together.

The novelist would later win the Nobel Prize, but he was already famous for his classic Southern epics like *The Sound and the Fury* and *As I Lay Dying*. When Warner Brothers offered him a contract to work on patriotic war films, he took it. He needed the money, and he was disappointed he couldn't go to war himself—for William Faulkner was a pilot. The First World War had ended before he completed his flight training, but he often wrote about combat pilots and aerial performers in his fiction. When the United States entered World War II, he tried to enlist as a navy pilot. But he was over forty years old by now, and wasn't accepted.

So working on *Battle Cry* was William Faulkner's way of contributing to the war against the Nazis. He could use his writing to inspire acts of patriotism and bravery. He could champion freedom and tolerance. He could still help win the war.

"Battle cry . . . rises from the throats of free men everywhere," he wrote, imagining the movie opening with a prophetic voice-over. "A defiance, an affirmation and a challenge . . ."

William Faulkner was excited to be working on a plot that starred men and women flying together to defeat the Nazis.

• • •

By the end of that hot July, the dry hills of California were the tawny brown of a lion cub that had been rolling in dust. In Los Angeles, thousands of people found their eyes and throats stinging with mysterious fumes. Terrified that the Germans or the Japanese might be targeting the United States mainland, a front-page headline in the *Los Angeles Times* blared on July 27, "City Hunting for Source of Gas Attack." Ironically, the real source turned out to be air pollution from cars and factories. It was LA's first serious battle with smog.

The weather didn't stop director Howard Hawks from getting the cameras rolling on *Battle Cry*. On July 28, forty actors spent twelve grueling hours filming scenes in a burning wheat field. Meanwhile, William Faulkner rewrote the Russian sequence of the film and typed up the full screenplay.

The Russian story for *Battle Cry* was based on a short radio play that had aired the year before as part of *Treasury Star Parade*, a weekly patriotic radio program featuring A-list stars in dramas of wartime heroism from all over the globe. In their play *Diary of a Red Army Woman*, writers Violet Atkins and William Bacher introduced their American audience to a fictional Russian female bomber pilot.

A woman flying in combat? This was something no one had ever heard of. Even though the war weighed on everyone's mind, the full scale of it still surprised people.

The full scale of World War II still surprises people today.

In the year following 1939, the German army, under Adolf Hitler, had taken control of almost every country in Europe. On June 22, 1941, Hitler broke a peace treaty and invaded the Soviet Union, sending his army storming across the huge nation in a battlefront that stretched for over a thousand miles. Hitler detested the eastern European Slavic peoples nearly as much as he detested Jewish people, and from the Baltic Sea to the Black Sea, the German invaders seized crops and burned communities, pushing toward the Soviet Union's major cities.

In *Diary of a Red Army Woman*, the fictional pilot Tania is furious about the German army's destruction of her village and the murder of her family. She joins the Soviet Air Force with her best friend, Nina, and they form a pilot-gunner team in a bomber plane. Together, the vengeful young duo fights to stamp out Nazi aggression in the Soviet Union.

At that time the Soviet Red Army was the only military in the world that officially allowed women to go into combat. American women spent years persuading the government to let them *deliver* military planes, but only Soviet women could fight air battles in them. Tania's fictional story on *Treasury Star Parade* gave American audiences a taste of how Soviet women were able to meet and kill the enemy in battle—not just on the ground, but also, incredibly, in the sky.

The original writers show Tania scoring kill after kill as she guns down German planes and drops her bombs on German troops. William Faulkner added his pilot's know-how to the scenario, getting technical as he described exactly what Tania would have to do to make her plane turn and swoop and dive.

On August 3, 1943, after more than a month of intense conferences, writing, and typing, William Faulkner put his own name on the cover page and delivered the full screenplay of *Battle Cry* to the Warner Brothers Story Department.

Battle Cry's Tania was fictional, but there were real women like her. While William Faulkner sweated in California trying to imagine what their lives must be like, hundreds of young airwomen were flying and fighting and dying over the battlefields of the Soviet Union.

• • •

One of these young pilots was twenty-one-year-old Lilya Litvyak. During that last week of July in 1943, literally on the other side of the world from California, Lilya was fighting for her life in the battle of Stalingrad.

Lilya was an eccentric beauty, a petite blonde who regularly sent her aircraft mechanic to pick up peroxide from a nearby hospital so she could bleach her hair. She flew combat missions with little bouquets of flowers stuck on her dashboard. But she was a deadly foe in the air. For nearly a year, Lilya had been flying for the Soviet Air Force in a single-seat fighter plane called a Yak-1.

Two weeks earlier, Lilya had been wounded in the shoulder and the leg. It had happened when she and five other Soviet fighter pilots had flown into battle against a swarm of three dozen German bombers and fighters. Lilya's aircraft was so badly damaged by gunfire that she'd had to crash-land it.

But that didn't stop Lilya. She got her injuries treated locally and refused to be hospitalized. Three days later, her closest friend was killed in combat. Even that didn't stop Lilya. The following week she was back in the air, in a desperate battle that ended with her having to parachute out of her crippled plane.

To be considered an ace, a fighter pilot has to shoot down five aircraft. By July 1943, Lilya was a *double ace*. In less than a year she'd shot down eleven enemy planes by herself, as well as an observation balloon. On August 1, 1943, with another pilot's help, Lilya added a "shared kill" to her score.

While most nations dragged their heels to let women to become transport pilots, how could Lilya Litvyak be shooting down German planes in aerial combat—in the same week, fighting the same war, even if it *was* on the other side of the world? What was so different about the Soviet Union?

It was partly because it was so new. "The Motherland" was a nation of ideals and contradictions. In 1917 the Russian Revolution had put an end to an empire that was centuries old and, after years of civil war, replaced it with a new system of government called communism. The idea was that the people of the new Soviet Union would share everything according to people's needs. In reality, it didn't work out that way at all—war always seemed to be on the horizon, and the changes forced on Soviet citizens were so harsh that millions lost their homes and starved to death.

But one thing that the new government got right was that it gave boys and girls a completely equal education. A generation of young people exactly the same age as the Soviet Union itself grew up expecting to have to go to war, and believing that young women would be able to fight alongside young men when they did.

The driving force behind Soviet women flying in combat was the world-famous pilot and navigator Marina Raskova. In 1938, she and two other Soviet women had splintered a world record in a long-distance flight they made across Siberia. When Lilya Litvyak was a teenager learning to fly, she'd admired Marina Raskova so much that she'd carried a picture of the Soviet record setter around in a notebook with her.

When the Soviet Union entered World War II in 1941, Marina Raskova took command of a thousand female aviators and trained them to fly in three separate bomber and fighter regiments. By the summer of 1943, these women were all fighting in combat against the German invaders.

Marina Raskova's regiments were the inspiration for Tania's story.

And *Battle Cry*?

Sadly, the epic project never got off the ground. That one hot July day of filming in the burning wheat field produced the only shots ever taken for the movie. It's not clear why, but it probably had to do with cost—the film was wildly over budget. It's also possible that Tania's *Diary of a Red Army Woman* sequence, which was full of Russian nationalism, was a little too controversial for American audiences.

But the real Tanias had to keep fighting whether or not Hollywood brought their story to the silver screen.

By the end of August, William Faulkner left California to return to Mississippi. His hard work on *Battle Cry* was a brief glimpse into the real-life drama that was happening on the other side of the world. Meanwhile, a thousand airwomen in the Soviet Union continued their battle against the Nazi war machine.

This is the story of those young women.

It's the story of three regiments of aviators, only three out of a thousand aviation units fighting for a common cause. Along with a scattering of individual women who served in the Soviet Air Force alongside men, the young aviators in these three regiments were the only women of any nation who flew combat missions during World War II.

Some of these soldiers flew as many as eighteen combat missions in a single night.

Some of them perished in flames.

Some of them worked in the dark, feeling their way blindly, in cold so fierce their hands froze to the metal tools they held as they made sure their companions were able to fly.

Almost all of them were in their teens when they went to war.

This is the story of a generation of girls who were raised in the belief that they were as good as men, and who were raised to believe that it was their destiny to defend their nation in battle.

It's the story of a thousand young women who grew up inspired by Marina Raskova and who were ready to follow her into the air.

It's the story of a generation of young people who learned to work with the wind—those who soared and those who came back to earth.

This is the story of a thousand sisters fighting and flying.

THE FUTURE WAR

THE EARLY LIFE AND TIMES OF MARINA RASKOVA, NAVIGATOR AND PILOT

A pilot has to work with the wind. You need to know which way it's blowing, and how strong it is, so you can take off and land safely. Birds do this without thinking about it. They even sit facing into the wind so that they can take off at any moment.

A flying aircraft is affected by the wind just the way a bird is. With a strong wind behind you, you'll fly faster; but if you fly straight into that same wind, it will slow you down. If the wind comes at you sideways, it'll blow you off track.

One of the most common poor decisions made by pilots is to continue flying into bad weather. Then, blinded by snow or cloud or fog, or with your wings heavy with ice, you can fly steadily into a mountainside and crash. Sometimes the wind becomes so violent or unpredictable that it tosses your plane into a deadly spiral dive. Even with twenty-first-century navigation improvements, a pilot is always encouraged not to continue flying into bad weather.

But in emergency situations, a coast guard helicopter crew risks their own lives to save the passengers of a sinking ship. Pilots might brave canyon winds to pull off a mountain rescue, or penetrate a blinding blizzard to rush someone to a hospital. The boundary of a weather pattern, often moving across an ocean or landmass, is called a "front," just like the line that marks out the edge of an invading army. Flying straight into either one is very likely to kill you; but in war, sometimes there is no turning back.

Navigating your way through life is like flying a small plane in a windy sky. To say that the wind is blowing with you or against you is too simple. Sometimes you need the wind behind you to speed things up; sometimes you need to head directly into the wind to help you take off.

Your life is influenced by the events and politics of your time. Your personality will be shaped by the world you grow up in. How you navigate that world will depend on how directly you face it at any given time.

Your future will depend on how you decide to adjust to the winds of change around you.

Aviation, the Soviet Union, and Marina Raskova grew up together. Marina would become an aviation adventurer, pioneer, and record setter; the wind was exactly right for her to lead her Motherland's young airwomen into battle in World War II.

And Marina Raskova was a good judge of wind.

MARINA RASKOVA

The airplane is probably the most exciting technological development of the early twentieth century. When the Wright brothers made their famous first powered flight on December 17, 1903, aviation fever seized the world.

Over the next ten years, all over the world, aircraft designers competed to make early planes safer, more powerful, and more efficient. And men and women everywhere took their lives in their hands for a chance to ride in these amazing machines, or better yet, to take the controls themselves. In August 1911, Lydia Zvereva became the eighth woman in the world—and the first woman in Russia—to get a pilot's license.

Less than a year later, on March 28, 1912, another Russian aviator came into the world. She was born into a family of musicians in Moscow, the second-largest city of the Russian Empire after Saint Petersburg. Her name was Marina Mikhailovna Malinina, and she was the girl who would grow up to be Marina Raskova.

When Marina was two years old, in 1914, Europe plunged into World War I. For the next four years, most of Europe's young men fought, and millions died, on the battlefields of France and Belgium.

The Russian Empire entered the war right away. But its army was badly equipped and Russia lost nearly two million lives, fighting mainly against Germany and the Austro-Hungarian Empire. Russians at home grew angry and unhappy, resentful of having to pour their lives and resources into this war. The capital of Russia, Saint Petersburg, was renamed Petrograd in 1914 because "burg" sounded too German. When the Russian Revolution started in 1917, a year before the end of World War I, it was partly in response to the awful wartime leadership of the imperial ruler, Czar Nicholas II.

For some years before the war started, women all over the world had been campaigning vocally and often violently for their own rights. Now, throughout Russia, young women felt that they ought to be allowed to fight in World War I alongside the nation's young men. *Thousands* of them enlisted—many in men's regiments, sometimes disguised as boys to reduce the possibility of being turned away or sexually assaulted. The Soviet Union didn't exist yet, but the actions of Russia's women in the world's first "Great War" led the way for the women who would fight for the Soviet Union in the "Great Patriotic War," the name for their part in World War II.

Maria Bochkareva, who'd married a soldier when she was sixteen, was desperate to play a part in the fighting. She joined a men's battalion and went into combat with them. A fierce and focused soldier, she was awarded a medal for rescuing fifty of her wounded comrades in one battle, and was even made a commander.

But Maria grew frustrated because the soldiers who fought alongside her were miserable about the way the war was going for the Russian army. She decided that a group of fighting women might embarrass these unhappy men and make them leap into action.

So Maria got permission from Czar Nicholas II to form her own regiment composed entirely of women. Terrifyingly, they were known as a "Death Battalion." Before World War I was over, four other Russian women's regiments formed based on Maria Bochkareva's battalion, along with many smaller units.

With so many Russian women joining the army as foot soldiers so they could fight in World War I, it's no surprise that several of Russia's first female aviators also went to war. A dozen nations were using the new technology of aircraft for bombing, for taking photographs of enemy troops, for shooting at soldiers on the ground, and for aerial combat against enemy pilots. Between 1915 and 1917, at least four Russian women—two of them princesses!—served as reconnaissance pilots (scouts who gathered information).

Nadezhda Degtereva, who disguised herself as a man so she could go to war, became the first woman to be wounded in air combat—though the medics who treated her wounds discovered her secret. One of the princesses, Yevgeniya Shakhovskaya, had been a flight instructor in Germany before the war. Like Maria Bochkareva, she went to Czar Nicholas II himself to get permission to fight. She persuaded the czar to let her fly for Russia as a military reconnaissance pilot, scouting out the best direction for soldiers on the ground to fire their guns. Though we don't know if she flew combat missions, she was without a doubt working as a pilot on the battle lines in a war zone.

Women of other countries served in World War I as nurses, ambulance drivers, and communications personnel. Their work was always dangerous and often dirty, and required endurance and bravery. But it wasn't *combat* work. Only Russian women went directly into battle to fight and kill other human beings. There weren't many of these women, but they paved the way for Marina Raskova and for the next generation—the generation that would fight in World War II twenty-five years later.

In 1917, Marina Raskova was five years old. She was probably too young to understand grown-up politics, even though she might have heard her parents talking about the terrible war news. But the war in Europe was only one part of Russia's troubles. Beyond the fragile security of the familiar walls of Marina's home, her Motherland was exploding.

Workers and intellectuals in Petrograd were hungry for political reform and for Russia to get out of World War I. They finally took matters into their own hands and took over the government, finishing off the three-hundred-year reign of the Romanov czars. The last czar, Nicholas II, resigned his power in March 1917.

That was the end of the Russian Empire.

The problem was that nobody agreed on who should run the country now, or on how to run it. A Provisional Government took the place of imperial rule in Petrograd and granted equality in law to Russian women, giving women the right to vote and to hold office. This made Russia the first country to give women the same legal rights as men.

But the Provisional Government didn't last long. In October 1917 the radical Bolshevik Party took advantage of people's anger over World War I and overthrew the Provisional Government. The Bolsheviks were led by Vladimir Lenin, a man of bold and energetic ideals who had been urging revolution for more than twenty years. Lenin's vision of a better future for the working poor was so ambitious that he hoped World War I would inspire everyone in Europe to get rid of their old-fashioned governments. That clearly wasn't going to happen, so Lenin did what he felt to be the next best thing for his own people: early in 1918, he negotiated a treaty with Germany to get Russia out of the war.

World War I didn't end for the rest of Europe until November 1918. Marina was six years old. In the same year that the Bolshevik Party carried out the murderous execution of the former czar, Nicholas II, and his wife and four children, Marina started going to elementary school and took lessons at the Pushkin School of Music in Moscow twice a week.

Around her, the Red Army of Lenin's Bolshevik Party was fighting to crush opposition groups that sprang up after the fall of the Russian Empire. Now, fierce disagreements within Russia itself over how to run the country began a bitter and bloody civil war.

The winds of change blew harshly around young Marina. When she was seven years old, her musician father was hit by a motorcycle and killed.

There is a Russian saying that people use with resignation at times like this: Life is life. Marina's widowed mother worked as the director of a boys' home near Moscow and then got another job in the city working at a child-care center, which made it easier for Marina and her older brother, Roman, to go to school. In 1920 Marina's mother managed to get a government-assigned room for her family in a shared apartment in Moscow.

So Marina must have known, from very early in life, that it is possible for a woman to be in control of her own destiny.

Marina was ten in 1922 when the last armed clashes of the Russian Civil War took place.

Her country's new leaders were now attempting to improve life with an untried system of government called communism, in which property, goods, and services are owned by the community and shared according to need. Their efforts weren't always made with the clearest of intentions or the best of success. An estimated one million soldiers, both men and women, fought and died to make these changes possible. Another eight million civilians perished because they were caught in the cross fire, or struck down by the starvation and disease that war brings with it.

Those numbers are so enormous they're almost meaningless, even to an adult. And Marina was only ten years old. She was just beginning further education in music at the Moscow State Conservatory, one of the most respected music schools in the entire world.

Marina's home city of Moscow now became the capital of a nation so new that it hadn't even given itself an official name yet. The scouring winds of the civil war, which had lasted five years and spread across two continents, left the population of her country struggling to feed itself and to rebuild its industries. From the ruins, the Bolshevik Party would become the Communist Party, and Lenin would emerge as the head of a new nation with a new form of government.

What was left of the old Russian Empire would become known as the Union of Soviet Socialist Republics—the USSR, or Soviet Union.[1]

Either way, it was still Marina's Motherland.

---

1. "Soviet" is derived from a Russian word for "assembly" or "council."

LEARNING TO FLY IN A NATION THAT'S LEARNING TO FLY

Marina Raskova's school years were bent and shaped by the harsh winds of change that swept her nation.

There were droughts in 1920 and 1921. The new government was unable to cope with its country's needs, and failed crops resulted in a horrific famine that lasted into 1922 and killed millions. Disease was everywhere. The streets of Russian cities were filled with homeless children Marina's age who hadn't been as lucky as her. They lived rough, their families torn apart by the events of the past ten years.

Also, Lenin now struggled with poor health. He died in 1924 at the age of fifty-three. Josef Stalin, who'd been the general secretary of the Communist Party since 1922, became the dominant party leader, though his official job title didn't change.

Lenin made a lasting impression on the people of the USSR. Even today he remains a cult figure. His body was preserved so that a continuous stream of mourners could view him lying in state in a special tomb on Red Square in Moscow. Five days after Lenin's death, Petrograd, the former capital of Russia, was renamed Leningrad in his honor. Marina, twelve years old in 1924, was no doubt aware of Lenin's passing; living in Moscow, she may even have been one of the tens of thousands of mourners who visited Lenin's tomb to get a glimpse of his eerily waxlike body in the weeks following his death.

Many of Lenin's modern ideals stayed in place as Josef Stalin first took over leadership of the USSR. Now Stalin and the Communist Party nailed together a haphazard structure for a country that, in principle at least, treated men and women with equal rights. One of the ways the Soviet government successfully put this into practice was through a school system that integrated boys' and girls' education. Although the design for this wasn't complete until the 1930s, the basic system was established during Marina's high school years.

In this respect, the United States was way behind the Soviet Union. In the 1920s in the United States, high school girls were given special classes in sewing, cooking, and hygiene, while boys learned woodworking and how to use tools. But in the years between the two world wars, children in Soviet schools were treated with complete gender equality, with girls and boys studying the same subjects. They were also encouraged not to settle for old-fashioned and "bourgeois" gender roles—"bourgeois" being a catchall term for the upper middle classes of Imperial Russia who'd aspired to wealth and luxury.

As a high school student, Marina decided her favorite subjects were biology and chemistry. But what she really wanted to be was a professional opera singer, like her father. She loved music and had talent, and she played the piano, sang, and performed, in school and at home.

When Marina reached the age of fifteen, the wind changed again for her.

This time, the wind that howled in her ears and that changed the course of her life affected her own young body: she came down with an inner-ear infection combined with a disease called paratyphoid. Marina had to stay in bed for two months. She was so sick that it affected her musical ability.

Even when your plane is flying in a windless sky, a mechanical failure can make it difficult or impossible to fly. It's always a good idea to keep a plan B in the back of your mind so you can get safely down to earth no matter what happens to you in the air.

Marina had dreamed of a musical career since she was six years old. When she had to give up on that dream, she fell back on chemistry. She was interested in it, and she knew it would be a good way to support herself and her family. And she wasn't wrong. When Marina graduated from high school in 1929, her focus on chemistry helped her find a job as an apprentice in a dye factory, and six months later she became a full technician.

Girls and boys growing up in the Soviet Union of the 1920s and 1930s, like Marina Raskova, felt that preparing for war was their duty, just like going to school. The "future war" would be their "test," as the civil war had been for their parents. In 1928, the Red Army's chief of staff, Mikhail Tukhachevsky, had published a report called *The Future War*. He recommended that the USSR build a strong military equipped with new aircraft and tank fleets, which he believed would be the key to a knockout victory in modern warfare.

And so, beginning in 1932, military training was built into the secondary education curriculum in the USSR. From the age of eight, both boys and girls studied the history of the Red Army, met and talked with veterans, learned to use a gas mask, and practiced shooting with a bow and arrow—an introduction to the rifle training they'd pick up at age thirteen.

In their free time, all boys and girls had to join a fitness or defense program outside school. These were run by the Communist League of Youth, or Komsomol, which sponsored clubs called Osoaviakhim[2] that gave military training to the Soviet Union's young people. You joined with your friends. It was fun, or at least it was challenging. You could earn badges and participate in competitions—just like in the Scouts.

You could learn to fly.

Even in powerful nations like the United States and the United Kingdom, only the very elite—or the incredibly determined—could learn to fly. In Germany, restrictions had been placed on their air force after World War I that meant they now had to train their military pilots in secret. State-sponsored flight training in Germany wasn't available until 1937, and of course even then it was only available to men. But in the USSR, by 1935 there were about 150 flying clubs that provided aviation tuition to any teenage girl or boy who was a Komsomol member. The training was free. You didn't have to pay for tuition or for fuel. *Anyone* could learn to fly if he or she really wanted to.

It wasn't a perfect system. The out-of-school activities didn't do as good a job of including girls as the schools did. It didn't seem as important for girls to learn to use rifles and fly planes as it was for boys, because only men were required by law to be on the military reserve list; women weren't registered in the reserves. A young woman could join the army, but she didn't *have* to.

Nevertheless, according to the Soviet Constitution of 1936, also called "Stalin's Constitution," Soviet women had voting rights and gender equality with men. In theory, they were even given equal pay to men—an issue

---

2. *Komsomol* is a shortened form of "**Kom**unistichesky **So**yuz **Mol**odyozhi," the Russian for "Communist League of Youth." The full name of the organization was the All-Union Leninist Communist League of Youth. The word *Osoaviakhim* comes from the Russian name for the Society for the Defense, Aviation, and Chemical Industries.

that wasn't dealt with in law until 1963 in the United States and 1970 in the United Kingdom. And in a country where men and women had equal constitutional rights by law, letting girls into after-school flying clubs fulfilled Komsomol requirements, so they couldn't be turned away.

Marina Raskova wasn't quite young enough to benefit from this program. But she was already on a career path that would soon turn her into one of her Motherland's most important and adored aviators of all time.

Marina was about eighteen when she married Sergey Raskov, another engineer she'd met at her first job in the Butyrsky Aniline Dye Plant; she took his name to become Marina Raskova.

Their daughter, Tatyana, nicknamed Tanya, was born in 1930. Marina stopped working while Tanya was a baby, but when her daughter was a year old, Marina found a new job. She became an assistant at the Aero Navigation Laboratory of the Zhukovsky Air Force Engineering Academy in Moscow, working with the academy instructor and director, Aleksandr Belyakov. She drafted drawings of new flight instruments and prepared them for testing. Air navigation became the focus of Marina's life, as music once had been. Dedicated, absorbed, and conscientious, she was soon promoted and began part-time studies at the Aviation Institute in Leningrad.

In our modern society, when a man works and succeeds at a skilled job, we expect it. When a woman does the same, we like to call her a "career woman," and if she happens to be someone's partner in a relationship and also a mother, we say she "has it all."

In the early years of the USSR, a woman was *expected* to have a job and also be a mother. Marina Raskova probably didn't think of herself as "having it all"; she was a hard worker, but in the Soviet Union of the 1930s, so was everybody else. Motherhood and jobs were both encouraged by the state.

MARINA RASKOVA AND HER DAUGHTER, TANYA

But it wasn't any easier then to be a working mother than it is now. Marina was able to manage because, in 1932, her own mother retired so she could look after Tanya.

The 1920s and 1930s are often called "the golden age of flight." Pilots flying new planes could provide swift transport over otherwise impossible distances and heights, perform glamorous stunts and dramatic rescues, explore new territory . . . and, of course, embark on dangerous acts of war.

That was the dark side of the world's obsession with aviation. Between 1929 and 1939, the world's great powers were in a race for air supremacy. In 1933 the Nazi government seized power in Germany under Adolf

Hitler, and by the mid-1930s the Germans were building an impressive modern air force of their own. They tested their new bombers in the Spanish Civil War, which began in 1936, using aircraft for brutal and ruthless attacks on civilians as well as soldiers.

The United States and the United Kingdom, though also powerful, were anxious not to repeat the horrors of World War I. They openly took pride in civil aviation achievements while keeping quieter about their military developments. But they were worried about what was going on in Germany. And the Soviet Union, Germany's geographic neighbor, was very worried about it. In the mid-1930s, even though the Soviet Union wasn't yet fighting the "future war" it dreaded and expected, it was already using its own air power to support countries who were at war, such as China and Spain.

No country, and certainly not one as vast and as aggressive as the new Soviet Union—nor one so close to Germany—was going to be without an air force. Stalin and the Communist Party encouraged ambitious designers, daring pilots, and mechanical experts to create an industry that was exemplary throughout the world.

While Marina was starting her adult life as a worker, wife, and mother, Stalin and the Communist Party launched the first of a series of fierce and brutal "Five-Year Plans" to modernize the nation, plans that would ultimately involve sacrificing the lives of the Soviet Union's own citizens.

Before the Russian Revolution, about 80 percent of the population were peasants who worked in the fields like their medieval ancestors. After the revolution, they'd claimed land and formed small shared farms. The first Five-Year Plan seized this land for the state under a program called "collectivization." The peasants still had to work on the same land, but instead of growing their own crops, they got paid in wages—they weren't allowed to sell or eat their own produce. Millions of other agricultural workers were told to move to cities to work in factories. Multitudes of people had to leave their homes, and the shock to traditional lifestyles was enormous.

The number of small farms merged into collectives was a number about equal to the current population of Texas. Imagine if every single man, woman, and child in Texas owned a farm—and then imagine that every single one of those farms was suddenly taken away by the government.

Not surprisingly, the collectives were spectacularly hated.

There was resistance to them everywhere, which the Communist Party crushed ruthlessly. In 1932 and 1933 it took away the food crop harvest and next season's seed in the Soviet states that produced most of the nation's grain—Ukraine, the Caucasus, and Kazakhstan. A police blockade was set up around the entire state of Ukraine so that no one could get out and no food could be brought in. The result was that an estimated four million people died of famine in 1933 in Ukraine alone—an area about the size of all the New England and mid-Atlantic states put together.

In addition to the collectivization of farms, the Five-Year Plans also aimed to industrialize the USSR. While agricultural workers starved in Ukraine, record numbers of laborers produced factory goods. Transportation routes expanded; workers dug the foundations and laid tracks for the new Moscow Metro subway system.

One of the major goals of the second Five-Year Plan was to multiply the number of civil air routes across the USSR, covering extreme distances and connecting the far-flung corners of the huge country. In 1933, at the age of twenty-one, Marina went along with her supervisor, Aleksandr Belyakov, as his navigator on a flight expedition sponsored by the Zhukovsky Academy. It was a national project to select landing sites for future passenger airports in the Crimea, Caucasus, and Sea of Azov areas. And it was a wonderful chance for Marina to use her new navigation skills over the enormous distances of the Soviet Union.

Marina Raskova and Aleksandr Belyakov, as navigators in the enticing and glamorous field of aviation, were helping the USSR become a leader in the aviation race.

In 1934 Marina graduated from the air navigation department of the Leningrad Institute of Civil Aviation Engineers. She was the first woman in the USSR to become a professional air navigator. She also became the first female lecturer for the Zhukhovsky Air Force Engineering Academy.

"WOMEN DON'T BELONG IN AIRPLANES"

Marina's work as a lecturer at the Zhukovsky Academy made international news. A story in the *Arizona Republic*, the state's largest newspaper (and one with traditionally conservative leanings), stated provocatively on June 11, 1936:

"Unlike American officials, who hold that women fliers aren't suited to arduous air duty, the Soviet gives women equality in aviation. Marina Mikhailovna Raskova, a young mother, has won a place in the Russian military aviation school as instructor of blind flying,[3] in which she is regarded one of the world's foremost experts."

Despite the popularity of celebrity female aviators such as Amelia Earhart, the general public in the United States felt that women should not be flying. The 1929 women's National Air Race was nicknamed the Powder Puff Derby, as if women couldn't take the controls of an aircraft without worrying about messing up their makeup.

---

3. "Blind flying" is what early aviators called air navigation using instruments in poor visibility.

Being the trailblazer for women in this field wasn't easy. Marina's first students were a group of older male officers. They refused to stand at attention when Marina entered the classroom, as they were supposed to do for a senior instructor, and had to be scolded by Marina's superiors. Only after she'd been teaching them for some time did they grudgingly admit that women aviators clearly *could* stand shoulder to shoulder with men.

As well as teaching, Marina also took her first flying lessons in 1934. Her employer, the Zhukovsky Air Force Engineering Academy, paid for her training at the Central Flying Club in Tushino, outside Moscow.

"Women don't belong in airplanes. That's a man's job," Edna Gardner White was told in 1928 when, even though she'd received the highest possible grade on her written aviation exam, she had to twist the examiner's arm to let her take her actual flight test for her license.

When an American female pilot was killed in an air race in 1933, women were banned from competition until 1935.

In 1927, when Charles Lindbergh made his groundbreaking first nonstop solo flight across the Atlantic, less than 1 percent of American pilots were women. By 1935, out of 13,949 licensed pilots in America, around 800 were women—about 6 percent of the total. (Believe it or not—and discouragingly—that statistic wasn't much higher in 2015, when women numbered only 7 percent of America's pilots.)

It's a sharp contrast that, by the end of the 1930s, somewhere between a quarter and a third of all pilots in the Soviet Union were women.

MARINA NAVIGATES

In the 1930s, the pressure on you to *belong* as a young Soviet was probably the most overwhelming pressure of your life. It wasn't just a question of being accepted by your peers, of wearing the right clothes or wearing them the right way or fixing your hair like everyone else's. Those are ordinary pressures we can relate to, the insistence of fashion or the approval of friends. Sure, you want to do well in school and you worry about your future in your community. But in the Soviet Union in the 1930s, the pressure to belong was literally a matter of *life and death*.

The reasons for this pressure are complicated, but they begin with the leader of the USSR, Josef Stalin.

Stalin was a complex, confusing man who was both powerful and paranoid. In the early 1930s, not only was he dealing with the industrialization of the Five-Year Plans and the forced starvation of millions of people on collective farms, but he was coping with the recent suicide of his wife (the official state announcement was that she had died of appendicitis). Stalin got his emotional support from his colleague and best friend, Sergey Kirov, the swashbuckling head of the Communist Party in Leningrad.

Things changed in December of 1934, when Sergey Kirov was suddenly shot and killed by a gunman waiting for him outside his office.

It's possible Stalin ordered the murder himself, but that's never been proved.

What's known is that Stalin set out to punish his friend's killer, and anyone else who might have been involved in the plot against Sergey Kirov—or against the Communist Party—or specifically against Stalin himself. Stalin called on the People's Commissariat for Internal Affairs or NKVD,[4] a military police force of spies and assassins, to root out treachery . . . whether it was real or possible or even fantastically impossible.

In the weeks following the murder, several thousand people were arrested in Moscow and Leningrad. There were so many of them that, to deal with them quickly, two hundred suspects were executed *every day* at the NKVD headquarters in Leningrad.

But Stalin didn't stop there.

He decided he needed to make absolutely sure that the people of the Soviet Union were loyal to him—or at least, that they behaved in all ways like loyal people.

In 1936 he began a series of random arrests and executions that touched every aspect of Soviet society. This horrific nationwide cleanup, which went on for two years, is now known as the "Great Terror" or the "Great Purge."[5] Hundreds of thousands of people—no one will ever be sure how many—were arrested, tortured, and forced to make confessions. Then they were thrown into jail, executed, or sent to prison camps in the frozen wastes of Siberia. People vanished *all the time* as they were arrested and killed or sent away.

No one was safe.

People tried to hide their identities, disguised their family histories,

---

4. NKVD stands for Narodnyi Komissariat Vnutrennikh Del in Russian.
5. The Russian for "Great Terror" is "Bolshoi Terror."

and even changed their names to protect themselves and their children. You could easily be accused of guilt just by knowing the wrong people. Teens weren't any safer than their parents.

A chilling example is what happened to Anna Popova, who was born in 1923 and was in high school during the Great Terror. Anna, like Marina, was destined for a career in aviation—she later became a flight radio operator on transport aircraft during World War II. Anna was arrested by the NKVD secret police, along with eight of her schoolmates, when they were only fifteen years old.

The reason for the arrests? Apparently some of the boys in the group had been signing their names in code when they wrote notes to their friends.

The teens were all put in prison in Minsk, the capital of the region of Belorussia (now Belarus) where they lived. Anna was kept in solitary confinement for six months before she completed ninth grade.

After a series of pleas and trials, most of the teens who'd been arrested with Anna Popova were released, but one unlucky boy was sent to prison for five years—for some uncomplimentary thing he'd said at school about the collectives.

So working hard at Osoaviakhim and Komsomol clubs wasn't just something you did to be like all your friends, or even because you were patriotic. Joining these groups was a practical way to protect yourself from suspicion. Komsomol-sponsored activities and paramilitary training through the Osoaviakhim helped young people to prove their Communist Party loyalty.

Anna, looking back on this terrifying time in her school years, commented bitterly that "the vigilant hawks of the Stalin regime . . . converted the whole great country into a big concentration camp of life-term inmates."

• • •

Somehow, Marina Raskova seems to have steered her way with brave and steady purpose through the Great Terror, avoiding any kind of suspicion.

Marina completed her pilot's license in 1935, just before the purges began. In the same year, she and her husband, Sergey, divorced. Their daughter, Tanya, was five years old, and Marina was only twenty-three when she became a single parent. Her own mother, Anna Spiridonovna, continued to care for Tanya.

Right after she got her pilot's license, Marina took part in a women's publicity expedition organized by the Experimental Aviation Institute. It was the first time she'd ever flown anything other than training aircraft, and it was her first time flying as a qualified pilot. For the stunt, Marina was one of six women, each flying her own plane, and each carrying another woman as a passenger. They were supposed to fly from Leningrad to Moscow, a distance of about 590 kilometers (370 miles). The six planes were supposed to travel together as a group.

They didn't make it to Moscow in one leg. Bad weather slowed them down, and as it began to get dark, Marina's group had to make the decision to come down to earth on a soggy airfield in the middle of nowhere.

No doubt Marina risked getting in trouble with her sponsor and the state, but she made the right decision. She was an inexperienced pilot in an unfamiliar aircraft, and she knew her limits. She landed short of her destination rather than continuing blindly into the storm.

You might think that being involved in the Soviet Union's great aviation achievements would help protect you from being accused of treachery, but you'd be wrong.

In June 1937, Stalin's minions tortured confessions of treachery out of Mikhail Tukhachevsky, the Red Army chief of staff who'd written *The Future*

War. He was tried, found guilty, and executed within hours of his trial. Not long after, most of the men who'd served as his judges were also shot. Now the Soviet Air Force became an unlucky target for Stalin's purges, because it had been a source of pride for Mikhail Tukhachevsky.

Less than a week later, Marina's mentor, Aleksandr Belyakov, made the first-ever air transit over the North Pole. He and two other pilots traveled from Moscow to Vancouver, Washington, in the United States, flying in a special long-distance plane designed by Andrey Tupolev. It was the first time anyone had successfully crossed the North Pole in flight—a triumph of international importance for Soviet aircraft designers and pilots.

But in October 1937, Andrey Tupolev and another leading aircraft designer, Vladimir Petlyakov, were arrested by the NKVD on typically flimsy charges of treason and sabotage. All the directors of the Central Aero and Hydrodynamics Institute, in Moscow, were swept up in the arrest along with them.

It might have been a strategic move by Stalin to keep a close eye on all the Soviet Union's top aviation specialists.

Andrey Tupolev would spend the next four years in prison, to be released on probation only after the USSR entered World War II. His work, like that of his colleague Vladimir Petlyakov, would be essential to Soviet wartime defense.

So what protected Marina from being arrested during the Great Terror, if hard work, success, and national glory weren't enough to keep you from suspicion? She was no doubt taking the political wind into account, navigating Soviet affairs of state as carefully as she navigated the skies. The fine line between safety and danger was probably all about lucky connections.

Marina was well placed. One fellow pilot believed she worked as a consultant for the NKVD, the organization that got rid of most of the Red

Army's officer corps, put the nation's leading aircraft designers in jail, and arrested fifteen-year-old Anna Popova and her friends. Whether or not this was true, Marina no doubt took advantage of her association with her boss at the Zhukovsky Academy, Aleksandr Belyakov. Record-setting flights were a good way to rally national support for aviation. Marina, following in Aleksandr's footsteps, now began pushing the limits of long-distance flight. In 1937, she placed sixth in a long-distance air race that called for sixteen hours of flying in a single day. Later that year, Marina teamed up with another daring and experienced female pilot, Valentina Grizodubova. In October they set a women's long-distance world record together.

Valentina herself was a deputy in the Supreme Soviet of the USSR, the highest branch of the government's legislature. Valentina detested the ferocious disregard for humanity of the Great Terror. Somehow, astonishingly, she managed to use her position of political influence to quietly help out an estimated five thousand people who might otherwise have been victims of Stalin's purges. If Marina really was working for the NKVD, it's possible she was assigned to keep an eye on Valentina.

In July 1938, Marina Raskova broke yet another distance record, this time navigating for pilot Polina Osipenko and her copilot, Vera Lomako. All three women were awarded the Soviet Union's Order of Lenin honor for their achievement.

Marina was perfectly placed to become a hero in the eyes of the people of the USSR, especially its youth. She had a flawless reputation for work and study; she was now a skilled and record-breaking air navigator; she had squeaky-clean connections. To the rising generation who would come of age in World War II, Marina Raskova was a young woman only a little older than they, someone they admired and aspired to be, a daring aviator and the loving mother of an eight-year-old daughter as well.

Marina was now twenty-six years old. Two months after the flight that earned her the Order of Lenin, the fateful wind behind her would make her an international celebrity.

THE FLIGHT OF THE
RODINA

Valentina Grizodubova, the pilot and politician who'd flown with Marina Raskova on their record-breaking trip in 1937, was about Marina's age. Her father was an aircraft designer who had taken her for her first flight when she was *two years old* in a plane he'd designed himself. Valentina had flown a glider alone by the time she was fourteen. After she finished her pilot's certification in 1933, she became an instructor herself—mostly teaching young men. From 1934 to 1938 she flew in a display squadron that performed thrilling aerobatic tricks. She was the first woman to be part of their team.

There were plenty of other pilots in Valentina's life, but not many of them were women. So when Valentina proposed to take off on another record-breaking journey, again she asked Marina to join her.

This time, Valentina wanted to fly across the vast double continent of the USSR, from Moscow to Komsomolsk-on-Amur[6] at the very eastern reaches of Siberia, covering over 6,500 kilometers (4,000 miles) in

---

6. The modern town was mostly built by young Komsomol members in 1932 and named in their honor.

a straight line. She hoped to set a new women's long-distance record for nonstop flight. Polina Osipenko, who'd flown with Marina earlier that summer, was going to be Valentina's copilot; Marina would be their navigator. And the government would pay their expenses.

The converted bomber aircraft they were going to fly in was another of Andrey Tupolev's designs. Valentina nicknamed the plane *Rodina*, the Russian word for "Motherland."

The flight was supported not only by the government but by Josef Stalin himself. Valentina spent two hours in a meeting with the Soviet leader and other highly placed officials as she described the route, how the crew would have to train, and what they needed to prepare for the flight. In July 1938, Premier Vyacheslav Molotov, another important Soviet dignitary, hosted a special reception for Valentina and her crew at his own summer house. Stalin showed up at the party.

And the Soviet press began a love affair with Valentina Grizodubova, Polina Osipenko, and Marina Raskova that would make the three women into household names and put their photographs into the inspired and admiring hands of every Soviet schoolgirl.

Meanwhile, in Europe, Hitler was already on the prowl for more territory. Early in 1938, Germany merged with its neighbor, Austria, to form a bigger and stronger state called "Greater Germany." Most Austrians were ethnically Germanic, and this wasn't an invasion of their country. It was a union that was popular with both Germans and Austrians. It wasn't so popular with the rest of the world, and European nations in particular watched uneasily as Germany suddenly got a lot bigger. Hitler's Nazi government was growing increasingly bold, and boasted that its air force was now second to none in the entire world.

A new long-distance flight record in a Soviet plane would make a fine political statement to the Germans: *our long-range bombers won't have any trouble reaching Greater Germany if war breaks out.*

Valentina, Polina, and Marina spent the summer training for the flight and familiarizing themselves with the *Rodina*. Their converted bomber was the only flyable plane of its type ever built, and that summer Polina made over a hundred practice takeoffs and landings in other types of bombers to get herself ready to fly it. In addition to their flight preparations, all three young women had to learn to fire pistols and hunting weapons in case they were forced to land in the Siberian wilderness.

But the flight of the *Rodina* had to be delayed because Marina was hospitalized with appendicitis. By the time she was back on her feet, it was late September. Now the planned flight would have to cross parts of Siberia where it might already be snowing. On September 23, a state commission canceled the flight of the *Rodina*.

Stalin, not a man to pay much attention to the wind, overruled the decision. The flight would go ahead as planned.

COPILOT POLINA OSIPENKO, PILOT VALENTINA GRIZODUBOVA, AND NAVIGATOR MARINA RASKOVA POSING WITH THE *RODINA*

Early in the morning on September 24, 1938, Valentina, Polina, and Marina, wearing leather jackets and fur-lined boots, took off from Moscow into a clear sky. Their nonstop flight would last more than twenty-four hours.

BLIND FLYING

Radar, which has so many uses in modern navigation, didn't exist in a practical form in the 1930s. It hadn't even been given that name yet. The early radio system used by aviators to find their way when they couldn't see the ground was called "radio direction finding."

Here's how it worked. An aircraft could send out a radio signal to a station on the ground. The controllers on the ground literally shifted their own radio around until they found the position where it was receiving the strongest possible signal from the air, and then they were able to tell which direction the signal was coming from. If two or more ground stations did this at the same time, they were able to compare their results. Then they could draw lines on a map and figure out a "position fix" showing exactly where the airborne plane was over the ground at the moment it had sent the radio signals.

Half an hour after takeoff, the fair weather disappeared. The trip had hardly started when the Rodina became surrounded by thick cloud.

The crew was flying blind. In the navigator's cabin up front in the nose of the plane, Marina could barely catch a glimpse of the ground to figure out where they were. By nightfall they were depending almost entirely on radio navigation, counting on people far away to relay their location to them in radio messages. After they'd been flying for sixteen hours and just before it got dark, Marina caught a brief glimpse of the river near Omsk, which was enough to tell her they were still on course. She sent a radio message back home to Moscow to let them know that all was well.

It wasn't just cloudy, though. It was cold—well-below-zero cold. Soon the aircraft became crusted with ice both inside and out. All three women

Once they'd figured out these details, the ground-based controllers could send a radio message *back* to the plane and tell its pilot exactly where she was—even if she couldn't see the ground she was flying over.

Navigating using instruments without being able to see the ground was known in the early days of aviation as "blind flying." We call it "instrument flying" now, and it's much more complex and reliable than it was in the 1930s.

At that time, if any of the radios failed on the ground or in the air, or there was any kind of interference with the radio transmission, the system didn't work. There usually wasn't a backup. The pilot was on her own. She'd either have to get out of the clouds, or land and wait for the weather to clear or for daylight to break. Otherwise she'd be flying blindly into the unknown.

knew that if too much heavy ice formed on the wings, the plane would become impossible to control. So Valentina climbed higher to try to avoid the damp cloud that was creating the ice.

But the higher she flew, the lower the temperature fell. Now they had *another* problem: the extreme cold froze the communication instruments. At about −35 degrees Celsius (−31 degrees Fahrenheit), both the radio and its emergency backup failed. So did the intercom. Marina and Valentina had to write notes to each other to communicate.

Valentina flew the *Rodina* higher still to get above the cloud, so that Marina could navigate by the stars. Now Marina had to hold her sextant out of the hatch of her cabin into the icy wind so she could calculate which direction they should fly. She had to take off her fur gloves to hold the sextant; the vapor from her breath made a thin crust of frost on her goggles. But she got the reading she needed.

Polina took over the flight controls for six hours so that Valentina could rest as they flew on through the subzero Siberian night.

As it grew light, the weather got better, and once again Marina was able to pinpoint where they were. They managed to warm up the radio enough to try to make one last transmission of their location to Moscow. But they didn't hear back—the freezing and reheating was more than the radio could take, and they weren't able to use it again.

They'd been flying without stopping for more than a day when the low-fuel light came on unexpectedly. It warned them they had only half an hour before they ran out of fuel.

This was the worst shock yet. They still had over an hour before they'd reach their destination, and they were supposed to have enough fuel for at least another 500 kilometers (300 miles). After all that preparation, how could they possibly have taken off without enough fuel? The fuel tanks had even been sealed shut back in Moscow so that they couldn't cheat and land somewhere along the way to fill up again. Valentina guessed that the mechanics back home must have failed to top up the fuel tanks after testing the engines.

In those tense minutes after the low-fuel warning light came on, Valentina and Marina discussed all the possible alternative destinations they could think of—but they didn't have enough fuel to get to any of them. All three women knew, with sinking hearts, that they were going to run out of fuel in the middle of the Siberian wilderness.

They were still flying over subarctic taiga, a seemingly endless landscape of conifer forest—in English this is sometimes called "snow forest." If any of the flight crew were going to survive, Valentina would have to land there. They were nowhere near an airfield, or even a village.

The navigator's cabin was by itself right up in front of the aircraft. If the plane crash-landed nose first, which could easily happen in an emergency, Marina would be crushed. According to the *Rodina*'s emergency procedure, Marina would have to escape from her cabin before Valentina tried to land the plane. Valentina told her to use her parachute to jump out.

Marina really didn't want to—she tried to convince Valentina that she'd be okay if she stayed as far back in her cabin as she could get. But Valentina was worried that if the hatch to Marina's cabin was crushed, Marina would be stuck in the forward cabin even if she survived the landing.

So Marina made her first-ever parachute jump, alone, into the middle of the Siberian forest.

The *Rodina* had lost its navigator.

With just enough fuel left to get them to the ground, Valentina and Polina managed to crash-land the *Rodina* in one piece. They didn't know if Marina had landed safely, but they hoped so, and after they'd climbed out of the aircraft, they fired shots into the air with their pistols to try to signal Marina to let her know where they were.

Marina had, in fact, survived her own landing.

Although her parachute had tangled in a fir tree as it came down, she had managed to cut herself free and made it to the ground. Alone by herself in the taiga, she heard the *echoes* of her companions' gunshots. But from where she stood, the echoes were louder than the shots themselves, and following the sound, Marina set off in the wrong direction.

It was days before she realized her mistake.

Marina was lucky it wasn't later in the year or she wouldn't have been able to survive the taiga's severe winter weather. As it was, the temperature dropped below freezing at night. After the frantic last-minute decision to jump out of the *Rodina*, Marina had accidentally left her emergency kit behind, so the only food she had on her was one and a half chocolate bars and some mints in her pockets.

For ten days, she survived on wild cranberries, mushrooms, and birch leaves. As she wandered in hungry frustration trying to find the shelter and supplies of the *Rodina*, she fell into the icy water of a swamp and became soaked. She had to wait for her clothes to dry before she could move on.

As the days dragged by, Marina began to hear and see planes passing overhead. So she knew that people were looking for her and for the *Rodina*. But she could also hear bears and lynx growling in the wilderness around her. To her horror, one evening, she got to meet the source of one of these eerie noises.

About fifteen meters (sixteen yards) ahead of her, a shape suddenly appeared out of the forest.

It was a black bear.

As it shuffled toward Marina, that extra training with firearms came to her rescue. She aimed her pistol and shot at the bear.

She didn't hit it, but she frightened it enough that it lumbered away and she survived the encounter undamaged.

Marina spent that night on the top of a hill, where she could keep a good lookout.

Meanwhile, fifty aircraft and thousands of people in motorboats, on foot, on horseback, and even riding reindeer were all searching for the missing plane and flight crew.

Eight days after the crash, a pilot named Mikhail Sakharov in a civilian aviation service seaplane finally spotted the downed *Rodina*. Two small figures stood nearby, Valentina and Polina, waving a white cloth at the small plane that buzzed over their heads in the wilderness. They still didn't know what had happened to Marina.

The Rodina had been found, but there wasn't any place for a rescue aircraft to land. Now that people knew where the plane was located, they had to figure out how to get to it on the ground. In the meantime, they dropped supplies to the crew by parachute.

During the rescue effort that followed, two of the search aircraft collided with each other. Horrified and unable to help from the ground where they waited, the pilots of the Rodina had to watch the terrible accident happen. Sixteen people were killed in the crash—including an air force commander and his chief navigator. It was years before this tragedy was made public. Nothing was going to stop the USSR from announcing that the flight of the Rodina was anything other than a phenomenal success.

For, in just over a day, Valentina Grizodubova, Polina Osipenko, and Marina Raskova had flown some 6,000 kilometers (about 3,700 miles).[7] The women's long-distance flight record, previously held by British pilot Elizabeth Lyon, had been smashed to smithereens. The Rodina had beaten the world record by approximately 2,000 kilometers (1,200 miles), in an aircraft that was an entirely new Soviet design.

The day after the crash site was located by the rescue team, Marina managed to make her way to the Rodina. She and her crewmates hugged each other, laughed, and cried, and Polina asked her what had taken her so long. Right away a doctor was summoned to treat her legs for bruises and frostbite, but Marina was especially grateful for hot tea!

---

7. They flew 5,908 kilometers (3,663 miles) in a straight line and 6,450 kilometers (3,999 miles) in total, in twenty-six hours and twenty-nine minutes.

Now the tragedy could turn to triumph. And not only had Marina Raskova played a key role in the phenomenal achievement, but she had an amazing story of ten days of wilderness survival to tell along with it.

What a woman! And a mother, too! When Marina was able to speak to her daughter, Tanya, on the telephone from the Far East, the call was broadcast by radio throughout the Soviet Union.

While the Soviet government was scrambling to launch the enormous rescue effort for their heroic women pilots, an event of global significance was going on without them in western Europe.

On September 30, 1938, while Marina was still lost in the taiga, government officials from Germany, France, Italy, and the United Kingdom met for a conference in Munich, Germany—the USSR wasn't invited. There, these "great powers" signed an agreement that gave parts of Czechoslovakia to Germany. This unfair treaty, called the Munich Agreement, shows just how desperate the European powers were to avoid the outbreak of a war against Hitler's Germany.

The timing of the Munich Agreement, which was made behind the Soviet Union's back and was certainly a blow to its pride, may partly explain why the Soviet government and media gave so much attention to the flight of the Rodina.

When the triumphant fliers got back to Moscow, they were swept up in a parade through streets filled with flowers and cheering crowds. Apparently Stalin himself greeted them with kisses when they reached the Kremlin, the palatial seat of Soviet government, and Marina and Valentina had a joyful reunion with their children. Valentina held her two-year-old son, Sokolik, while she gave a speech; at a reception at the Kremlin, Marina's daughter, Tanya, sat with Stalin and the premier, Vyacheslav Molotov, who'd hosted the *Rodina*'s crew at his summer house in July.

The flight of the *Rodina* was reported all around the world. Marina and Polina were each presented with a second Order of Lenin award, and they and Valentina were all given the Gold Star of Hero of the Soviet Union— the nation's highest honor. They were the first women ever to receive it. Marina, mother and aviator, was a worldwide star.

"A GENERATION NOT FROM THIS UNIVERSE"

Two days after the flight of the *Rodina* was celebrated as a success, the commander-in-chief of the Soviet Air Force wrote a comment for *Komsomolskaya Pravda*[8], the newspaper for the youth branch of the Communist Party. He said that the central air force headquarters had already received more than a hundred letters from young women begging to be admitted to military schools. Every single one of them mentioned the *Rodina*'s crew as her inspiration.

But the women who'd made the record-breaking flight in the *Rodina* weren't just dazzling celebrities: they were also *safe* role models. Of course, Marina was young and attractive, a skilled career woman in an exciting industry, an educated academic, and an adored mother; but most important of all to her success, she was admired and supported by Josef Stalin. So were Valentina Grizodubova and Polina Osipenko. When Polina died in

---

8. Pravda, or "truth" in English, was the name of the main Soviet newspaper. It's commonly used as a name for Russian news sources even today. *Komsomolskaya Pravda* means "Komsomol Truth" (the *skaya* ending turns a noun into an adjective).

a crash in May 1939, only seven months after the record-breaking flight, Stalin was a pallbearer at her funeral. Polina was buried in the wall of the Kremlin just behind Lenin's tomb.

Here's what's so hard for us to understand today: The ruthless, paranoid Josef Stalin, by then the uncontested leader of the USSR, commanded a bizarre and absolute power over his people. If you were a young person in the Soviet Union in the 1930s, you were unable to separate your fear of Stalin and his henchmen from your genuine patriotic fervor for your Motherland.

It may be impossible for us to understand how the Great Terror could have prepared these youthful, idealistic minds for the incredible hard work and the enormous sacrifices that lay ahead of them in World War II.

But though we can't relate to it or understand it, this mix of fear and patriotism helps to explain why the youth of the Soviet Union fought so ferociously and relentlessly against Hitler's Germany and Nazi fascism. Fascism, which we associate so strongly with the Nazi Party[9], is a form of government rooted in nationalism, in which democracy gives way to a dictator. It's used to describe political movements that whip up hate and fear against outsiders and try to disguise them as patriotism. During World War II, the people of the USSR referred to the Germans as "fascists" more than they used the term "Nazis." Soviet citizens felt that they themselves were real patriots, fighting a war against the false patriotism of fascism.

The Soviet name for the fight to drive the German army out of their nation during World War II is the "Great Patriotic War." Today's Russians still use that name.

And the youth of the Soviet Union were ready for a patriotic war. In June 1935, eighteen-year-old Anna Mlynek gave a high school graduation

---

9. "Nazi" is the shortened name for the German *Nationalsozialistische Deutsche Arbeiterpartei* (NSDAP), or National Socialist German Workers' Party.

speech that was reported in *Komsomolskaya Pravda*; addressing both the young women and young men of her generation, she concluded, "Each of us will become a hero when ordered by our country." A whole generation of teens was anticipating having to become soldiers.

We don't know all their stories. We can only look at the ones that have been recorded, and consider what it must have been like for others in their generation. It is baffling for us to imagine how frightening life must have been for these teens, yet how much they seem to truly have felt they were working to improve their nation—their Motherland—and how desperately they struggled for safety and acceptance so they could live ordinary productive lives.

Stalin often managed to shrug off the blame for his actions onto his subordinates or the Communist Party itself. People revered him as much as they feared him; they were just as anxious to prove themselves worthy party members as they were to avoid arrest.

Another teen who suffered as a result of the Great Terror was Lidiya Vladimirovna Litvyak—or as she was known all her life, Lilya. She was born on August 18, 1921, and her birthday just happened to be Soviet Air Fleet Day or Aviation Day. For Lilya, this must have felt like destiny, because she wanted to be in the air more than anything else in the world.

Lilya was one of millions of young people almost exactly the same age as the USSR itself, educated entirely in those Soviet schools that were now so free of gender bias. She made her first solo flight, in the sky on her own, when she was fifteen years old. She was seventeen and already training as a flying instructor when Marina, Valentina, and Polina made their record-smashing flight in 1938. Like the rest of the nation, Lilya was probably glued to the radio as reports told of the *Rodina's*

adventures in the Siberian wilderness. Lilya
cut out newspaper articles and photographs of the brave and resourceful
crew members and carried them
around with her in a notebook.

In 1937, when Lilya was sixteen,
her father, Vladimir Litvyak, was
arrested, for crimes he'd supposedly
committed against the Communist
Party. Lilya never saw him again. After
his arrest all trace of him simply van-

LILYA LITVYAK

ished, and Lilya and her mother and eight-year-old brother, Yuri, could
only guess what had happened to him. They never even found out how
he died.

When he got older, Yuri changed his name. He dropped his father's
family name, Litvyak, and replaced it with his mother's, Kunavin, so that
his identity wouldn't be associated with his father's arrest.

Lilya didn't change her name. She felt fiercely that she had to make
up for her father's criminal disloyalty, if it had existed, whatever it might
have been. She was determined to devote her life to flying in support of
her Motherland, both for her own protection and to redeem her missing
father.

Again, it's hard to know how honest individual storytellers are about their
feelings for Stalin, even with themselves. Lilya's story is told in hindsight—
she didn't live long enough to be able to reflect on her youth, and much
of our knowledge of her thoughts is filtered through the memories of her
friends.

Antonina "Tonya" Khokhlova, who became a tail gunner in the 587th Bomber Aviation Regiment, tells a different story about how she felt about the leader of the USSR. Fifty years later she admitted frankly, "I hated Stalin throughout my life, beginning with the murder of Kirov. I was fifteen then, in sixth grade, and I said, 'That's Stalin's deed!' . . . and I hated Stalin when the war started."

Tonya was the coxswain for a young men's rowing crew, and they all went to enlist as soldiers together when the war started—"eight boys and myself," Tonya said. She told them that fighting "[for] the motherland is all right, but why should I fight for Stalin? He's a man—let him fight for himself!"

An outburst like that could have actually killed her. But none of her friends told on her.

"I was not brave, I was lucky," said Tonya; "like all fools I was lucky. If someone had turned me in, of course I would have been shot, shot on the spot."

Irina Rakobolskaya, who was born in 1919 and who became the second-in-command of the 588th Night Bomber Aviation Regiment during World War II, expressed how hard it is to understand these young people through the lens of hindsight.

"We are a generation not from this universe," she said.

We don't know Marina Raskova's personal take on the Great Terror. But while in the past she'd been a civilian working on the edges of the military, now she made a positive decision to follow a military career herself. Early in 1939, she began a two-year course at the M. V. Frunze Military Academy.

Marina had seriously injured her legs during her wilderness adventure after the *Rodina* crashed, and it took her several months to recover. But she'd been rewarded with a pile of cash and a new two-room apartment for her role in the record-breaking flight, and now with time on her hands, she became a writer. She wrote a full-length autobiography, *Notes of a Navigator*. It was published by the Central Committee of the Komsomol in 1939, and anybody who couldn't get hold of the physical book could read it as a serial through the hugely popular program Newspaper Novels. Marina also worked at answering her steady stream of fan mail.

Young aviators throughout the nation adored her. All over the USSR, young women were taking to the skies and trying to join the Red Army so they could be like their modest and hardworking hero, Marina Raskova.

Meanwhile, Adolf Hitler was steering Europe headlong into World War II.

"NOW EUROPE IS MINE!"

To the Soviet Union, which had been left out of the Munich Agreement, the rate at which Germany was gobbling up European territory was seriously alarming. So Stalin's government decided to make its own deal with Germany. On August 23, 1939, Soviet Premier Vyacheslav Molotov, the same official who'd hosted the *Rodina's* crew at his summer house, signed a treaty with Germany's foreign minister, Joachim von Ribbentrop.

In the new treaty, called the German-Soviet Nonaggression Pact[10], the distrustful neighbors pledged not to go to war with each other for at least ten years. To sweeten the deal, they also secretly agreed to divide up parts of Poland, the Baltic States, Finland, and Romania, as if European nations were a box of candy.

Hitler was so delighted when he heard the results of this agreement that he is said to have exclaimed, "Now Europe is mine!"

Feeling confident, happy, and hungry, Hitler sent his forces to invade Germany's half of Poland on September 1, 1939. The United Kingdom and

---

10. The German-Soviet Nonaggression Pact was also called the Molotov-Ribbentrop Pact, after the men who signed it.

France, finally shocked into action, declared war on Germany two days later.

And the USSR sent its forces to take over its half of Poland in the middle of September.

World War II had begun.

As soon as the United Kingdom had rallied its military and told civilians to prepare for war, the British government set up a new aviation service called the Air Transport Auxiliary (ATA). The ATA allowed nonmilitary pilots to ferry aircraft from factories and maintenance units during wartime. With civilians doing this unglamorous but necessary transport work, Britain's fighter and bomber pilots could concentrate on flying into battle against the Luftwaffe, the fearsome second-to-none German Air Force.

In November 1939, a respected and diplomatic British pilot named Pauline Gower was allowed to choose eight highly qualified women to join the ATA's initial forty-three men. At first, these women were restricted to flying obsolete training aircraft. Despite those regulations, in February 1940 the British ATA became the first organization in the world to officially allow women to fly aircraft in wartime.

Thousands of miles across the Atlantic, the United States was still trying hard to stay out of the war. But it too was preparing new pilots—just in case. In 1939 a Civilian Pilot Training Program began to offer sponsored flight instruction to young Americans. For the first two years of the program, one in ten of these flight students was a woman. Most Americans, however, like the British, still objected to the idea of women flying. By June 1941 women were banned from the Civilian Pilot Training Program to make room for men.

Meanwhile, in the USSR—which, thanks to the German-Soviet Nonaggression Pact, wasn't under attack—young women across the nation were continuing their state-sponsored flight training and flight instruction as though nothing had changed. By now, one in every three or four pilots in the Soviet Union was a woman.

For most Soviet citizens at home, 1940 remained a period of uneasy peace. But the thunder-rumble of war was ominous. The Red Army tested its strength by invading the states on its western borders that the USSR had divided up with Germany. After he'd taken over half of Poland, Stalin had a go at invading Finland in the winter of 1939–40. The Soviet soldiers involved in this war found themselves in an icy stalemate, freezing and starving to death. The USSR backed off and signed a peace treaty with Finland in March 1940.

Meanwhile, Nazi Germany became bolder and bolder. In April and May of 1940, Hitler's armies snapped up western European nations including Denmark, Norway, Belgium, the Netherlands, and finally, in June 1940, France. Next on Hitler's list was the United Kingdom.

But the United Kingdom is separated from the rest of Europe by the English Channel and the North Sea. The closest the German troops could get to the island of Great Britain was at Calais, France, about thirty-three kilometers (twenty miles) from England. And Britain's Royal Air Force, in a gallant and furious fight against the Luftwaffe, turned out to be a stronger opponent than Germany had expected. By September 1940 it became clear that the German invasion of the United Kingdom was not going to happen.

Europe's invaded countries set up governments in exile in London, the capital of the United Kingdom, to make war plans as a group of "Allied" nations fighting together against German aggression.

Hitler immediately turned around and made a treaty with Japan and Italy, creating his own group of allies known as the "Axis" powers. By the end of September 1940, Hungary and Romania had also joined the Axis nations—both countries shared borders with the Soviet state of Ukraine, and hoped Germany would help protect them from the Soviet Union. And now Germany sent troops into Finland, which was still mad at the USSR for their "Winter War" earlier that year.

Hoping to soothe Soviet anxiety about all this military might sitting right on its doorstep, in October Germany invited the USSR to join it as another Axis power. But the Soviet government was suspicious. It came up with all kinds of conditions that Germany didn't want to let it have. Months went by, and the waffling was still going on, and then in April 1941 the USSR signed a nonaggression treaty with Japan without consulting Germany.

Hitler had had enough. He didn't actually have anything to gain from another treaty with Stalin, and he was annoyed with the nitpicking negotiation. He detested the Slavic people of eastern Europe with a murderous racist hatred similar to what he felt for Jewish people, and was greedily eyeing the Soviet Union's enormous agricultural areas, such as Ukraine.

So Hitler decided to invade the Soviet Union.

For all Stalin's preparation for the "future war," he seems to have had some kind of mental block against believing that Hitler was really going to attack him. In the spring of 1941, the Luftwaffe regularly sent spy planes over Russian troops and Russian cities. Nobody close to Stalin dared to give this adequate attention. Soviet informers sent their chief of intelligence nearly a hundred warnings of a planned German invasion. Winston Churchill, the British prime minister himself, sent warnings based on captured German codes to the Soviet government. Again, nobody dared to take action.

People were scared to bring Stalin bad news, and he was sure he couldn't be tricked. And of course it must have seemed that even the army of Nazi Germany couldn't possibly manage to launch an invasion into a country whose border with eastern Europe was over twenty-five hundred kilometers (over fifteen hundred miles) long.

But they did.

The entire length of that border was about to become a battlefront.

Hitler's plan was to sweep across the USSR in a lightning-swift strike that would capture its agricultural and industrial resources, its important cities, and its capital. His code name for the invasion was "Operation Barbarossa," after the great twelfth-century tactician and emperor Frederick Barbarossa, who unified many European kingdoms under German rule as leader of the Holy Roman Empire.

In the early hours of the morning on June 22, 1941, the German forces hurled themselves at the Soviet Union. Hitler's invasion of Marina Raskova's Motherland blazed into life.

PART II

THE GREAT PATRIOTIC WAR

THE FIRST YEAR: 1941–1942

THE STORM OF WAR BREAKS

June 22, 1941, was a Sunday, and it happened to be Olga Yakovleva's day off. The young flight instructor was dozing in the sun after a swim in the river when she heard a radio announcement coming from a nearby stadium.

She couldn't tell what the announcer was saying. But from the strangely urgent tone of his voice, she could tell it wasn't an ordinary broadcast. Olga scrambled up, gathered her things, and ran home to listen to her own radio.

That's how she discovered the terrible news—the war had begun.

The next thing she did was to go straight to her flying club to volunteer as a fighter pilot.

She wasn't alone. All over the USSR, citizens raced to defend their Motherland. They stood in long lines outside recruitment offices, hoping they'd be able to join the Red Army and immediately get sent where the fighting was fiercest.

One shocking feature of the Germans' early-morning attack on June 22 was that they destroyed hundreds of Soviet aircraft *on the ground*. The Soviet pilots were so taken by surprise, they didn't even have a chance to get into their planes and fight back. The Luftwaffe aircraft swooped in low, bombing and gunning the easily targeted empty planes where they stood parked in rows on the Soviet airfields.

Meanwhile, German troops were marching and motoring forward along a line running from the Baltic Sea in the north to the Black Sea in the south—about the length of the entire East Coast of the continental United States. When the Red Army met the invading Germans to fight back, the concentrated force and fury along that line became known as World War II's Eastern Front.

Imagine, if you can, three million armed soldiers and an army of tanks and guns and bomber aircraft, all hurling themselves in a ferocious attack across the United States from Maine to Florida. Imagine them fighting, burning, looting, and bombing every city and farm in their path until they reached the Great Plains. That's what the Soviet Union was facing and fighting: destruction on that scale.

Early on, supplies became so short and the fighting so chaotic that

A VILLAGE BURNS AS THE GERMAN ARMY INVADES THE SOVIET UNION.

many Red Army soldiers were reduced to wearing rags and going barefoot. In desperation, they resorted to tactics such as strapping small bombs to dogs' backs and sending them to blow up German tanks.

The Germans first stormed through the cities of the Soviet states of Belorussia and Ukraine. The Red Army correspondent Vasily Grossman's notes give a vivid snapshot of a Belorussian city under attack: "A cow, howling bombs, fire, women . . . The strong smell of perfume—from a pharmacy hit in the bombardment—blocked out the stench of burning, just for a moment." Traveling with the Red Army to the front, Grossman saw the panicked population as people left their homes and tried to escape the German army. They traveled in carts and herded livestock on foot, carrying children. When Grossman tried to interview the refugees, they would begin to cry when he asked them a question. Ripe grain went unharvested; unpicked orchard fruits were left in trees to rot as communities fled from the invaders.

For the Germans, the big targets were the cities of Leningrad, the old imperial capital in the north, which had been the birthplace of the Soviet Union, and the new capital in Moscow. In 1941, Leningrad had a population twice the size of modern Manhattan; Moscow was bigger than Los Angeles is today.

Twenty-year-old Mariya "Masha" Dolina was a flight instructor at the Dnipropetrovsk Flying School when the war started. The club was part of the Soviet Air Army, and Masha and two other women—another pilot and a navigator—wanted to join the club's military division along with the men. Their commander agreed to let all three of them sign up.

In every town and village the Germans invaded, they took over and set up their own soldiers and government to occupy and replace the Soviet system. Masha's first wartime assignment was to fly her club's aircraft away from the enemy's grasp, and to make sure the Germans couldn't use the airfield when they got there. So before the flight school pilots left their airfield for the last time, they had to get rid of all the fuel they couldn't take with them and destroy the hangars where the aircraft were kept.

Masha ferried three planes away from the advancing front that night. Before she took off for the last time, she and her companions set fire to the flying club's hangars and even to her own house—a building she and her friends had built, Masha said, "with our own hands, where we had lived so happily." A dreadful scene lay below her as they left the airfield. "When I flew over that night the river was burning with oil, and everything on the ground was burning," she said. "It felt as though even the air was on fire."

As the Red Army mobilized its soldiers to fight for the USSR, civilians had to do all the defensive work they could. They got to work digging trenches that might slow down the German tanks. Emergency laws added three hours to the workday and banned vacation days and public holidays. There weren't any air raid shelters in Moscow; when the Luftwaffe planes got close enough to bomb the capital, women and children would have to hide in dugouts that they'd built themselves, covered with dirt and wooden boards. People in Leningrad also worked frantically to build makeshift defenses.

And all over the country, teens and young adults who had grown up believing they would come of age in wartime rushed to military posts and recruitment offices to volunteer to defend their Motherland. Everybody wanted to be sent to the front, and young women who had grown up firing guns and flying planes in clubs and schools were just as ready to fight as the young men were.

But because military enlistment had only ever been a requirement for men, the USSR didn't have a system figured out that would suddenly allow thousands of young women to sign up for active service. Sure, flying clubs had allowed female pilots to become instructors, but not to move directly on to military flying schools. Masha Dolina, whose first wartime job was to fly aircraft away from her burning airfield, was one of only a few lucky women whose commanders found a place for them right away.

Most young Soviet women found themselves struggling against the inconsistency of the Communist Party's approach to gender equality. Olga Yakovleva, who'd been sunbathing when the war started and then ran straight to her flying club to volunteer for the air force, was stunned to find that instead of being sent into battle at the front, she was going to be assigned to train a group of girls to replace the flying club's male instructors, who'd now be going off to war.

Olga wasn't alone. All over the USSR, women who could fly were now assigned to train new pilots—many of them young men who'd be flying off to combat missions. Lilya Litvyak, born on Aviation Day, had already trained forty-five pilots at the Kirov Flying Club in Moscow. At eighteen, only a month before the war began, she'd been praised in the Soviet Union's *Airplane* magazine for carrying out a record number of training flights in a single day (over eight hours of flight time). She wanted desperately to take part in the fight against the enemy. But when Lilya tried to sign up for military duty, she too was rejected.

At the beginning of the war, women who successfully signed up with the Red Army were only sent to the front as nurses, or in communications or antiaircraft gunner units. The government didn't like the idea of women fighting in frontline combat.

For an entire generation of young women who felt they'd been preparing for war all their lives and who knew they *already* had a skill that could be put to good use in defense of their country, the first few months of the war were incredibly frustrating.

Polina Gelman, who'd taken up flying in ninth grade, was in her third year of a history degree at Moscow University on June 22, 1941. When she and a group of students and professors went to volunteer for the war, she was told that the army didn't draft women.

"We were brought up to believe that women were equal to men, and we thought that we should be allowed to go into the army, too," Polina argued. She didn't get anywhere. She had to spend the summer of 1941 digging trenches around Moscow and putting out fires started by German bombs.

Zoya Malkova and two of her friends visited the local military recruitment officer at least three times, begging him to assign them to combat duty. Her friend Anya Shakhova told the officer: "But we are indeed capable of serving in the army! . . . We can do anything: cover 50 kilometers [over thirty miles] on foot per day, fire a rifle, drive a motorcycle, and sleep in the snow."

The man told them they'd be called up when they were needed. To let them know he was done talking to them, he bent straight back to his paperwork while the three young women were still standing in front of his desk.

In August 1941, Stalin issued a fearful rule known as Order 270. It stated that anyone who surrendered or was captured by the enemy would be considered a traitor to the Motherland. Even family members of these so-called traitors could be arrested or imprisoned. In such desperate times, you'd think that anyone who *volunteered* to fight for the Red Army would be welcomed. But most of the women who hoped to join the military were at first turned away.

These young people had grown up during the Great Terror. They understood how dogged patience and persistence could pay off. All over the USSR, young women like Olga, Lilya, Polina, and Zoya would find their way to the front by making appointments and writing thousands of letters to those in authority, offering their skills and their lives.

And Marina Raskova would lead them there.

"DEAR SISTERS! THE HOUR HAS COME . . ."

arina Raskova was also persistently looking for war work.

When the Germans launched their surprise attack on June 22, 1941, Marina, too, tried to sign up to fight at the front. She was already a military officer as well as a national hero who'd been awarded the country's highest honor. But like so many thousands of other women who volunteered for battle, even Marina Raskova's application was rejected.

Meanwhile, young women across the nation were sending Marina thousands of desperate letters begging her to help them go to war. Pilots and navigators, many of them already experienced flight instructors, were all sure that the famous Marina Raskova might be able to influence the highest levels of government in a way that they could not.

They were right.

As the USSR lay under siege from the German army, and the front line swept closer and closer to the capital city of Moscow, Marina approached Josef Stalin with the idea of forming a women's aviation regiment as part of the Soviet Air Force.

She offered to lead it herself.

It's not clear how Marina got the green light to form her group of women aviators. It's very likely that the Central Committee for the Komsomol came up with the idea, and Marina Raskova was the obvious person to put in charge. Nina Ivakina, who became the Komsomol organizer for the 586th Fighter Aviation Regiment, told a journalist in 1975 that Marina took the bull by the horns and marched into the Defense Ministry armed with a briefcase full of the letters all those pilots were sending her.

It's possible she even made the suggestion to Stalin herself. Yevgeniya Zhigulenko, who eventually flew with the 588th Night Bomber Aviation Regiment as both a navigator and a pilot, said that Marina told her regiments about a conversation she'd had with Stalin. According to Yevgeniya, Stalin warned Marina, "You understand, future generations will not forgive us for sacrificing young girls."

And Marina answered him: "They are running away to the front all the same, they are taking things into their own hands, and it will be worse, you understand, if they steal airplanes to go."

Yevgeniya knew this was no exaggeration. In fact, it had happened in her own flying club. She said, "There were several girls who had asked to go to the front, and they were turned down. So they stole a fighter plane and flew off to fight. They just couldn't wait. . . ."

We don't know how much access Marina actually had to Josef Stalin. Women in general, and Marina in particular, weren't his number one concern when he faced up to the enormous reality that his country was at war.

In his first wartime radio speech to the nation, on July 3, 1941, Stalin promised that the USSR would be allied with "the peoples of Europe and America" against "enslavement by Hitler's fascist armies." He urged everyone in the Soviet Union to "defend with their lives their freedom, their honour and their country in this patriotic war against German fascism."

But Stalin didn't mention any specific role for women. In fact, in none of his wartime speeches did he *ever* mention women in the military, though nearly a million Soviet women would eventually fight in the Great Patriotic War. Throughout the war, there were never many formal organizations for women soldiers. By luck or persistence, either women took roles right beside men or they joined volunteer regiments known as "people's corps" that sprang up all over the nation and later merged with the Red Army.

Even Marina's aviation regiments weren't organized by the military. They were run by the Komsomol. And although the women of Marina's regiments were trained as strictly as any soldiers, they didn't receive military status until their training was complete.

Whatever actually happened, sometime during the summer of 1941 Marina Raskova must have had direct contact with Stalin and received a sympathetic ear. It took several months, but in the end Stalin liked the idea of forming aviation regiments for women.

At the end of the first week in September 1941, as the German army surrounded the city of Leningrad, Marina gave a speech at a "women's antifascist meeting" in Moscow. It was broadcast over the radio and printed in major newspapers—even mentioned in American newspapers. In the speech, Marina called on women to volunteer to go to war. She wasn't reaching out to airwomen in particular, but she was certainly including them, as she urged the youth of the Soviet Union to fight for their Motherland. "Dear sisters! The hour has come for harsh retribution! Stand in the ranks of the warriors for freedom . . . !"

The USSR was the first nation in the world, and the only nation in World War II, that allowed women to fly and kill in combat.

There's been a lot of discussion among scholars and military experts as to why Stalin's government allowed this to happen.

People often assume there was a shortage of men to fly the available aircraft. This wasn't so. There were hundreds of Soviet flight regiments in 1941. Most consisted of two squadrons of ten aircraft apiece; Marina Raskova's three female regiments were not going to change the outcome of an air war on this scale.

Stalin may have felt that Marina's air regiments could eventually be used for publicity. Marina Raskova was already a folk hero. She was a working woman and a single mother. Her daughter, Tanya, was a girl to be proud of, a ballet student at the famed Bolshoi Theater in Moscow.

Marina's leadership would be an example to the people of the USSR. The patriotism of her young flight crews would be an inspiration to women serving the Motherland in a host of less glamorous roles—as snipers, tank drivers, antiaircraft machine gunners, technicians, cooks, or launderers. And the participation of Marina's aviators in the war effort would help present a picture of the nation as equal in all ways.

But the formation of the women's air regiments was kept quiet at first, because very few other women were being taken into the army in combat roles yet. Thousands of rejected volunteers would have been outraged if they'd found out that an exception was being made for aviators. But at the same time, the creation of the air regiments meant that the mostly educated young women who volunteered their aviation skills would feel their voices had been heard, even if they weren't accepted.

On October 8, 1941, the People's Commissariat of Defense issued Order 0099 to form a combat group of female aviators, including commanders, pilots, navigators, mechanics, armorers, and ground staff, to be created and led by Marina Raskova.

To give Marina the authority she needed, she was promoted to the rank of major. An official order was made for women pilots from civil aviation and Osoaviakhim to report to an assembly point in Moscow, where Marina would take charge of them.

For most of the women who joined Marina Raskova's ranks, this was exactly the chance they had dreamed of. They were wildly enthusiastic. They felt ready to head straight to the front to fly into deadly combat against the invading Nazi fascists.

That didn't happen for a long time—nor did everyone who joined Marina Raskova's aviators end up flying as combat pilots.

The German army was now closing in on Moscow, and hundreds of thousands of Red Army soldiers were desperately trying to hold back the invaders. A massive and chaotic evacuation of the city was under way in the middle of the autumn mud season, called the *rasputitsa*. The mud was caused by heavy snowfall overnight that completely melted during the day, and it was the wettest and muddiest *rasputitsa* in living memory.

There were trucks and motor vehicles carving tracks in the road, which froze overnight and then turned to mud again during the day. There were construction projects going on as people built barricades in the mud. There were extra trains coming in and out of Moscow's station carrying soldiers to the front and civilians to the distant countryside in the east, where they hoped they'd be safe. Museum staff were frantically packing up valuable artworks to remove them from harm's way—even Vladimir Lenin's embalmed body was evacuated to the distant stretches of Siberia to keep it safe, leaving on a special refrigerated train reinforced with shock absorbers. German aircraft flew over dropping bombs; there were dead bodies lying on train station platforms.

In the midst of all this, the young women who wanted to fly for the

Soviet Union had to travel in to Moscow before they traveled out.

Yevgeniya Zhigulenko was a horse rider, an aspiring actress, a night-glider pilot, and a college student. She flew at the club where the pilots had stolen a plane to take to the front when the war started, and she'd had a frustrating summer trying to figure out a legitimate way to get to the front herself. Finally, in October 1941, she and a friend named Nina found the telephone number of a high-ranking air force officer at his Moscow headquarters. The young women called up this important official and told him they had a secret they could only reveal to him in a private meeting.

When, not surprisingly, they didn't get an appointment, Yevgeniya and Nina called him again and again, driving him crazy for a whole week. Fed up with being pestered, at last the officer agreed to let Yevgeniya and Nina visit him at work! The two took their passes and found their way through the long corridors of a big concrete building. Finally they were admitted to the man's office.

When they told him they were going to refuse to leave until he signed them up to fight at the front, he burst out laughing and said, "Marina Raskova is forming female flying regiments; she is to be here in a few minutes, and you may personally talk with her."

And Marina really did turn up. The young women were "spellbound" when they found themselves face-to-face with their national hero, who personally invited them to join the others signing up at the Zhukovsky Academy meeting point.

There wasn't any kind of media announcement about how to join the women's flight regiments. All the information was spread through word of mouth, mostly by the Komsomol.

Irina Rakobolskaya, who grew up in the "generation not from this universe," was twenty years old and in her third year as a physics student at Moscow University when the Great Patriotic War broke out. She wasn't particularly fascinated by aviation—her other interests were theater and poetry. But she'd attended a parachute school and made several jumps just to find out what it was like.

Irina was on duty in the Komsomol room of Moscow State University on October 9, 1941, when she received a telephone call from the party headquarters. The caller gave her information about what sounded to Irina like a request for women to go to the front. The recruiter was looking for twelve volunteers from Moscow University.

IRINA RAKOBOLSKAYA

Irina immediately signed herself up—then quickly found others to fill out the list.

When she and her friends went to the assigned meeting place the next day, the room they met in was crowded with eager young women who'd received similar calls. Now everybody discovered that the call to arms was being led by the famous Marina Raskova, and that she was specifically looking for airwomen.

No one who heard the summons could resist.

THE 122ⁿᵈ AIR GROUP

For the young women who answered the Komsomol call for volunteers on October 10, 1941, their transformation from civilians to soldiers was abrupt. Many of them came straight from digging defensive trenches, carrying only a small bag of essential items with them. No one who volunteered that day went home that night.

The women from Moscow who joined Marina's group were all sent to an assembly point where they were fed and assigned to barracks in the old Petrovsky Palace. They wouldn't be on their own for very long. Throughout the huge nation, members of the Osoaviakhim and civil air clubs had received the same order, and were sending their women aviators to Moscow.

The young women were thrown into military drills first thing the next morning. One of them, when Marina assigned her to guard duty, struggled to look like a soldier by standing with stiff dignity—a tall order for someone who happened to be wearing a green ski suit and high heels!

On October 14 the girls were given military uniforms—men's military uniforms. For socks, they had to wear portyanki foot wraps, squares of linen cloth like those used in the Russian army since the seventeenth century.[11] For nearly two years, the young women would have to struggle with men's boots and oversize, ill-fitting clothing, made for men "right down to the underwear." Even in 1943, when they received skirts as parade dress uniform, they weren't issued with stockings. One woman remembered that when a pitying male commander ordered new clothes for her regiment, he sent them high-heeled shoes, of no use whatsoever to a pilot flying into battle or a mechanic working on a plane!

After the recruitment drive, the next step would be to sort the volunteers by their skills. But it couldn't happen in Moscow anymore, because now the German forces were only 120 kilometers (75 miles) away. Stalin began

---

11. Portyanki foot wraps were still used in the Russian military right up until 2013.

COMBAT BOOTS

The Soviet women who fought in uniform in the Great Patriotic War had to struggle to adapt to clothes made for men. When Marina Raskova's aviation recruits were first given their oversize men's uniforms, many of the young women were still in their teens—the men's boots were so big that their feet moved around inside them. Klavdiya Terekhova, the 122nd Air Group's Communist Party secretary, said that in one drill, when Marina Raskova commanded everyone to turn, one young woman's boots stayed facing forward as her feet swiveled sharply to the right!

But the young recruits were forbidden to alter the boots in any way.

to evacuate the Soviet government and told foreign embassies to leave as well. Then, on October 16, 1941, a Moscow radio broadcast announced that German tanks had broken through the Red Army's defenses and were about to storm the city.

Everybody panicked. It was a frigid October night, with temperatures below freezing, but people left their homes and poured into the train station with all their belongings, looting food from abandoned stores on their way, desperately trying to get out ahead of the German army. During that single chaotic night, 100 trains carrying 150,000 people left the station in Moscow.

Aboard one of those trains were nearly four hundred young women who were about to become combat aviators.

Marina's recruits had to wait until after midnight for a track to clear so their train could leave. They didn't have any idea where they were going,

They wrapped their feet in extra cloth, filled the gaps with balled-up pieces of newspaper, and wore the boots.

Forcing female soldiers to wear men's boots isn't unique to the Red Army in World War II. Combat boots in women's sizes for British soldiers were introduced in the United Kingdom only in 2012. In 2015, after American women soldiers stationed in Afghanistan complained that the army still did not provide boots in women's sizes, the United States Congress suggested it might be time for a more up-to-date policy. American soldiers receive an allowance for their uniforms, and it is now possible for American military women to purchase approved boots made to fit their feet.

and they wouldn't be told until they were on their way. Their train was made up of freight cars, each heated by a stove in the middle, and the young women kept themselves busy making beds with the mattresses and pillows they'd been issued for the long journey.

At the station, in the freezing darkness lit only by antiaircraft searchlights looking for Luftwaffe planes to shoot down, one young woman was on patrol. Marina had appointed Militsa Kazarinova as her chief of staff. Right now Militsa was checking up on the recruits she'd assigned to guard the group's equipment and luggage.

Militsa was a career military officer like Marina, an Air Force Academy graduate who'd already taken part in several Moscow air shows and even had some training as an attack pilot. She was cool, organized, and efficient, and used to working mostly with men. She wasn't pleased when she found that the young women she'd assigned as sentries had made a cozy bunker for themselves in a pile of mattresses!

Marina was understanding, though, and laughed when she heard the story. She assured her new chief of staff that they'd go over field service regulations with the new soldiers when the train started to move.

In the dark hours after midnight on October 17, 1941, along with many other eastbound trains carrying soldiers and refugees, the train carrying Marina Raskova's aviation volunteers crawled away from Moscow.

In total, nearly a thousand young women answered the Komsomol and Osoaviakhim summons to join Marina Raskova's aviation unit. All of them would make their way to Engels, a town on the Volga River about 800 kilometers (500 miles) southeast of Moscow, where there was a military flight school. There, they would train for several months before they were assigned to combat regiments.

It took nine days for the Moscow group to travel to Engels. Their train moved slowly and often had to wait at stations or stop to let other trains pass. Marina and Militsa took positive action to get priority for their train, which sometimes meant crawling under a dozen other stopped trains in the dark to get to a platform where they could talk to a railway official.

During the long trip, Marina went from freight car to freight car visiting with the young women, chatting and interviewing them personally. She made time for everyone.

And the recruits started to make friends. Yekaterina "Katya" Budanova led the others in singing to pass the time. Lilya Litvyak, friendly and curious, talked to anyone who'd listen. Yevgeniya "Zhenya" Rudneva, an astronomy student from Moscow University, had a head crammed full of poems and stories. She provided nonstop entertainment for the other young women.

You didn't have much choice about getting to know each other, because the trains didn't have any toilets. People had to hold on to your arms while you leaned out the door of the moving rail car! One young woman lost her footing and nearly fell out of the train in the middle of a toilet break, but fortunately her friends hung on to her. Everybody collapsed in laughter when they were safely back inside.

There wasn't a lot of food available. Most of it was bread, herring, and porridge. At one station there was a pile of cabbage, and some of the recruits jumped off the train and stole it. They were so hungry they started to nibble it right off the head, "just like rabbits," said Valentina "Valya" Kravchenko. "Then Kazarinova discovered us and made us take it all back."

Stolen food wasn't the only thing Militsa disapproved of. At one station, a pair of the new recruits jumped off the train at a run. But they stopped when they saw Marina and Militsa, and asked permission to mail bundles of letters their companions had given them. Pleased that the recruits were beginning to recognize her authority, Marina let them go, and they ran for the mailbox holding hands, their long hair flying in the wind behind them. Long hair, often braided into crowns, was stylish with Russian women of the time.

"Service personnel must cover their heads," Militsa commented, and suggested to Marina ominously, "and something should be done about the hairdos. The permanents of many of our girls have turned into mops." Militsa was no-nonsense about her own appearance, and already wore her hair in a man's short haircut. Marina filed this comment away in her head for later.

There were no lights showing when the train arrived at Engels on October 25, 1941. It was dark and wet, and no one was waiting to meet the young women. Militsa, who'd graduated from the Engels Flying School herself seven years ago, led the group between the clay houses of the town to their new home. Their hearts must have lifted a little when they arrived at the entrance gate with its decorative blue propellers!

The gymnasium of the Red Army Officers' House had been transformed into a dormitory for the recruits, with bunks made out of wooden planks and straw mattresses. But when Marina was given a private room with a double bed and flowers, she was disgusted. "Is this some kind of a boudoir? Take the bed away. Exchange it for two ordinary cots. My chief of staff and I will share this room. Take the carpet and the flowers away, too. After all, the girls don't have them either!"

Now a military representative called Colonel Bagaev met with Marina Raskova and confirmed that the formal name for her aviation unit would be the 122nd Composite Air Group.

When they finished training, the 122nd would be split into three regiments. The numbers for these future aviation regiments had already been assigned. They would be called the 586th Fighter Aviation Regiment, the 587th Bomber Aviation Regiment, and the 588th Night Bomber Aviation Regiment of the Soviet Air Force.

Colonel Bagaev asked Marina if she was sure she wanted to go ahead with the project.

She definitely did.

"NOW I AM A WARRIOR"

Marina hadn't forgotten Militsa's comments about the young recruits' lack of military polish, and the first order that she gave at Engels was for them all to get men's haircuts.

For Olga Yakovleva, the sunbathing flight instructor, it was a shock. The haircuts drove home to everyone that they were in the military, not on a Komsomol-club-sponsored winter camping adventure. Even though they were totally dedicated to defending the Motherland, having to "part with their braids" was so traumatic that many of the recruits cried about it.

At first, headstrong, talented Lilya Litvyak downright refused to get her hair cut. When all the other recruits had had their long hair shorn off, the air group's Communist Party secretary, Klavdiya Terekhova, anxiously had to report Lilya's disobedience to Marina Raskova.

Marina was determined: She'd given an order and it was going to be obeyed. So Klavdiya, nearly in tears herself, went back to Lilya and begged her to cooperate.

Lilya did, but that wasn't the end of her insurrection, or of her battle to maintain her femininity.

When the young women of the 122nd Air Group were given winter uniforms, of course once again it was standard military issue meant for men. Lilya had reluctantly cooperated with the regulations about haircuts. But now she couldn't bear to be forced to wear still more oversize and unflattering clothing. In a move that caught everyone's attention, she cut the woolly lining out of her men's boots and sewed it onto her coat to make a decorative collar.

When she turned up at the next morning's roll call, Marina must have had a hard time keeping a straight face.

She asked Lilya to step forward. Lilya did, and her companions burst out laughing.

"Litvyak, what do you have on your shoulders?" Marina asked.

"A goatskin collar," Lilya answered innocently. "Why, doesn't it suit me?"

Marina had to admit that it did. But she couldn't let such an outrageous violation go unpunished. Regardless of Lilya's fashion sense, the bottom line was that her feet needed to be protected from the below-zero Russian winter cold. Marina ordered Lilya to spend the next night sewing the lining back into her boots!

Hanging on to their femininity was something that remained important for most of these young women throughout the war, and often something that brought them together. In fact, many of them grew their hair back after that initial haircut, and no one tried to stop them. But in the beginning, Marina felt she had to play strictly by the book. She still had to train her recruits and prove that they could make their mark as serious combat teams.

• • •

Marina divided the young women into pilots, navigators, and technicians. But one of the first problems she ran into was that everybody wanted to fly fighter planes. Anyone who was already a pilot was convinced she should be flying straight into combat.

And it was absolutely impossible for everyone to be a fighter pilot. Only one of the three proposed regiments would be equipped with single-seat fighter aircraft. The other two regiments were to fly planes that would need a navigator to go along as part of the aircrew; Marina was going to have to appoint nearly as many navigators as pilots. Other women would have to become gunners.

To avoid argument, Marina made the decision that the women who would become pilots had to have already logged a minimum of five hundred hours' flying time. Very few of the young women had training as navigators, so some of the recruits were going to have to retrain. Marina gave these assignments to women who'd been to technical college or other higher education, such as Polina Gelman, the Moscow University history student who'd been digging trenches and putting out fires all summer, and Yevgeniya Zhigulenko, the aspiring actress who'd badgered the air force officer with telephone calls. Women with physical strength were assigned positions as mechanics or armorers.

Many of the young women were bitterly disappointed with their assignments. But it didn't stop them getting to work. They began lessons immediately—ten classes and two hours of drilling every day. Theory in the classroom included the principles of flight, aircraft and weapons mechanical instruction, and navigation skills. And in addition to classes, in weather that grew colder and stormier every day, the pilots were given flight tests to decide which aircraft they'd be best suited for.

MEMBERS OF THE 588TH NIGHT BOMBER AVIATION REGIMENT POSING WITH A PO-2 AIRCRAFT. FROM LEFT, MARIYA SMIRNOVA, DINA NIKULINA, ZHENYA RUDNEVA, IRINA SEBROVA, NATASHA MEKLIN, AND SERAFIMA AMOSOVA.

Inna Pasportnikova worked hard at the daily routine set for the recruits.

"Our days were filled with intensive training. Reveille was at 6 a.m., and then we were marched off to breakfast; the trip to the canteen and back was utilized for drill training. An order would ring out in the frosty air: 'Sing!'"

When they sang, it always seemed to warm everyone up.

Sometimes, to get people used to combat conditions, they'd have unexpected drills in the middle of the night. Then they had five minutes to leap into action, get dressed, and line up outside.

On November 7, 1941, less than a month after they'd been recruited and on the official anniversary celebrating the Russian Revolution, Marina Raskova's 122nd Air Group took the Red Army oath. Marina spoke to the young women herself during the ceremony, telling them, "Let's vow once more, together, to stand to our last breath in defense of our beloved homeland."

After taking the oath, Zhenya Rudneva finally confessed to her parents that she was off to war. She wrote to her mother, "Now I am a warrior . . . not studying at university as you think, mummy, but getting ready for the front . . . mastering a fearsome weapon."

Less than a month later, on December 5, 1941, Hitler decided to postpone his attempt to seize Moscow until spring. The Red Army had held the invasion back from the Soviet capital, but it was the wretched Russian winter that really turned the tables. On December 6, Soviet soldiers began to push the frozen and exhausted German troops away from the city. Most of the western Soviet Union was in German hands, but its largest cities still hadn't fallen, and the Red Army was still fighting. Operation Barbarossa had failed.

This was Germany's first defeat on the ground since the outbreak of war over two years earlier.

UNITS OF MEASUREMENT

Military language has its own systems for naming different groups.

In World War II, in the USSR, nearly twenty *air armies* were stationed throughout the country. The air armies were set up in *divisions*, each with its own job—for example, bomber, fighter, or ground attack.

Within the divisions, there were any number of individual *regiments* like Marina's 586th, 587th, and 588th. There were usually about twenty or thirty aircraft to a regiment, with a similar number of pilots to fly them. By the time you added in navigators, gunners, mechanics, armorers, communications technicians, Komsomol organizers, and cooks, a full regiment was likely to have at least 250 people in it—all living together, and often dying together, in improvised dugout shelters or abandoned

Meanwhile, another ferocious wind was rising in the Pacific. On December 7, 1941, the Axis power Japan surprised the United States with an air attack on the naval base at Pearl Harbor in the territory of Hawaii[12]. Furious, the United States at last joined the global conflict by declaring war on Japan the next day.

The world's nations rushed to choose sides, and within a day, eighteen other countries, including the United Kingdom, also declared war on Japan. Hitler was long since fed up with the Americans undermining his battle against the Allied nations while claiming to be neutral, and on December 11, 1941, Germany declared war on the United States, which declared war right back.

Six months behind the Soviet Union, the United States had also entered

---

12. Hawaii would not become a state until 1959.

bunkhouses or hosted in local homes.

A regiment was usually divided into three *squadrons* of ten planes, with a squadron leader and deputy assigned to each. A squadron could be split into *flights* of three aircraft for smaller missions, too.

If you do the math, it turns out that there would rarely be more than about thirty pilots flying for each regiment—sometimes as few as twenty, if the regiment was made up of only two squadrons. In the beginning, of Marina Raskova's thousand recruits, only about fifty of them could count on starting out as pilots.

But by the end of the war, well over a hundred women flew planes for Marina's regiments.

World War II. The two huge nations, so different from each other, were allied against Germany.

While the United States was still reeling from the surprise attack on Pearl Harbor, on December 9, 1941, under an order of Stalin, the first of Marina Raskova's aviation regiments was created. Marina chose Militsa Kazarinova's sister, Tamara, as its commander.

MILITSA AND TAMARA KAZARINOVA

Marina also assigned commanders to the other regiments. She herself would take charge of the 587th Bomber Aviation Regiment. She planned to keep Militsa as her chief of staff there, and her deputy commander would be Yevgeniya "Zhenya" Timofeyeva. People liked Zhenya, whose husband was fighting at the front. Their two small children, left with their grandmother, were trapped in a town that had been taken over by the Germans during the summer of 1941.

Marina chose Yevdokia Bershanskaya to be the commander of the 588th Night Bomber Aviation Regiment. Yevdokia wasn't happy about this at first. She wanted to be a fighter pilot, and she was worried that she wasn't going to be able to live up to the responsibility. But Marina wanted her to take charge, because Yevdokia would be the oldest member of her regiment as well as the most experienced. In time, she would become the only woman to remain in command of a women's regiment for the entire war—and her regiment would turn out to be the only Soviet military unit of the war made up entirely of women.

YEVDOKIA BERSHANSKAYA

Yevdokia's second-in-command and chief of staff in the 588th Night Bomber Aviation Regiment was Irina Rakobolskaya, the physics student who'd taken that first recruitment phone call from the Komsomol office. Irina had gone to war without even telling her mother—she was pretty sure her parents would have objected. Now, when Marina Raskova told her that she was going to be given a position of command, Irina started to cry. She wanted to fly.

Marina's response? She reminded Irina that she was in the army. The Soviet Union, and all the world, was at war. Orders and regulations must be obeyed, and Irina would have to do her duty whether she liked it or not.

In any case, no one in Marina's aviation regiments would be doing any fighting until their training was finished. And they would have to complete it during the most terrible Russian winter on record.

WINTER TRAINING

The winter of 1941–1942 was the coldest winter of the twentieth century. The *average* temperature in Leningrad that winter was −14 degrees Celsius (7 degrees Fahrenheit), and in Moscow it was even colder at −15 degrees Celsius (5 degrees Fahrenheit). But Engels, where the 122nd Air Group was training, beat them both. It sat in the middle of an empty plain offering no protection from the bitter wind, with an average temperature that winter of −16 degrees Celsius (3 degrees Fahrenheit). And the young aviators were training in open-cockpit biplanes, with the wind biting at them. They covered their faces with masks made out of mole fur, but they ended up with spots of frostbite anyway.

MOLESKIN MASK BELONGING TO LARISA ROZANOVA

Throughout that fearsome winter, the young women of the 122nd Air Group lived and breathed flight training, cramming a three-year military program into six months. Sometimes new volunteers arrived at Engels and joined them. The students flew every day as long as the weather let them, working on flight skills and cross-country navigation. Veteran combat pilots trained the recruits in air combat tactics.

Beginning in January 1942, some of the young women who'd never flown before but who were training as navigators took their first flights. They went in groups in a big four-engine heavy bomber, to give them experience calculating unplanned routes. Training in wartime meant that in the middle of an exercise, the plane might land in a snow-covered field where the navigation students would have to help refuel it by carrying buckets back and forth from a tank truck that couldn't drive through the snow. Then they'd be escorted back to Engels by armed fighter planes ready to protect them if the enemy tried to shoot them down. The skies that the young pilots and navigators were learning to fly in were already unsafe.

The harsh winter would give the young women a taste of the trials that lay ahead of them, although of course they could have no idea that they'd be fighting for over three more years.

Zoya Malkova would soon become a mechanic for the 586th Fighter Aviation Regiment. Here's what a typical day of her training at Engels was like:

"It was early morning and still dark. A strong wind knocked you off your feet. Dry snowflakes pricked your face like needles. Dressed in quilted pants and jackets, girls bustled around an aircraft. . . . Flying practice was about to commence, but the aircraft['s . . .] lubricating system malfunctioned. . . . And again (for the umpteenth time) we take off the pump and check the lines and the tightness of the nuts. It is cold. The wind penetrates to the bone marrow, and hands freeze to the metal."

When one of the young women began to cry with cold and frustration, another started to sing, and soon Zoya would be singing along with them.

"Other girls join in. Now they are no longer tired. Glancing at the smiling faces of your girlfriends, you immediately forgot your swollen hands and the cold, and somehow you found new strength."

The young airwomen truly did *adore* their commander.

Because Marina Raskova was at least five years older than most of them, and in some cases ten years older, they thought of her as a teacher and an authority. She had the wonderful ability of being able to make all who knew her feel that they were special to her as individual human beings. Everyone who flew with her spoke of her beauty, her love of music, her love of children, and her dedication to her work. They'd admired these aspects of her personality from a distance before they actually met her, but now that she was living and working with them in the flesh, she was their ideal leader.

She hummed along to Rimsky-Korsakov on the radio; she'd take a moment to sit down at the piano in the evening if she got a chance. She played duets with Ekaterina Migunova, her deputy chief of staff and an old friend from the Zhukovsky Academy. At the end of the day's training and briefings, Marina would suggest, "Let's sing!" Years later, when war veterans who'd been under her command gathered together, they'd inevitably end up singing a favorite of Marina's—"The Dugout":

A fire's aflame in the stove,
Teardrops of pitch on the logs.

The accordion sings in the dugout
To me of your smile and your eyes.

MEMBERS OF THE 122ND AIR GROUP IN WINTER UNIFORM

And she had a sympathetic ear. Masha Kirillova, Yekaterina "Katya" Fedotova, Alexandra "Sasha" Yegorova, and Antonina "Tonya" Skoblikova were a group of friends working together at the same flying club when war broke out. The four of them had written a letter *together* begging Marina to help them become combat pilots, and they joined the 122nd Air Group together. When it came time to divide the women into separate regiments, knowing how close these friends were, Marina assigned them all to the same squadron.

Some of the women, like Irina Rakobolskaya, were young mothers and had left small children in the care of family or friends. If Marina knew that someone's child had fallen ill, she'd find a way to send medication and, on occasion, an air ambulance. She even granted leave to one pilot to visit her child, and she reached out in person to comfort a parent whose child had died.

Marina had sent her mother, Anna, and her daughter, Tanya, to safety in a town far up the Volga River when war had first broken out. Their only way of keeping in touch was by writing letters. No wonder she was sympathetic to the other young mothers.

The one thing Marina didn't make time for was rest. She was so busy she'd sleep in her uniform, or fall asleep at her desk.

Years later, when other men and women who'd served in the military in the Soviet Union's Great Patriotic War referred to their units, they'd call them by their official name or by their regiment number. But the women who trained in the 122nd Air Group, though they split into three separate units when they went to war, would say that they belonged to "Raskova's regiments."

GROUND CREW

Marina took advantage of the loyalty she inspired and used it to get her recruits to cooperate. Some of the women who'd volunteered for her aviation regiments were going to have to face disappointment, because they were going to have to do jobs that kept them on the ground.

SERGEANT LIZA TEREKHOVA LOADING AMMUNITION FOR THE 586TH FIGHTER AVIATION REGIMENT

All those pilots, navigators, and gunners in the air were going to need support from dedicated teams working as aircraft mechanics and weapons technicians. All the regiments would need armorers to load bombs and machine guns, and the fighter and dive-bomber regiments would also need radio technicians and parachute packers.

It's true that many of the young women who imagined themselves soaring through the sky as they chased away Nazi aircraft over the heads of Soviet soldiers were sorely unhappy about their assignments.

But for Marina, they accepted their tasks determined to make her proud. *Somebody* had to do it, after all.

Irina Favorskaya was a student at the Moscow Institute of Geology when the war started, and like many other young women her age, she'd spent the summer of 1941 digging fortification trenches. She and her friends had marched off to enlist without packing anything, and the only clothes they had with them were the dresses they were wearing when they jumped into the trucks that drove them to the distant outskirts of Moscow. All summer they dug in their underwear to save their dresses.

Irina was assigned to become an armorer, loading bombs and guns and doing necessary maintenance work. Training days at Engels when the cold dropped to −35 degrees Celsius (−31 degrees Fahrenheit) were especially brutal. "We had to fix instruments on the aircraft with our bare hands, our skin stuck to the metal, and our hands bled," Irina said. "I wrote to my mother saying that it was unbearable to work with bare hands, and she sent a parcel . . . with a pair of pink silk ladies' gloves! I wore them, and all the girls laughed and made fun of me."

Zinaida Butkaryova came from a peasant family. As a child in 1931, when Soviet farms were being collectivized during the first Five Year Plan, she'd gone to live with relatives in Moscow because her parents were worried that if she stayed in her home village, she'd starve to death or be killed. Zinaida had worked in a textile factory for five years before joining the 122nd Air Group, and she was assigned to become a parachute packer for the 586th Fighter Aviation Regiment.

With little higher education, Zinaida had known all along that she wouldn't be flying. But she couldn't keep the tears back when she realized she wasn't even going to get to work on aircraft.

She soon found that her assignment was anything but boring—for one thing, she had to make a few practice jumps herself before she learned to pack parachutes. On Zinaida's first parachute jump, one of those too-big men's boots slid off in the air, taking with it the cloth she'd wrapped around her foot to fill out the boot. She landed with one bare foot, causing a lot of laughter among her fellow trainees! And wonderfully, after that, the young women were finally allowed to find ways to alter their boots to make them fit better.

It was a job that had its rewards, too. "When one of our aircraft was shot down and the pilot jumped with the parachute I had packed, I felt proud because it was also the result of my job that the pilot got down safely," Zinaida said.

She received a medal for it.

When you look at the faces in the photographs of Marina Raskova's regiments, the first impression is that most of these young women share a wholesome, rosy-cheeked appeal—their grins are brave and eager as they ham it up for the camera, like the resourceful heroines of Russian folktales.

They also look as though they pretty much all come from the same eastern European background, and it's true that these young Soviet citizens weren't a diverse group by modern standards. Most of the women in the 122nd Air Group were from Russia, even though the USSR was made up of fifteen different states sprawled across Europe and Asia, all with unique cultural traditions and even their own separate languages.[13] Some of the women of the 122nd Air Group were from Ukraine and Belorussia (now

13. All fifteen Soviet states, including Russia, are today individual independent nations.

Belarus). One, Khivaz Dospanova, was from a town in Kirghiz (the town is now part of Kazakhstan), in central Asia. Another, Polina Gelman, was Jewish. Based on the records we have access to, these ethnic differences don't seem to have affected the way the airwomen got along.

The women of Raskova's regiments were from a wide range of educational and economic backgrounds. Some were from peasant families, some were the children of intellectuals, some were the children of factory workers and had worked in factories themselves. Some were from tiny villages in the middle of nowhere, while others were from the big cities of Leningrad and Moscow. Only a third of one percent of Soviet women attended universities at this time, so the education level of many of Marina's recruits was off the scale by ordinary standards.

In an ideal world, communism is supposed to create a society without class. Its utopian aim is to give equal opportunities to all people. In theory, goods are shared according to the level of contribution people make to a society, which means that hard work gets rewarded.

In the reality of the USSR, millions of people were tortured and starved to death in the first years of the Communist Party state. Of those who managed to live ordinary lives, some already had more education than others, or their parents were peasants, or they came from a small village or a big city. No matter how noble the ideal, some people had better jobs or nicer apartments whether or not they had earned them. All these differences contributed to a distinct class awareness, and even snobbery, in some of the young women who joined Marina Raskova's regiments. Zoya Malkova, the aircraft mechanic who described the bone-chilling training routine at Engels, called the students from universities and aviation institutions "elitist"—including herself.

There's no doubt that Soviet pilots, navigators, and commanding officers were privileged during the war. Life was harder for ground crew than for aircrew. Their living conditions were worse, and because of the way the Red Army gave out rations according to rank, the ground crew was not as well fed as the aircrew, even though they worked every bit as hard. Some of the mechanics, who had been pilots before the war, struggled not

KITCHEN DUTY: ANOTHER FORM OF ELITISM

Family, culture, race, religion, wealth, and education can all affect your social status, even in a society that makes an effort to ignore these things. In the USSR, gender equality in law didn't always mean gender equality in everyday life.

Valentina Petrochenkova was so inspired by the flight of the *Rodina* that she'd faked her own birth certificate so she could take her flight test early. But when the war started, Valentina was told she couldn't join the air force because she was a woman. She had to keep working as a flight instructor.

Then, after months of training pilots, she was told she had to train parachutists. And first, Valentina would have to take a parachuting course herself, which she did during that bitter wartime winter. After jumping, when the students touched down on the icy airfield, the wind in their billowing parachutes would take them sliding across the ice—"and only the instructors in the bushes could stop us!" said Valentina.

When she'd finished her course, she was told she had to train sixty men before she'd be allowed to volunteer for combat duty. And she did, and at last she was offered a place as a pilot with the 588th Night Bomber Aviation Regiment.

to feel bitter about it. There was bickering and quarreling that sometimes ended in tears and even name-calling.

The young women who'd been assigned as Komsomol administrators had the unlucky job of trying to patch things up. In these early days of learning to live with a thousand strangers under harsh conditions, the

Valentina insisted on becoming a fighter pilot, and made her application to a male commander.

He told her, "No! No women!"

"I will go nowhere, I will fly fighters," Valentina said, and refused to get up from the chair where she was sitting.

"All right, you can sit here!" said the commander. Then he left.

Valentina spent the entire night sitting in his office. When he came back the next morning she was still sitting there.

Finally she wore him down, and Valentina was allowed to stay with the all-male fighter pilot training regiment. She was given her own little private plywood cabin in a corner of the dugout where the other pilots slept. But she wasn't allowed to fly.

Valentina had over ten times more flying hours than the rest of the students, so there wasn't any point in putting her through the paces in the training aircraft with the young men.

Instead, she was given kitchen duty—but the commander promised that when the fighter aircraft arrived, she could be the *second* person, after the top male student, to try one out!

Valentina would finally get to join Marina Raskova's 586th Fighter Aviation Regiment late in 1943.

pilots and mechanics had a hard time getting along—especially when the shortages were so extreme that there weren't enough forks and spoons to go around, and even the officers had to try to scoop up watery porridge with their fingers!

Klavdiya Ilushina, the chief engineer for the 588th Night Bomber Aviation Regiment, was at first annoyed at the working-class rough edges of the mechanics, who'd mostly had no higher education. Having to work closely with these women helped Klavdiya overcome this prejudice.

"After I was in closer contact with the girls," she said, "we all became like sisters."

Anyone who came of age in the Soviet Union during the 1930s was not going to let class awareness affect her commitment to the urgent demands of war.

THE AIRCRAFT ARRIVE

Late in December 1941, Marina inspected three beaten-up Sukhoy planes that the 587th Bomber Aviation Regiment was supposed to train on. The first thing she noticed about them was the nasty smell.

These battered Sukhoys were stinky and smoky and inefficient. They burned a lot of fuel, and they used castor oil, which leaked and splattered all over the cockpit after a few flights. Pilots would climb out with their clothes covered with castor oil, and the smell didn't wash off. If you weren't careful, the plane's nose dipped as you landed it, and then the whole plane would flip over onto its back. The young women of the 587th were miserable in these planes.

So Marina made a special trip to Moscow to check out new planes for the regiment she was going to command.

Remember Vladimir Petlyakov, one of the aircraft designers who'd been arrested during the Great Terror and spent three years in prison? He'd been released from prison in 1940, and for his fantastic work on the Petlyakov Pe-2, a brand-new dive-bomber and fighter, he was awarded the Stalin Prize in 1941.

These Pe-2s were the planes Marina ordered for her dive-bomber regiment, and by the end of the war the 587th loved this aircraft so much that they, and other pilots throughout the USSR, gave it an endearing nickname: "Peshka." It means "pawn" in Russian, but it's also a cute way to say "Little Pe-2"!

The design was so new that the planes wouldn't be ready to roll off the production line for another six months. The 587th Regiment would have to keep on training in the stinky Sukhoys. But at least they wouldn't be stuck with them forever.

The aircraft for the 588th Night Bomber Aviation Regiment were much easier to get hold of. They were Polikarpov Po-2 biplanes[14], the same aircraft that all the Soviet flying clubs used. Almost every pilot in the 122nd had learned to fly in a plane like this one.

It was a flimsy thing made of plywood covered with fabric, with two cockpits that were open to the wind and rain and snow. In daylight, the Po-2 was an easy target for enemy fighter planes because it was so slow. But at night, believe it or not, this was actually an advantage. The Po-2s were hard to see in the dark as they bumbled along, and the German fighters couldn't fly slowly enough to get an easy shot at them.

Dozens of Soviet Air Force regiments, all men's except the 588th, flew these planes. They were already being used at the front for communications, as ambulances, and for clobbering German troops. Every night the Po-2s dropped thousands of pounds of explosives behind the front lines, destroying enemy camps and supplies and not allowing the enemy soldiers a wink of sleep throughout the entire war.

---

14. The Polikarpov Po-2 biplane training aircraft was called the Uchebnyy-2 or U-2 until 1943; uchebnyy simply means "training." To avoid confusion it's called the Po-2 throughout this book.

A PO-2 BIPLANE

"It sounded like a sewing machine," said Sergeant Artur Gartner of the German Luftwaffe. "But they were nasty because we couldn't sleep as long as the Po-2s approached."

The Germans absolutely hated them.

The Soviet women hated the Germans right back. Polina Gelman, who became a chief squadron navigator for the 588th Night Bombers, said, "We hated the German fascists so much that we didn't care which aircraft we were to fly; we would have even flown a broom to be able to fire at them!"

As for the 586th Fighter Aviation Regiment, Marina ordered them brand-new single-seat Yak-1s. The Yak was a sleek and speedy Soviet plane, easy to fly and easy to fix, and it could stand up to the deadly Luftwaffe fighters.

Marina pulled some strings to get twenty-four new Yaks. She had help from I. S. Levin, a friend who was the director of the Saratov Aviation Factory where the Yaks were made, just across the Volga from Engels.

The male technicians at the factory were angry. Why should they build the hottest design in Soviet fighters for a few women, when men already in battle at the front desperately needed new planes?

Marina decided to introduce the factory technicians to the pilots who'd be flying their planes.

She sent a group of women from the 586th to visit the Saratov fac-tory, which wasn't far away. Lilya Litvyak, overflowing with enthusiasm and oozing personality, was one of them. "Our aerodrome kids were transformed," said I.S. Levin, the factory's director. "Exhausted, fatigued from sleepless nights, from stressful work in the freezing cold, they somehow at once pulled themselves up." After they'd met the women pilots of the 586th in person, the young men put extra effort into Marina's order!

YAK-I ASSEMBLY LINE

It wasn't long before the splendid Yak-1 fighter planes were delivered to Engels. They were painted in white winter camouflage and had skis instead of wheels so that they could take off and land from the snow-covered airfield. It was a clear and sparkling day when the Yaks arrived, and the young pilots of the 586th were thrilled at the dangerous beauty of their new snow-white planes against the snowy landscape.

Those fighter planes only had room for a single pilot. She would have to act as her own crew, doing her own navigation and gunning at the same time as she flew the plane. The new Yak-1s all came with radios, but only the planes for the squadron commanders had *transmitting* radios that would let one person talk to others in flight.

Marina wasn't happy about the radio situation, and neither were the women who were supposed to fly the Yaks in formation. In fact, they refused to fly unless they were able to talk to each other in the air. So the factory sent radio equipment over to Engels, and one of the first real jobs for the women training as aircraft mechanics for the 586th Fighter Aviation Regiment was to install radio transmitters in the new Yak-1s.

They had to do this "outside when the wind was blowing and the temperature was forty below zero," according to Galina Drobovich, who became the 586th's chief aircraft mechanic. "When we touched the metal of the engine our skin would stick to it, and some of it came off on the metal. Our cheeks and foreheads were frozen too. On returning to the barracks our hands would be a deep blue color."

There was a world of difference between working on models in the classroom at Engels and having to go to work on the real thing.

Once the radios were installed, the 586th Regiment loved their new Yaks and couldn't get enough of flying in them. Soon the young fighter pilots at Engels were practicing shooting at targets and working on aerobatic loops and rolls. They weren't supposed to fly more than three loops in a row,

A YAK-1 FIGHTER PLANE

but Anya Demchenko got in trouble for doing six!

Lilya was full of energy and excitement over the new plane when she wrote her next letter home. "The machine is splendid! What a speed! A few times I fell into a spin, but in the end I learned how to turn."

NOT QUITE READY FOR WAR

The women of the 122nd Air Group who were going to be fighter pilots and dive-bomber pilots had to learn to fly new planes before they went to war. But even the future night bomber pilots who would fly the familiar little Po-2s had a big challenge to face. They had to learn to fly at night.

Hardly any of Marina Raskova's pilots had ever flown in the dark, so the women of the 588th Night Bomber Aviation Regiment had to pick up this skill very quickly when their planes arrived in February. The Po-2s didn't have to fly in formation and would never be equipped with radios, so the navigators couldn't use radio signals for blind flying. The only way to get anywhere was to use your eyes in the dark.

But when you're in the sky at night, fields and forests and villages all look the same: dark. According to pilot Raisa Zhitova-Yushina, a conversation during a nighttime training flight might go like this: "You see this? I cannot see it! Do you see this? I cannot see it! This is a road. I cannot see it!"

It took three or four flights before you could pick out the subtle shapes of the land when you were high in the sky in the middle of the night. A clear sky, or a moonlit night, made it easier. But a dark and cloudy sky could be deadly—even without the Luftwaffe.

On March 9, 1942, it was deadly for the 588th.

That night, several of the flimsy open-cockpit Po-2s took off from Engels on a practice bombing mission—dropping concrete "bombs" on a parade ground at another airfield. Yevdokia Bershanskaya, the 588th's commander, was flying with them. The dark sky was clear when they started out, but as the flight went on, the wind picked up—and then it began to snow.

Soon the young women on the training mission couldn't see a thing. They couldn't see the horizon, so they couldn't even tell which way was up—without a visible horizon in the air, speed and centrifugal force make your brain believe that the bottom of the plane is always down. The only thing they could see was the faint light of the instruments in the cockpits. If a light winked through the darkness outside the plane, they couldn't tell if it was a star or a light on the ground.

Yevdokia said, "It was like flying through milk."

Unable to see the other planes and without any way to communicate with them, Yevdokia turned around and flew back to Engels. There was nothing else she could do except to hope that the other pilots would do the same.

After Yevdokia landed, Marina stayed up late, waiting for the other aircrews to come home. It was past midnight when a frantic telephone call came in from the site where the practice bombing was supposed to take place.

There had been a crash.

It's not clear what happened that night, or how many planes were involved—different people tell different stories. The rookie navigators might have been lost in the bad weather, or the rookie pilots might have run out of fuel. It seems that two planes collided, unable to see each other in the dark. Yevdokia's plane was the only one that made it back.

When Marina and Yevdokia organized a search party the next day, they found the wreckage of the Po-2s and the broken and twisted bodies of their pilots and navigators. Four young aviators had been killed—even before they'd had a chance to fly into combat.

Back at Engels in the days that followed, Marina's recruits organized a funeral themselves for the four young women who had died, placing flowers alongside their bodies and lifting their coffins into the truck that would carry them to the burial site. The young women sobbed broken-heartedly during the ceremony.

"My darlings, my girls, squeeze your heart, stop crying, you shouldn't be sobbing . . . ," Marina told them. "These are our first losses. There will be many of them. Clench your hearts like a fist. . . ."

The incident shook everyone, but the 588th Night Bomber Aviation Regiment took it hardest. They were supposed to be the first of Marina's regiments to leave for the front. Now they were grieving for their friends and it was clear they didn't have enough night flying experience to go to war yet.

Because of the accident, the 588th was given another two months of training before they left Engels to fly into combat.

The 586th Fighter Aviation Regiment must have been nervous and excited—it was the end of March 1942, and the newly trained combat pilots in their fast and dangerous solo Yak fighters were eagerly awaiting their first wartime assignments.

Lilya Litvyak wrote home on March 29, "We are having remark-able summer-like flying weather every day. . . . It is very warm aboard fighters—not like in the [open Po-2]. The cockpit is heated; sometimes, it is even too warm in it." She finished up with assurance, "I am very confident and completely grown-up." She was twenty years old.

But before they could go to war, the 586th first had to fly to Moscow to get the skis on their Yaks replaced with wheels now that the snow was gone. This was a tedious assignment, as they ended up waiting around for days and days with nothing much to do. Bored and frustrated, Katya Budanova led the others in a constructive project—they scrounged some planks to build themselves a private wooden hut around the hole in the ground they had to use for a toilet, and decorated it with leaves and twigs!

At last the wait was over, and their Yak-1s were fitted with wheels. But when the 586th's assignment came, they were disappointed to find that they weren't being sent to the front after all. Instead, they'd be protecting the strategic city of Saratov on the banks of the Volga River. It was hardly any distance from Engels, where they'd been training for the last six months. This wasn't going to be the heroic heat of battle they'd been hoping for.

PILOTS OF THE 586TH FIGHTER AVIATION REGIMENT

But an assignment was an assignment, and there wasn't anything they could do about it. On April 16, 1942, the women of the 586th flew to their first base, in a village called Anisovka. They would live here in wooden summer houses until February 1943; the airfield itself was just two wooden huts and some dugouts that the women had to dig themselves. Skylarks sang in the fields around them, but every night the air raid sirens wailed in the darkness as the Luftwaffe planes tried to bomb the nearby city.

The 586th's main mission in their dangerous Yak fighters was defense. They were going to protect Saratov's bridges and railways from enemy bombers, and to guard the Saratov Aviation Factory, the very factory where their own planes had been built. Sometimes they also had to deliver urgent messages, or provide a fighter escort for important officials who needed protection in case they encountered armed German aircraft.

In addition to being disappointed that they weren't flying into battle, the young pilots didn't like the food at their new air base—they knew that frontline soldiers were getting better rations than they were. And there was another problem: they weren't crazy about their commander.

Marina had appointed Tamara Kazarinova to lead the 586th. Six months earlier Tamara had been badly injured in an air raid with a compound fracture to her left leg, which left her with a permanent limp. She didn't join the others training at Engels until February 1942, which meant she didn't get to share the ups and downs of becoming soldiers or making friends during the first few months there.

Most of the women under Tamara's command found her hard to like. The highest praise you could get from her was that you'd done "fairly well" or that you were "not bad." Tamara didn't often fly along when the 586th was given assignments, either because of her leg injury or because she wasn't familiar with the high-performance Yak-1 fighter aircraft. She probably lost a little respect from her regiment because she stayed on the ground while the rest of them were risking their lives in the air.

This would all cause trouble later, but for now, the young pilots of the 586th were busy getting used to flying real combat missions—even if they weren't at the front.

Soviet fighter pilots were alone in their single-seat planes, but they typically flew in pairs. They kept their planes close together so they could look out for each other in a fight. Three of the 586th's fighter pilots, Zoya Pozhidayeva, Anya Demchenko, and Mariya Kuznetsova, became close friends almost immediately, and Zoya and Anya flew together as a pair. So did Galina Burdina and Tamara Pamyatnykh.

Lilya Litvyak and Katya Budanova also became inseparable friends. Katya, like Lilya, was a natural pilot, and like Lilya, she'd been a flight instructor before the war. She wasn't as flashy as Lilya, but she was every bit as confident. Neither one of them was happy about not being at the front yet.

"So May has almost ended . . . ," Lilya wrote to her mother. "We are training a great deal now and this fills us with enthusiasm, since it brings us nearer to . . . [our] goal—to fight at the front. Virtually no one amongst us wants to live in wartime as peacefully as we do now. . . . All of us are thirsting for battle, especially me."

The 122nd Air Group's limited military career so far hadn't done a thing to reduce that thirst for battle. They had joined Raskova's regiments so they could fight for their Motherland, and they must have felt very cut off from the rest of the world during the time they spent in Engels. They knew there was a world war going on: It meant that they were cold and hungry, separated from family and home—some of them even from their own children. It meant that they were working and studying day and night to cram a three-year training course into six months so that they could fly into battle as combat pilots, which they were eager to do. But beyond the grubby clay-and-straw houses and the concrete official buildings that surrounded them in Engels, beyond the daily flights and mechanical drills, what was going on in the world?

Ever so briefly, this is what much of the world looked like in the spring of 1942:

There were now more than twenty-five nations allied against the Axis powers.

The Americans were fighting an air and sea war against the Japanese in the Pacific.

The British were everywhere: they were fighting the Japanese in Burma, and they were fighting the Germans in North Africa. Back home in the United Kingdom, food, clothes, coal, gas, and electricity were in such short supply they had to be rationed.

Throughout Europe, Hitler was beginning his murderous holocaust of Jewish people and other ethnic groups—he wanted to wipe out the entire population of Poland to clear the land for German citizens. His disregard for humanity was fierce and random. In the first half of 1942, the terrible machinery that formed the horrific Nazi death camps was grinding into action, beginning to exterminate hundreds of thousands, and eventually millions, of men, women, and children.

As the snow began to melt in Russia, Leningrad was completely surrounded by German troops. Its three million people were slowly starving to death. Hitler's plan was to keep them blockaded and wait till everyone dropped dead; it would be cheaper and easier than fighting to get into the city.

But Moscow was still free. And now that spring was here, the Soviet Union tried to strike back against the German forces. In March, the Red Army began fighting in Crimea, a huge peninsula in the Black Sea on the southern edge of Ukraine, the Soviet state that produced most of the nation's food. The German troops wouldn't budge.

This was the area where the 588th Night Bomber Aviation Regiment was about to be sent on their first combat missions.

Operation Barbarossa, Hitler's attempt to take over the USSR in a speedy lightning invasion like those he'd won throughout western Europe, had failed. But he was nowhere near ready to give up.

Encouraged by the warm weather, Hitler decided to try attacking the Soviet Union from the south. If German forces could control the huge Volga River, it would create chaos for Soviet shipping, and cut off the USSR from its own oil supplies. Hitler's new target was Stalingrad[15], a large industrial city on the Volga—and the one that bore Stalin's name, an insult to Stalin himself. Once the Germans captured the Volga River and destroyed the Soviet Union's defenses, they could head north to get at Moscow. The new strategy was called Operation Blue.

There was no end in sight to the conflict that was slaughtering so many people. It had been the hardest winter since records began; the Red Army was stretched even thinner than it had been at the beginning of the war. And for Marina Raskova's young aviators, the real battle was only beginning.

---

15. Stalingrad's modern name is Volgograd.

PART III

THE GREAT PATRIOTIC WAR

THE SECOND YEAR: 1942–1943

THE 588th: IN COMBAT AT LAST

In May 1942 it was the 588th Night Bomber Aviation Regiment's turn to get their first taste of combat. In their open-cockpit Po-2s, their number one job would be to harass the enemy. They were going to work all night to ensure that the German invaders didn't get a wink of sleep.

The 588th was sent to help prevent the Germans from taking over the Caucasus region between the Black Sea and the Caspian Sea, an important source of oil for the USSR. If the Germans seized this area, the Soviets would run dangerously low on fuel.

Here, along with a men's night bomber regiment, Marina's recruits would fly low over the German troops in the dark, bombing their head-quarters and ammunition and supply depots on the southern end of the front.

Marina Raskova's young aviators were thoroughly excited about finally being able to do the enemy some real damage.

Marina flew with the 588th as they traveled to their new base, which was only twenty-five kilometers (fifteen miles) away from the fierce fighting on the front lines. She led the regiment's pilots and navigators in twenty Po-2s on a two-day journey, including an overnight stop at an airfield on the way. The rest of the staff made their way more slowly in trucks on the ground.

THE 588TH NIGHT BOMBER AVIATION REGIMENT. IRINA RAKOBOLSKAYA IS ON THE FAR RIGHT IN THE FRONT; COMMANDER YEVDOKIA BERSHANSKAYA IS THIRD FROM THE RIGHT IN THE CENTER OF THE FRONT ROW. ZHENYA RUDNEVA KNEELS BETWEEN THE BACK ROW AND THE THIRD ROW, WITH HER FRIEND GALYA DOKUTOVICH ON HER LEFT IN FRONT OF HER.

Ten minutes before the planes of the 588th arrived at their new airfield, a squadron of speedy fighter aircraft joined the regiment in the air. Navigator Raisa Aronova, flown by her pilot, Katya Piskareva, in their fragile Po-2, saw the red stars of the Soviet Air Force painted beneath the wings of the fighter planes and assumed they were there as a protective escort for the new regiment—which they were.

But the pilots of the fighter squadron decided they'd have a bit of fun with the rookies. Instead of flying along with the Po-2s, they wove and dived around them. Most of the 588th pilots had no idea what was going on. They didn't have much experience identifying other aircraft in the air, and some of them didn't see the red stars that Raisa and Katya had noticed—it's very difficult to spot details of an aircraft in flight. Most of the young women thought they were under attack from enemy fighter planes. Panicking, the 588th pilots broke formation and tried to escape.

When the squadron of fighter planes saw the chaos they'd caused by scattering the Po-2 regiment, they didn't have any choice but to fly on to the airfield alone.

One by one, the pilots and navigators of the 588th eventually straggled into their new airfield. Below them as they came safely down to land, the surrounding orchards were foamy with white apple and cherry blossoms, in spite of the bloodshed so close by. When the young women climbed out of their cockpits, they were teased mercilessly by the men who were now waiting for them to turn up. "Hey, spineless, can't you tell a star from a swastika?"

The 588th Night Bomber Aviation Regiment was not off to the best start.

Once again, the young women's morale and nerves were badly shaken. Because of the errors they'd made in reacting with panic to potential danger, their first taste of combat was pushed back yet another two weeks, into June, so they could have still more time to train. Adding insult to injury, they also now had to have their flight skills checked by male pilots.

They proved themselves up to the challenge, though. The pilot who checked out Mariya Smirnova wrote in her logbook that her performance was "excellent"!

Before Marina flew back to the training center at Engels, she gave the young women of the 588th Night Bomber Aviation Regiment a pep talk. They crowded together in a room stuffy with the heat of early summer. She told them that their job wouldn't be easy, but she knew they'd be able to overcome the difficulties—including male pilots who didn't take them seriously. She wished success for the young aviators and told them she hoped they'd earn the honorable name of "Guards" for their regiment—a special title awarded to elite military units.

In the middle of Marina's speech, the noise of bombs at the front could be heard clearly through the open windows. Natalya "Natasha" Meklin, one of the 588th's flight commanders, wondered what the future held.

"Standing shoulder to shoulder, we all thought and felt the same," she said. "A new chapter was opening up in our lives."

On June 10, 1942, three Po-2s of the 588th Night Bomber Aviation Regiment finally braved their very first combat mission at the front.

The 588th's commander, Yevdokia Bershanskaya, flew the lead aircraft herself, with Irina Rakobolskaya as her navigator. The two other planes were flown and navigated by the regiment's squadron commanders. As they approached the target area under cover of darkness, there was nothing to light their way but the smoldering glow of burning coal mines.

They were surprised that no one seemed to be shooting at them.

Pilot Serafima Amosova and her navigator didn't have any trouble finding their way in the dark. When they got to the target, they circled it twice in their small plane, heavy with the weight of the bombs hanging beneath its fabric wings. Still no one fired at them, so for the first time, Serafima's navigator released the catch that held the bombs in place.

Suddenly the night was full of explosions. It wasn't just the bombs Serafima and her navigator had dropped—now the German antiaircraft guns began firing up at the small Po-2. Long, eerily pale beams of light swept back and forth across the dark sky as the Germans on the ground tried to find the aircraft that were attacking them.

The surrounding landscape grew covered with smoke, and it was even harder to find the way home than it had been to get to the target in the first place. Back at the 588th's airfield—about fifteen minutes' flight away—there were only three small lights to guide the returning Po-2 down to the ground.

But Serafima and her navigator made it. The rest of the regiment were all sitting on the airfield in the dark, waiting anxiously for their commanders to return. "When we landed, our fellow pilots began hugging and kissing us," Serafima said.

But for Lyuba Olkhovskaya's squadron, the excitement and triumph of that night slowly turned to apprehension, and eventually to grief. They waited and waited, but the plane flown by Lyuba and navigated by Vera Tarasova didn't come back.

In the days that followed, the regiment pieced together what had happened to Lyuba and Vera.

After they'd dropped their bombs, those guns that were firing from the ground had torn through their fragile aircraft. Wounded and bleeding, Lyuba managed to land her plane in the dark. But she and Vera didn't have the strength to climb out, and neither one of them ever set foot on the ground again. After they landed, they both bled to death in the Po-2's cockpits.

The Germans found and searched their bodies, then left the dead aviators for local villagers to bury.

Once again, the 588th had to cope with a shocking loss.

But this time they weren't going to let it delay them one day more. This time they were on their own and they were at war at the front. They must have remembered and repeated to themselves all the things that Marina had said to encourage them, and above all they must have looked forward to being able to take action—to being able to *do something* at last.

Serafima said, "We painted on . . . our planes: Revenge to the Enemy for the Death of our Friends."

Lyuba's squadron had to fly their own first combat mission the next night, even though they'd lost their commander. Mariya Smirnova, the pilot who'd had the "excellent" comment written in her logbook after her flight test, became their new commander.

For most of the summer, the young women of the 588th Night Bomber Aviation Regiment stayed at their first base in the village among the orchards. They slept in the homes of local residents and they had a mess area with tables under a grove of trees. And all summer long, the German army fought and burned its way relentlessly toward the city of Stalingrad.

Yevdokia Bershanskaya turned out to be a good commander for the 588th. She was decisive without being bossy and didn't easily get angry. She didn't talk down to people. She didn't praise you, but she didn't criticize you, either. She encouraged the young women under her command to think about the effects of their own actions.

Yevdokia didn't have Marina's natural warmth, but she was understanding. She tried to balance military discipline with human kindness to help the young women of the 588th manage enormous physical and emotional stress. When they were on duty, they had to call each other by their ranks and surnames; off duty, they could use their first names—or even sweet or funny nicknames. Tonya Rudakova, who was tiny for a mechanic, was called Ponchik—"Doughnut"!—by her friends.

Yevdokia was always there on the dark airfield to give instructions to the women who were flying that night, and to hear their reports when they returned. She'd have a few cool, calm words to speak to each pilot before she took off.

"Be careful."

That was enough to reassure the young women that their commander was thinking about them as they flew out into the dark and the antiaircraft fire.

The 588th settled into a routine. They used two airfields at the same time: one, the home field, was the place where they ate and slept and took care of their aircraft. The other was about fifteen kilometers (nine miles) closer to the front, where they were able to land and refuel and reload their bombs between missions at night. Fuel and explosives were brought there in trucks. There wasn't any need for shelter at this temporary airfield, because everyone here was awake and working all night. In the morning, all the ground and aircrews would drive or fly home to their base to repair damaged planes and get some sleep.

The advantage of this second field was that it wasn't obvious from the air. There weren't any buildings nearby, and no aircraft were parked there during the day. If a German scout plane flew over it in daylight, all the pilot would see was an empty green field. The night bombers didn't need paved surfaces or even runways; the pilots just pointed their planes into the wind and took off from the dirt or the grass.

Zhenya Rudneva, the astronomy student and storyteller, became the 588th's chief navigator. She makes the navigator's job of releasing bombs sound perfectly simple:

"You point your plane at the target and press the bomb release catch. The bomb is released and lands on the heads of the damnable Germans. God, how I hate them!"

The release catch wasn't entirely reliable, though. If it got stuck, the navigator had to climb out of her cockpit onto the plane's lower wing in the dark sky full of gunfire and jiggle the bomb free with her own two hands.

When Zhenya wrote a letter home five days after her squadron's first flight, her tone was full of enthusiasm. She told her parents, "I am not in the least afraid when I am flying. . . . Well, the only difference between training and combat duty is that antiaircraft guns are sometimes firing at us. Above all, don't worry about me. . . . After all, it is so wonderful to fly!"

Of course Zhenya's breezy tone was partly meant to reassure her anxious parents.

Flying in the dark was a constant danger. Once, a returning aircraft accidentally landed on top of one that was already on the ground, killing three of the four crew members involved.

Another sobering accident happened in the dark when Galina "Galya" Dokutovich, one of the navigators, returned from a nighttime flight mission that summer. The plane she'd been flying in had been damaged, so while she was waiting for another plane to be readied for her next mission, she lay down to rest right there in the tall grass on the edge of the airfield. A truck was hurrying on its way to refuel the planes. The driver didn't see Galya and ran over her in the dark.

She survived, but with a serious back injury that kept her hospitalized for six months. As Galya lay on her stretcher about to be carried away, she made Irina Rakobolskaya promise that when she came back to the regiment, she'd be allowed to fly again.

The darkened nighttime airfields were dangerous to people in the air as well as on the ground, but there wasn't anything the night bomber regiments could do about it. They couldn't use bright lights to guide them in to land, because any kind of permanent airfield lighting might have been spotted by enemy aircraft. Sometimes they got a vehicle parked on the ground to quickly switch its headlights on and off. Otherwise, their regular landing lights were kerosene lanterns you could only see from one direction—they called them "flying mice"!

The pilots joked, "Soon we'll be expected to land by the light of our commander's cigarette."

They were getting used to working in the dark.

DIVE-BOMBERS FOR THE 587th

Back at Engels, late in the summer of 1942, the new Pe-2 dive-bombers that Marina had ordered for the 587th Bomber Aviation Regiment finally arrived.

The challenging, powerful Pe-2 dive-bomber, with its aircrew of three, was one of the most sophisticated aircraft the USSR built during World War II. So before the pilots of the 587th could go anywhere else, they had to learn how to fly it, and the maintenance teams had to learn how to take care of it.

PE-2 DIVE-BOMBERS IN FLIGHT

It wasn't an easy plane to fly. The Pe-2 had twin tails and twin engines, one engine on each wing. Hardly any of Marina's pilots had flown using two engines before, and now they had to learn how to balance these engines, and how to land out of balance on one engine in case the other failed. The plane was hard to take off, and once it was in the air at last, it was also tricky to land.

Some pilots in other regiments called the Pe-2 a "flying coffin." It would be a while before the 587th liked it enough to call it their little "Peshka"!

Katya Fedotova, one of the four friends who'd begged Marina to let them fly together, said that "the control stick was heavy to move, and our arms and legs were so short we had three folded pillows behind our backs. The navigators helped us by pushing on our backs as we pushed on the stick to get the tail up for takeoff."

Marina Raskova was less experienced as a pilot than as a navigator, and as the commander of the 587th Bomber Aviation Regiment, she too had to learn to fly this difficult plane. Katya was there to see Marina Raskova's first solo flight in a Pe-2. Things seemed to be going fine until, high in the sky, Marina tried to turn. Suddenly a white plume of steam trailed from the starboard engine and it stalled.

Katya and the other pilots on the ground watched breathlessly, willing Marina to keep her speed up and turn the controls toward the working engine, as they'd been taught.

Marina did exactly what she was supposed to and then made a faultless landing. As the young women came running across the airfield in relief to welcome her back to earth, a smiling Marina climbed out of the plane.

She told them calmly, "Never mind, girls, this machine mustn't be trifled with, but certainly is airworthy."

• • •

The challenging Pe-2 dive-bomber's aircrew of three included a pilot, a navigator, and a tail gunner. The pilot sat in the main cockpit with the navigator standing behind her. According to pilot Yelena Malyutina, there wasn't any seat for the navigator. The navigator also acted as bombardier, releasing the bombs over the target. In the back of the aircraft there was a separate compartment for the tail gunner, whose other job was to operate the radio.

Now Marina ran into an unexpected problem. She didn't have enough recruits to crew and care for these complicated planes, and she didn't have the time to train reinforcements. So Marina recruited men from the air force reserves to fill out her staff shortages. When the 587th Regiment finally went to war, most of its tail gunners were men, because the machine guns in the Pe-2s required so much strength to recharge. But all the 587th's pilots and navigators were women.

We don't know much about how these men felt when they were first told they were going to work in a women's regiment. But we do know that the mixed aircrews quickly became reliant on each other and worked together loyally.

Tonya Khokhlova was one of a very few women who was a tail gunner in a Pe-2. Because of the strength it took to load the machine guns, she'd started as their only female tail gunner; she'd been a gymnast, a rider, and a rower before the war and had great upper body strength. Crouched in her little canopied compartment in the back of the aircraft, Tonya could see in all directions, and there she was responsible for two machine guns that would protect her crewmates from enemy aircraft.

Tonya said that it was so hard to recharge the machine gun that she couldn't do it on the ground—"but in the air it was one, two, and it was recharged!"

It was difficult for the armorers who had to load these guns, too, and the women who ended up doing this work weren't at first particularly interested in bombs or guns or even in engineering. Often, they ended up being recruited for jobs that had nothing to do with what they were good at, just because there was a gap to be filled.

The Pe-2 dive-bomber contained five machine guns. As a bomber, of course, it also contained bombing gear and bombsights, and all of this needed maintenance and loading. One young woman was responsible for all the weapons on a single aircraft. When the regiment was flying combat missions, the armorers had to service the aircraft two or three times every day.

Galina Volova, the regimental armament engineer, called their duties "unspectacular but difficult and important." They worked covered with sweat in stifling enclosed cockpits in the summer. They worked without gloves in well below freezing temperatures in the winter. Natalya Alfyorova, another armorer in the 587th, said that during combat "the guns became very dirty inside, choked with smoke and burned particles. We had to lift them; they weighed sixteen kilograms [about thirty-five pounds] and were two meters long [about two yards]. We were all so small and thin—what was Raskova thinking about when she chose small girls for such jobs?"

It was a rhetorical question, of course. They did the work without complaining.

"NOT ONE STEP BACK"

Spirits were very low in the USSR in the summer of 1942. Although Marina's aviators were excited to be finally engaged in combat, most people weren't rushing to defend their Motherland with the same energy and passion they'd felt the year before.

In the areas that hadn't already been taken over by the Germans, cities were on fire. People were starving. Those who were fighting were dying in what seemed like hopeless battle. They were tired and hungry, and their resources were scarce. Refugees fled frantically ahead of the German troops, and when they got stuck at river crossings, the German Air Force swooped down overhead and fired their machine guns into the waiting crowds. The Soviet Air Force didn't have enough fighter planes to fight back.

Back in August 1941, right after war broke out in the USSR, Stalin's Order 270 had ruled that if you surrendered or were captured by the enemy—or even just ended up behind enemy lines—you were a traitor. This iron-handed law was supposed to encourage people to fight to the death. Sonya Ozerkova, the chief engineer of the 588th Night Bombers, accidentally ran into real trouble because of this policy when she got stuck in German-occupied territory while she was working on a damaged plane. The Germans moved in so swiftly that she had to run away, leaving the plane behind, beginning a three-week adventure on foot that included shooting a German soldier herself.

But when she finally made it back to Soviet territory, she didn't get anything like a hero's welcome. Sonya was immediately arrested by her own people, interrogated for treason, and sentenced to be shot. In shock, she had to let her captors shave her head while she awaited execution.

She was rescued at the last possible minute. An officer whose battalion included the 588th found out what was going on by a chance comment from his driver. He told the commander of the Southern Front, who ordered Sonya to be released. Sonya, stunned and traumatized by the events of the past weeks, was able to return to her regiment.

You'd think that this kind of terrifying treatment would be enough to keep everyone in line, but with the terrible losses of 1942, people weren't fighting with the enthusiasm and commitment they'd shown in the beginning of the war. So on July 28, 1942, the Soviet government issued a new order, with an even more fearsome message than Order 270. Stalin's Order 227, "Not One Step Back" (Ni shagu nazad), made it a crime even to retreat. Now it became illegal for soldiers to stop fighting.

Imagine you are someone with a dangerous job—let's say a firefighter. Now imagine that the law says no matter how fierce the fire, if you don't successfully put it out, you'll be executed. If you back out of a burning building, even if the fire is too far out of control for you to do anything, you'll be shot the next day for turning back. But if you stay in the burning building and die and nobody ever identifies your ashes, the official verdict will be that you probably tried to get out. So even though you died fighting that fire like a hero, no one can prove it. Your family won't get any survivors' benefits, and you won't even be given a memorial.

That's exactly what the Red Army soldiers faced under Order 227.

The order had chilling consequences. Prisoners of war faced instant execution the second they were freed. If there was no hard evidence that a soldier had been killed rather than captured—for instance, if a pilot's body was charred to cinders in a shot-down plane, or if her plane crashed and was never found—that pilot couldn't receive military honors and her family would receive no compensation for their loss.

Lilya Litvyak's greatest fear as a fighter pilot was that her Yak would be shot down over enemy territory and that she'd die there, or that her body wouldn't be found. Her own father had vanished in the Great Terror, and Lilya knew all too well how hard life was for the family of a "traitor." She dreaded this happening again to her mother and young brother, because of her this time.

And yet the Soviet forces were taking such a beating that it was impossible not to retreat. Colonel Dmitry Popov, the commander for the military division that the 588th Night Bomber Aviation Regiment was part of, wisely and desperately drew his forces back after the 588th had been at war for only a few weeks.

"I remember a night when I flew with tears on my face," said navigator Polina Gelman. "[The Germans] were advancing so fast that we had not time to change bases. We didn't even have maps. It was August and September, we could not harvest grain, so they burned it. And so I was crying. Because it was my country and it was burning."

From August to December 1942, just after the issue of Stalin's Order 227, the 588th Night Bomber Aviation Regiment was based in the Caucasus Mountains, for their harassment missions in their open-cockpit Po-2 planes. They were part of the effort to keep the Germans away from the

Soviet oil fields, which were so necessary to keep the gears of industry moving.

It's hard to fly in a mountainous area. Wind blows in unexpected downdrafts and updrafts as it moves over mountain peaks, and this can slam a small plane into the ground. The mountains also create wind shear, which is when the wind suddenly changes direction, another deadly hazard to flight.

The still, quiet hazards of fog and mist can also be deadly. Some nights in the Caucasus were so foggy that the 588th's ground crew had to fire flares to show the pilots where to land when they came back from their missions. The mechanics on the ground would listen for the noise of a Po-2's engine as it flew closer, and then send up a red flare to show where the runway began, or a green flare if they thought the pilot wasn't in the right place for a safe landing.

It's incredible that these young pilots coped with such extreme conditions and survived. Landing at night is hard, but if there is a light on the ground, at least you can *see* the ground. In fog, you have no idea where the ground is. Darkness and fog are a deadly combination. On a foggy night in England in February 1941, twenty-two British bomber aircraft crashed after returning from a combat mission. More than thirty British bombers were lost and crashed in fog after a single mission in December 1943, an event known as "Black Thursday." Even with modern instruments, pilots of commercial aircraft today need to be able to see the runway before they can land, even if they've been flying in cloud nearly to the ground.

But fog didn't stop the pilots of the 588th. *Not one step back*, right? Experience made them bold. "Landing in thick fog, I would enter that milky sheet and when the cockpit began to darken, it was a sign that the land was close," said squadron commander Mariya Smirnova. "Then I would pull the nose up and sink to the ground for a landing."

Not every landing ended safely. One night, returning from a mission in thick fog, two Po-2s collided in midair. Both crews were killed. In an even more terrible incident, four aircraft collided, two landing and two taking off. Seven of the eight pilots and navigators in those planes were killed.

"When they hit the ground some of them were still alive and were crying out for someone to save them because their aircraft were on fire," said armorer Olga Yerokhina. "No one could help them. They couldn't escape from the cockpits, and nobody could come close to the planes because of the fires. They exploded, one after another."

The horror of that night was unforgettable.

Far more horrific was the German army's assault on Stalingrad, which began in August 1942. The Germans destroyed most of the city's antiaircraft defenses in a single day, their bombs setting fire to oil storage tanks and demolishing buildings. It was the beginning of a ferocious and bloody battle that would last nearly six months and cost two million people their lives. In addition to being one of the most significant battles of World War II, it was probably the biggest battle in *history*.

THE
BATTLE OF
STALINGRAD

The journalist Vasily Grossman groped for words to describe the horror he saw in Stalingrad as the assault began. "Stalingrad is in ashes. It is dead. People are in basements. Everything is burned out. The hot walls of the buildings are like the bodies of people who have died in the terrible heat and haven't gone cold yet. . . . Bombing again, bombing of the dead city."

The 586th Fighter Aviation Regiment was still based at Saratov, using their fast and dangerous solo Yak fighters to defend and protect supplies and transport on the Volga River north of Stalingrad. Up till now, most of their flying had been by day, and unlike the women of the 588th Night Bomber Aviation Regiment, they'd had no training to fly at night. They ended up learning the hard way.

In August 1942, squadron commander Tamara Pamyatnykh was assigned to lead two other pilots on a long flight to deliver a message to the Stalingrad Front. But it grew dark while they were in the air—and none of the three pilots in Tamara's squadron had done any night flying in fighter aircraft at all, not even in training. By the time they got to their destination, it was so dark they couldn't see the front lines or even the airfield itself. All they could see ahead of them were the flames and smoke of the burning city of Stalingrad, red against the night sky.

The pilots hadn't even turned on the lights on their planes, for fear of attracting enemy gunfire. But the ground crew below must have heard their engines, because suddenly a firework flare from the airfield burned brightly for a moment to give them an idea where they should land.

"I was afraid that one of the other two planes would land on top of mine, so I turned on my lights for just a minute, even though I had no permission to do it," Tamara said. "Galina Burdina told me that if I hadn't done that she would have landed on top of me! We all landed safely—our first night landings."

Should they have turned back while it was still light, when they realized they were going to have to land in the dark?

Physically, it would have been the safest thing to do.

But Stalin's Order 227 didn't take darkness into account. So Tamara and Galina couldn't, either. They didn't dare fail at what they'd been sent to do.

Not one step back: in a world at war, the fear of Stalin's directives was a threat more terrifying than dying in battle.

BATTLE OF THE SEXES

Beyond the borders of the USSR, western Europe had now been at war for three years. Far to the west of Saratov and Stalingrad, across the English Channel, British women—and a few from other Allied nations as well—were also flying planes to support the war effort.

By the middle of 1942, the Air Transport Auxiliary in the United Kingdom let women ferry every single type of aircraft that the men of the Royal Air Force flew. That included their fighter planes and heavy bombers. Most of the ATA women were in units made up of both men and women at a dozen different airfields, although there was one completely female unit. Even though they weren't flying combat missions, the air work that British women were doing was so impressive that the Americans decided they needed to check it out.

American women still didn't have any way to serve their country in the air. Two remarkable pilots, Jacqueline "Jackie" Cochran and Nancy Harkness Love, were working on separate plans to change that. Nancy was organizing a squadron of women who could fly aircraft to the United

Kingdom and the Soviet Union through the Lend-Lease program. Jackie Cochran had another idea.

PILOTS OF THE BRITISH AIR TRANSPORT AUXILIARY (ATA) WITH AMERICAN VISITOR JACKIE COCHRAN, CENTER. NEXT TO HER, FOURTH FROM LEFT, IS PAULINE GOWER, HEAD OF THE WOMEN'S SECTION OF THE ATA.

Jackie was an ambitious and accomplished pilot. She'd won the 1938 Bendix Air Race flying a fighter plane from Los Angeles to Cleveland, and later in life she would become the first woman to break the sound barrier. When World War II started in 1939, looking ahead, Jackie had asked Eleanor Roosevelt, the president's wife, for help to create a program to train American women pilots for ferry flights. That way, American men could be freed up for combat work.

In the spring of 1942, Jackie brought a group of twenty-five American women, all with years of flight experience, across the Atlantic to join the British ATA. Jackie herself had no intention of staying with them, though. She was on a research trip. She wanted to study what the ATA was getting right, so she could go back to the United States and set up a similar pro-gram for women pilots in her own country.

It must have been incredibly frustrating to know that you had such a valuable skill to share in wartime, and not to be able to share it. Even after nearly three years of conflict, most women aviators were struggling to make use of their talents, all across the world.

In the Soviet Union, where women were lucky enough to have Marina Raskova's regiments to fly for, after all their training they now had to prove that in the air they were just as good as men.

Tamara Kazarinova, the commander of the 586th, still struggled to get along with the most talented pilots in her defensive regiment. People found it hard to take commands from someone who seemed inexperienced at flying the Yak fighters. Early on, Tamara transferred eight of the 586th's finest pilots to other regiments to try to ease the friction. She might even have been told to do it by a superior commander.

Lilya Litvyak and her friend Katya Budanova were two of the women Tamara had trouble with—they didn't like taking orders from someone "who didn't know how to fly a fighter." In September 1942, Lilya and Katya, along with Raisa Belyaeva and Mariya Kuznetsova, moved to the men's 437th Fighter Aviation Regiment. The 437th was based on the Stal-ingrad Front and had already lost several pilots and even more planes in the now furious battle. Marina Raskova flew over to Anisovka so she could talk to the 586th Regiment herself and let them know how important it was to help the pilots at Stalingrad.

Lilya, Katya, Raisa, and Mariya would now be the only women in a regiment made up entirely of men.

The women who didn't get to go were envious. Anya Demchenko, the pilot who'd been in trouble for showing off and flying six loops and who was Mariya's good friend, took off and flew to Stalingrad on her own after the others. She wasn't allowed to stay.

When the pilots flew to the new airfield in their single-seat Yak-1s, their ground crew had to be transported together in a larger aircraft meant for heavy bombing. It wasn't equipped for passengers—the young women had to ride in the bomb bays in total darkness. Most of them weren't used to flying, and almost all of them got airsick. When the technicians got to their new base, the bomb bay doors opened and they tumbled to the ground—some of them were so stunned by the experience that they couldn't even get up.

But they didn't get a moment to recover. The airfield was in the middle of an enemy attack. Gunfire and shells were going off around them, and the airfield was peppered with ugly little antipersonnel mines people called "frogs," which would explode if you stepped on them. The technicians from the 586th hadn't ever been under fire before. They were terrified. They had no idea where to go or what to do.

The men who were already stationed on the airfield ran to push the newcomers into the defensive trenches, protecting them with their own bodies. No one was hurt; but the terrible reality of Stalingrad was a shock after looking forward to this moment for so long.

Arkady Kovacevich, a squadron commander for the 437th Regiment, was not happy when he was told he had to include four young women in his group of elite combat fighters.

"Whyever me? Why me?" he complained.

The division commander told him, "Understand this very clearly: you will lay your head on the block for the safety of these girls."

Arkady answered, "Cut my head off right now—just take the girls away from me!"

The 437th Regiment was stationed near Stalingrad in a plain

surrounded by watermelon fields. A camel named Pashka carried water to the base from the Volga River. Lilya, Katya, Raisa, and Mariya had to adapt quickly to their new surroundings, and they also had to prove that they were capable of flying with the men of the 437th.

The regimental commander arranged a mock dogfight, an air battle that would take place between the new pilots and the veterans—two men against two women. The men were flying complicated Lavochkin-5 (La-5) fighter aircraft, and they thought the Yak-1s that the young women had arrived in were inferior and underpowered. They expected it would be an easy win.

Katya and Raisa took off determined to prove that, in the air at least, they were as good as any man.

Speeding after the other planes in the air, Raisa managed to chase close behind one of the men's La-5s, a successful attack position, even though she wasn't going to shoot at him. It was the first "victory" score of the contest, and the women had already pulled ahead.

But Raisa's triumph didn't last long, because at that moment actual Luftwaffe enemy fighter planes appeared in the air above the competition. Suddenly the danger became very real. The Germans had the advantage of height, and the four competing Soviet aircraft weren't prepared for battle. They had to fly away and land somewhere else—Raisa, Katya, and the others couldn't get past the Germans to land safely on their own field!

Mariya and Lilya watched it all from the ground. "These two girls proved that in their Yaks they could fight the men in the more sophisticated aircraft," Mariya said. "Everything depended on skill."

If everything depended on skill, Lilya Litvyak was as skilled a pilot as any man.

In September 1942, Lilya flew into battle for the first time as the wingman[16] for the commander of the 437th Regiment, supporting her leader in the air. When they spotted a group of German bombers, Lilya followed her leader straight into such a forceful attack that the Luftwaffe aircraft scattered. In the mayhem that followed, Lilya and the commander each blasted a German bomber out of the sky.

Before they'd even had a chance to return to the airfield, Lilya saw that Raisa Belyaeva was dogfighting with a Luftwaffe fighter plane. Raisa had run out of ammunition. Lilya flew to her rescue and damaged the enemy fighter so badly that the pilot had to abandon his plane in the air and take to his parachute.

---

16. In the language of aviation in English, there is no feminine form of the word "wingman" yet. Because it's used in the Soviet pilots' translated memoirs, it's being used in this book.

A HEROINE OUT OF THE SPOTLIGHT

A few female pilots were transferred into Marina Raskova's unit against their will. For example, Kseniia Sanchuk had been flying supply and medical missions on the front lines since the beginning of the war; she was insulted to be sent to Marina's new group for "training" purposes.

Some people, some women included, felt that women should not be segregated into separate regiments from the men. Valentina Grizodubova, who'd piloted the *Rodina* on its record-breaking flight, was one of these.

When the Great Patriotic War broke out in 1941, Valentina immediately found air work as a captain with the Moscow Special-Purpose Air Group. Through her connections in the Soviet government, she managed

Three days after her arrival at Stalingrad, Lilya Litvyak had become the first woman in the world to shoot down enemy combat aircraft on her own—not one, but two in the same flight.

The story goes that the German fighter pilot she'd shot down was captured on the ground. He turned out to be one of the Luftwaffe's most celebrated and deadly flying aces, and he wanted to meet the pilot who'd shot him down.

Lilya Litvyak was only too happy to oblige. When she stood before him, small and blond and pretty, less than a month past her twenty-first birthday, the German ace thought his Soviet captors must be making fun of him.

But using her hands as planes, Lilya was able to describe the maneuvering of their aerial dogfight blow by blow, and the German pilot had to admit that this novice fighter had defeated him. He was so impressed that

to get Stalin to approve her position as the commander of a new long-distance bombing regiment. In doing so, she became the only woman to lead an entirely male regiment for the USSR during the entire war.

The 101st Long Range Air Regiment, as well as bombing, helped bring supplies by air to the blockaded and starving city of Leningrad. Eventually they also made hazardous supply flights to the partisans, the guerrilla groups who were fighting against the Germans in the Bryansk Forest near the Russian border with Ukraine.

Valentina flew more than 1,850 of these missions, and evacuated around 2,500 orphaned children and wounded partisan fighters. She flew more missions during the war than most male commanders.

he tried to give her his wristwatch, but she disdainfully refused it!

Confident and cocky as always, Lilya wrote to her mother: "The Germans don't fly here. The girls say, 'they are afraid of us.'"

At last Lilya was getting a chance to quench her thirst for battle.

TROUBLE IN THE 586th

Back in Anisovka, the fighters of the 586th weren't feeling as satisfied as Lilya about their combat flights. They wanted to use their dangerous solo Yak fighters for something more obviously heroic than defense.

The male pilots fighting on the Stalingrad Front were exhausted and were running out of planes—but of course the Soviet newspapers reported thrilling patriotic stories about the glamorous and deadly air battles of "Stalin's Falcons," and the women of the 586th felt that they were really missing out. While Stalingrad was burning, they were cooling their heels in the fragrant fields of the Russian steppes, surrounded by sagebrush and birdsong. It made the whole regiment cranky and frustrated.

Shockingly, the first death in the squadron was a suicide. One young pilot, Lina Smirnova, shot herself in the head after a rough landing in July. She'd been flying Raisa Belyaeva's plane before Raisa left the regiment, and Lina seems to have dissolved into a panic attack over how Raisa was going to react to finding that her Yak had a bent propeller. Lina's death must have had a terrible effect on the mental state of the other young women in the regiment—and was probably one of the reasons Raisa was transferred.

The 586th's first flight loss came about a month later. In September 1942, Zoya Pozhidayeva and Olga Golisheva took off from the airfield at Anisovka and lined up to fly side by side to protect a railway and bridge from an enemy attack. When they got back to their base, on the same day, they were assigned a training flight over the airfield.

And then Olga lost control of her plane. There might have been a mechanical failure in the aircraft—or it could have been an error Olga made herself, perhaps failing to pull out of a dive. But for some reason, Olga's aircraft suddenly went plummeting earthward.

Zoya, in the air with a full view of what was about to happen to Olga, called to her friend over the radio: "Jump!"

But Olga didn't respond, and she didn't use her parachute, and she never pulled out of the dive.

Her aircraft plowed into the ground—Olga was killed by the impact.

Zoya was heartbroken, and not just for her friend. She said, "I felt so terrible—it was not only my first loss but the first loss of the regiment."

At the same time that the 586th's fighter pilots were dealing with frustration and grief, they were also getting their first taste of battle, and some of them were having to do it in the dark.

On the night of September 24, 1942, a call came in to tell the 586th that a group of German bombers was heading toward Saratov. Yevgeniya "Zhenya" Prokhorova and Valeria "Lera" Khomyakova ran for their Yak-1s, scrambled in, and took off into the dark to chase away the enemy planes.

Nina Slovokhotova, the 586th's chief of chemical services, watched and waited tensely that night with the rest of the regiment. Sirens wailed and the antiaircraft guns rumbled like thunder. Nina saw the pale searchlights sweeping across the sky, hunting for the German aircraft. Finally one of the grasping fingers of light snatched at the tiny, distant silhouette of a plane. Within seconds, the other searchlights caught it in a web of light.

The women watching from the ground saw the gleaming red bursts of tracer bullets[17] across the dark sky. Then they heard a distant explosion.

A breathless messenger came running from headquarters, where Commander Tamara Kazarinova was giving radio directions to her pilots from the ground. The messenger told the excited regiment, "According to the Air-Warning Service posts, the enemy [bomber fell] to the south of the railroad bridge and blew itself up on its own bombs!"

When Zhenya landed, she was in tears and furious—her weapons had jammed and she hadn't been able to use them. That meant that it was definitely Lera who'd shot down the German bomber. Her mechanic, Yekaterina "Katya" Polunina, came running up to Lera and kissed her. Katya exclaimed, "You darling, you've just shot down a Heinkel!"

The next morning, Nina went by truck while Lera and Tamara flew overhead to check out the crash site. What they found there was sobering.

"Near the bridge, in the willow thicket on the river bank, lay the broken-up machine with a black spider of a swastika on its tail unit," said Nina. "Beside the dead German aircrew were their unopened parachutes." Not realizing how low they were in the dark, the Luftwaffe crew had jumped out of the plane seconds before it hit the ground, and were killed by the impact.

---

17. Tracer bullets are bullets that are on fire so that they are visible to the person doing the shooting. They are visible in daylight as well as at night.

As well as being Lera's very first nighttime combat, this was the first air victory for the 586th Fighter Aviation Regiment.

They were jubilant. Lera was given a pay bonus and a special victory breakfast of vodka and watermelon. The regiment even got a splashy full-page story in the youth magazine *Ogonyok* (Spark). Lera Khomyakova had become the first female pilot in history to shoot down an enemy aircraft at night.

But Lera was one of the pilots Tamara Kazarinova didn't get along with. Now she'd become a celebrity, the first woman ever to shoot down a bomber at night. Lera received a medal for her history-making victory, and she had to travel to Moscow to go to the awards ceremony. When she returned from the long trip, before she had a chance to rest, Tamara assigned her to night duty. Lera was supposed to fly a routine patrol, searching for enemy planes.

Lera managed to snatch a short nap on the ground while her mechanic, Katya, started the engine of her Yak-1 for her. When a messenger came to wake Lera and told her it was time to take off, she leaped into action. She raced for her plane, jumped into the cockpit, and took the controls.

But she didn't give herself enough time to adjust her eyes to the dark.

Lera's plane sped down the runway, which was purposely unlit so that German aircraft couldn't find it. She misjudged her takeoff. She turned too steeply as she was climbing, and instead of lifting off into the sky, her plane crashed a little way beyond the airfield, killing Lera. She wasn't found until the next morning.

As commander, Tamara Kazarinova was blamed for the chain of events that led to Lera's death.

Soon afterward, she was dismissed from her command.

Tamara had only been in charge of the 586th for six months when she was fired. It's not entirely clear why she left, though it may have been related to Lera's crash. Or it might have simply been that Tamara's leg injury was keeping her from flying with her squadron. There were also probably personal or political issues going on that we don't know about. It's even possible that some of the other pilots—including Lilya Litvyak, Katya Budanova, and Raisa Belyaeva—may have gone behind Tamara's back to ask for a new commander.

For a few days, she was replaced with a temporary commander. Then, either because someone felt the 586th needed a firmer hand or simply because there weren't any qualified women available for the job, the command of the women's 586th Fighter Aviation Regiment was assigned to a man, Major Aleksandr Gridnev.

Aleksandr Gridnev had troubles of his own. He'd been arrested earlier that year while in charge of another air force regiment, for endangering the life of a top government official by failing to fly with him through a dust storm. Aleksandr Gridnev was never brought to trial, but throughout the war and for years afterward he had to worry that he might be. He may have thought that being put in charge of a women's flight regiment was his punishment.

When Aleksandr Gridnev showed up as the new commander of the 586th on October 14, 1942, the rookie fighter pilots were still frustrated at being "stuck at Anisovka." Aleksandr suggested that he run a training program for them along with their flight duties that fall. Once he was satisfied that they were ready for it, they would be sent to the front.

The young pilots were thrilled by this response and asked Aleksandr how long he'd be staying with their regiment.

"Forever," he told them.

• • •

COMMANDER ALEKSANDR GRIDNEV WITH (FROM LEFT) 586TH FIGHTER AVIATION
REGIMENT PILOTS KLAVDIYA PANKRATOVA, ZINAIDA SALOMATINA, MARIYA KUZNETSOVA,
OLGA YAMSHCHIKOVA, ANYA DEMCHENKO, AND ZOYA POZHIDAYEVA

Aleksandr Gridnev took his role as commander of the 586th very seriously.
As time passed, the women of the regiment grew to like him so much they
began affectionately to call him Batya—"Dad." It was a contrast with how
they'd felt about their previous commander.

In the fall of 1942, the two squadrons of the 586th were joined by a
third squadron of male pilots, along with their ground crew. These men
flew and fought beside the women of the 586th as their equals, but there
isn't much on record about them. According to Katya Polunina, the senior
mechanic who became the regiment's historian, the women often flew in
pairs with a male pilot because the men had more experience.

Aleksandr Gridnev got to work right away on the training program
he'd promised. In the fall of 1942 the 586th practiced formation flying,
navigation, target practice, and night flying using radar. Even while they
were training, they were on alert in case of nighttime attacks by the enemy.

A couple months after Aleksandr Gridnev took over, half of the pilots
who'd transferred under Tamara Kazarinova's command came back.

The 586th Fighter Aviation Regiment was back on its feet.

⤕· 20 ·⤔

"LIFE IS LIFE"

Even at war, people need food. They need a place to sleep. They need water and soap to wash with every now and then, or else they have to struggle with parasites and diseases. They need clothes, especially in winter. Women need extra underwear when they get their period. All these things need to be produced: crops have to be grown and distributed, soap must get boiled, cloth has to be woven. In wartime, this has to happen at the same time as factories produce aircraft and tanks and trucks, while other factories refine the fuel to keep those vehicles moving on the ground and in the air.

The necessities of daily living were often hard to come by in the Soviet Union under Stalin's iron grip in the 1930s, and they were even harder to come by after the Soviet Union went to war with Germany. Leningrad, Russia's old capital, was under attack and had been blockaded by the German army since September 8, 1941. It would stay that way until January 27, 1944, nearly two and a half years later. It was almost impossible to get supplies into the city. In the fall of 1942, people in Leningrad had nothing left to eat but wallpaper paste and broth made of boiled leather. Nearly a million of the city's inhabitants would starve to death before the war was over.

The suffering in Leningrad was extreme, but no one in the USSR was living in luxury. Food was scarce; in a nation at war, much of it occupied by enemy troops, it was difficult to grow and gather crops. When the harvest was in, goods were hard to transport. Everyone's food was rationed. Those serving in the military were given rations according to a strict order of rank and importance.

Pilots were at the top of that ranking system. Zinaida Butkaryova, the parachute packer, did her best to be polite when she summed up the difference between the ground and aircrew of the 586th Regiment: "Our ration was a soldier's, and the pilots had their own rations." Pilots got butter and cheese with their bread—mechanics did not, and had to survive on a steady diet of porridge (they called it "blondie"). If they were stationed near a village, they could exchange soldier's luxuries such as tobacco, cigarettes, and sugar for milk and eggs. But they couldn't count on it. Once, when the German forces cut off their supplies for several days, the ground crew of the 586th ate nothing but herring.

The pilots were supposed to get better rations than the ground crew, but they didn't always eat well, either. Even Aleksandr Gridnev, the 586th's commander, looked forward to an unexpected treat from the supply chain every now and then: "When they sent us the American food, it was a feast—canned meat, dried eggs, canned milk." Even that must have been delicious when they'd eaten nothing but herring for three days!

Throughout the war, ground personnel lived in underground dugouts they built themselves, no more than trenches covered with logs and soil—or even just with canvas. It could get so cold in these dugouts that sometimes your hair would freeze to the wooden planks of your bunk while you were sleeping. The only heat came from a *pechka*, a small woodstove, or a *burzhuika*, a fireplace made from an oil drum. The word *burzhuika* comes from the same word as *bourgeoisie*—the middle class who liked luxury. A good fireplace that actually gave off heat was a luxury!

Water trickled into the dugouts when it rained. Sometimes everybody's pillows, sheets, and mattresses would be soaked; the person who slept nearest the entrance was in charge of checking how deep the water was getting while the other women rested. "When . . . there was so much water in the trench that everything was floating, we would jump up and go out in our underwear to ask the men on the truck with a pumping machine to come and pump out the water so we could go back to sleep," said Valentina Kovalyova, a mechanic for the 586th.

There was never enough soap, and sometimes not even enough water. In the 588th, the women might have to wash with water from puddles or melted snow. About once a week a truck would turn up for the 587th with a box of cold water on it for them to bathe in. And in the 586th, every couple of weeks the regiment could get a truck ride to the nearest town so they could bathe in a public bathhouse, common throughout the Soviet Union. But the women had to share the bathhouse with the men of their regiment, so they hung a sheet between them for a little privacy!

Yelena Kulkova-Malutina, who became a Pe-2 pilot for the 587th Bomber Aviation Regiment, ran into a different kind of problem. She spent the first part of the war training male pilots—out of eighteen instructors, she was the only woman. "It was in an open airfield, and there was no place for a ladies' room," she said. "Everything was open, to find a place I had to go behind a bush, where I could be seen by everyone, and there were only men. I was so shy and embarrassed that I didn't even have a gulp of water in order not to go to the ladies' room behind a bush. And the cadets insisted on asking our commander why I didn't ever have breakfast!"

Lack of soap and water and toilet facilities weren't the only problems that the Soviet soldiers faced in terms of hygiene. The steppes, the flat grassland of southeastern Europe, crawled with rats and mice. When the rodents migrated, they could stop trains—the wheels would get jammed with their crushed bodies. In November 1942, one fighter pilot of the 586th found mice in the cockpit of her Yak-1 while she was flying. Zhenya Prokhorova had taken off one night for a training flight when Commander Aleksandr Gridnev noticed that she was flying erratically. Aleksandr assumed there was something wrong with Zhenya's aircraft and called out the emergency vehicles. When she landed, leaped out of the cockpit, and ran, people thought her plane was about to explode.

In fact some mice had been nesting in the plane and had fallen onto Zhenya's head while she was flying. She'd been a member of the state aerobatic team before the war, but she'd never had to deal with rodents landing on her head in flight before!

In our modern civilizations, we don't really think of bathing with soap and water as being gendered. We have similar expectations for what counts as cleanliness in men and women alike. But being afraid of mice is a gendered expectation in many people's minds. It would probably surprise us more, and be an even funnier story, if the mice in the cockpit had upset Aleksandr Gridnev rather than Zhenya Prokhorova.

And this highlights a theme that runs through almost every Soviet female soldier's story of the Great Patriotic War: War is gendered, and it is not feminine. No matter how valiantly a woman proves herself in battle, her experience of war will always differ from a man's experience, *because* she is a woman. Dressing in men's clothes and using the same equipment as men does not turn a woman into a man.

The young women of the Soviet Union who fought in World War II clung to their feminine identity with consistent determination, and if one single item could represent this individual battle, it's underwear.

Soviet stores had never sold much in the way of pretty underwear, and most Soviet women at the time made their own. In wartime, being forced to wear men's underwear drove them crazy. It didn't fit, it was ugly and uncomfortable, and they all hated it. Soviet women soldiers waged a private battle against men's underwear the whole time they were fighting their invading enemy, the German army.

Maybe your mother could send you some panties. If you were lucky enough to get hold of a piece of German parachute silk, you could transform it into panties yourself. Then you could trade your sturdy military men's underwear with local people in exchange for potatoes or milk. If you got caught, you'd end up having to spend a few days in the guardhouse. But since your "guards" were friends from your own regiment, you could usually get someone to sneak a book into your cell.

Two armorers from the 588th Regiment were sentenced to ten years in prison because they'd taken little parachutes off unused flares and made silk panties out of them. Their sentences were put off so they could continue to fight, and eventually they were both retrained as navigators. One of the women was killed in action—but the other had a row of medals by the end of the war. She didn't have to go to jail over silk panties after all.

It might seem silly and insignificant to us now, but the silk panties *mattered*. Hanging on to femininity was a concrete way to express your womanhood. It was especially important when other physical markers disappeared—your long hair, dresses and shoes that fit properly, limited access to makeup and soap. Under so much physical stress, many women stopped having their periods throughout the war, which meant that even their bodies didn't seem to be functioning like women's bodies anymore. This wasn't just confusing and upsetting—it could be frightening, too. These young people didn't have a women's health clinic they could consult. They didn't know what might be causing this change. But suddenly they had to live with the possibility that they might not ever be able to have children.

Making strong statements about their womanhood helped them to cope with these issues.

"We wanted to make ourselves look pretty and attractive and womanlike, in spite of the uniform," said Nina Shebalina, a mechanic in the 586th Regiment.

"We were sick and tired of the men's boots, and once I decided to put on these slippers I knitted for myself," said Mariya Kaloshina, an armorer for the 587th. "From other people's point of view, it was ridiculous when I appeared in my slippers in uniform!" Another young woman in the 587th, who'd been a hairdresser before the war, used a metal rod for cleaning guns as a curling iron. One pilot in the 586th got in trouble for keeping perfume in the cockpit of her fighter plane.

Don't forget: the pressure to conform was a matter of life and death in Stalin's time. Nobody openly challenged gender boundaries—in spite of the wartime crew cuts and men's underwear. The young women of Marina Raskova's regiments treasured the thought of finishing the war and living ordinary lives, drawing heavily on Marina's model of perfection as a soldier, a woman, and a mother.

"We dreamed of our grooms, marriages, children, and a future happy, peaceful life," said 588th pilot Yevgeniya Zhigulenko. She even claimed that "after a night of combat we never forgot to curl our hair"! Yevgeniya felt that keeping herself pretty was good not just for her own morale; it was also encouraging to anyone she met.

While they were in training at Engels, Marina Raskova assured them, "After the war you'll wear white dresses and pretty shoes, and we'll have a big party. Don't worry; we're going to win the war."

But some of the young women felt it was unpatriotic to fuss over their appearance during wartime. Galya Dokutovich, the navigator who'd been run over, thought that people who wore makeup and daydreamed about boys were good for nothing but a "bride's fair." One of the mechanics in the 588th told aircrew who wore makeup while on missions, "You've gone out of your minds!" When an important pair of major generals came to inspect the 588th, one of them gave a speech and told the regiment that they were "the most beautiful girls in the world." He added, though, according to Zhenya Rudneva, that "beauty lies not in lipstick or a manicure, not in clothes or a hairdo, but in what we actually do." Zhenya told her parents, "And he is right."

Lilya Litvyak's friend Katya Budanova was Lilya's polar opposite as far as her appearance was concerned. Katya kept her hair short. She even went so far as to use a male name, Volodka, as her nickname in the 437th Regiment, where most of the other pilots were male. If the regiment held a dance and local girls got invited, Katya would introduce herself as Volodka and get them to dance with her. On one occasion, she walked one of these girls home—but made an escape when, still thinking Katya was a boy, the girl tried to kiss her.

When boyish Katya went to visit her sister in Moscow, she dressed in a stylish woman's coat and hat. We can't assume anything about Katya's sexuality from her behavior, or anybody's. Soviet culture at the time essentially demanded everyone to accept heterosexuality as the norm. None of these women talk about any other kind of romance.

But it's tempting to read between the lines and wonder if some of their intense friendships were more than just friendships. Zhenya Rudneva makes it clear in her diary entries about her dearest friends that she loved them deeply and passionately. She didn't keep it secret, either, and it made some of them uncomfortable—for example, when she gave Galya Dokutovich a story she'd written about two girlfriends with a deep love for each other, one of whom she'd named "Galya."

No one seems to question the urge of these women to form intense friendships, though, or to explore more deeply what those friendships might mean. To complicate our understanding even more, Zhenya was also passionately in love with a young man in a tank crew named Ivan Slavik, with whom she exchanged letters more than once a week—and whom she kissed and cuddled on the rare occasions that they met.

From our much more broadminded twenty-first-century North American viewpoint, it's important to remember that identifying yourself as male or female doesn't necessarily have anything to do with your sexual orientation. These women were all doing what's considered to be a man's job and were forced to dress and behave like men. Regardless of their sexuality, most of them liked to remind themselves that, yes, they still identified as women.

There was one pretty, feminine thing available for free throughout the war—flowers.

Lilya Litvyak wasn't the only one who flew combat missions with a small bouquet stuck on her control panel—Yevgeniya Zhigulenko liked to have a bunch of lilies of the valley in her Po-2 when she was dropping bombs.

Even in winter when nothing was blooming, people made flowers out of gauze or newspaper or hung up pictures of them.

PILOTS OF THE 586TH FIGHTER AVIATION REGIMENT READING, WRITING, AND EMBROIDERING—IN A ROOM FULL OF FLOWERS

When flowers were in bloom, the women of Raskova's regiments—along with the other women soldiers of the USSR—filled their living spaces with fragrant blossoms. Tulips, dandelions, daisies, and poppies were favorites as they came into season; roses were prized. When women shared an airfield with male pilots, they put bunches of flowers on the wings of their own planes to mark them.

They did it out of pride, too. Those flowers on the wings of an aircraft at rest boasted: *I am a woman and I am a combat pilot.*

At about this time in the war, the female fighter pilots of the 586th found another visual way to take pride in their role: they began to mark their dangerous Yak fighter planes with a white stripe, which was easy to spot even when they were aloft. Now when they teamed up with other Soviet pilots in the air, everyone would know there were women flying with them. Lilya Litvyak got her ground crew to paint something even more personal on her Yak: a white lily, of course.

Creative outlets were another way to express yourself as a woman. The creative urge doesn't go away just because you're at war; we need to use our imagination almost as desperately as we need to eat. Making things seems to satisfy some deep inner need for us. One pilot who joined the 587th as a reinforcement, Antonina Bondareva, worked on a piece of knitting in between flights. She kept it in her plane—she'd take it out and knit until she was given a combat assignment and then she'd tuck it behind her parachute.

Needlework was all the rage among Marina Raskova's aviators—something that you could scrounge the materials for. The armorers of the 587th made pillows out of their foot cloths and decorated them with planes. "Everybody embroidered the Pe-2 on their pillows," said Yekaterina Chujkova. In the 588th, people embroidered their foot cloths with flowers—using blue thread pulled out of their regulation men's underwear again! One day when Irina Rakobolskaya came into a flooded dugout to inspect it, she found someone standing on a table to get closer to the light, calmly embroidering while water streamed down the walls around her.

Music, song, poetry, and literature also raised everybody's spirits—and could be used to express determination and to show patriotism. Most of the pilots and technicians of Raskova's regiments were educated at least to high school level, and many of them had some university education as well. They read, they wrote—and published—poetry, they put on shows, and they produced newsletters. The 588th produced their own literary magazine, and the infinitely creative navigator Zhenya Rudneva sometimes gathered everyone around her at the airfield while she recited fairy tales. All the women liked to keep track of what the other aviation regiments were doing, so they wrote letters to friends they'd made while they were training at Engels.

Music, especially singing, was deeply important to them all. One Po-2 pilot for the 588th, Klava Serebryakova, always had her mandolin waiting for her back on the ground. The 586th held talent shows. Their mechanics took a record player with them as they moved from base to base; one of them, Sonya Tishurova, organized a group who performed national dances from different states in the USSR. When an airwoman for the 587th gave a concert for her companions, her comrades made her a white silk dress out of parachute fabric to wear while she sang.

Everybody *loved* to sing. The armorers for the 587th sang as they fixed bombs to aircraft. Nina Yermakova, an armorer in the 586th, got nicknamed the "USSR Honorable Singer" by her regiment. She said, "Lieutenant Colonel Aleksandr Gridnev would call out, 'Yermakova, sing out!' and I would start the song, and then the rest of the regiment would join me."

"You heard them singing all over the place: in the dugouts, on the airfield, in aircraft, and in the evening during amateur talent performances," said Lina Yeliseyeva, the deputy commander for political affairs for the 587th Regiment. The 587th performed in hospitals. They made up their own songs as well as poems that others set to music. Once, on a day when they didn't have to fly, they helped local peasants to harvest a field full of rye. At the end of the day they sang together as they marched back to the airfield.

"When weather caused the cancellation of a mission, everyone stayed at the airfield and danced," said Irina Rakobolskaya. "It would never come into any man's head to do that, while waiting for permission to fly."

WOMEN OF THE 588TH NIGHT BOMBER AVIATION REGIMENT PERFORMING AN IMPROMPTU FOLK DANCE BETWEEN MISSIONS

• • •

And no matter where they were, everyone always found ways to try to make life feel more ordinary. The pilots and navigators of the 587th kept a long-running volleyball competition going whenever they got a free moment, with the two flight squadrons making up their opposing teams. No matter how harsh their living conditions, no matter how hungry they were, the young women of Raskova's regiments were living life to the fullest.

In November 1942, the commander of the Southern Front turned up to present thirty-two members of the 588th with commemorative watches as a reward for their service, and medals to ten others. When he told the regiment about the first Soviet victories at Stalingrad, the young women all started cheering and clapping.

The 588th's chief navigator, Zhenya Rudneva, wrote in her diary on December 2, 1942, "This is silly, a complete paradox: after all, the war is going on, there is so much horror and spilled blood all around, yet I am convinced that for me this is the best time of my life."

And Galya Dokutovich, the navigator who'd been run over while lying on a landing strip in the dark, came back to the 588th late in 1942. She was supposed to be on sick leave—she hadn't fully recovered. But she didn't want anyone to know that. She wanted to fly. On December 20 she wrote in her diary, "I am back in my regiment. I doubt whether it would be possible to get a better reception anywhere else. It was like going home to my own family! I hid the leave authorization in one of my pockets. I'll rest and get better after the war."

She was going to have her work cut out for her, because now the Soviets were on the offensive again.

WINTER COMES EARLY

By December 1942, as another harsh Russian winter began to settle in, the Soviets managed to get the German army surrounded at Stalingrad. Then they began to starve them. Now the Germans could only get supplies

FROM LEFT, NATASHA MEKLIN, RAISA ARONOVA, AND KATYA RYABOVA OF THE 588TH NIGHT BOMBER AVIATION REGIMENT WEARING WINTER FLIGHT GEAR

by air, and the Soviets shot down their lumbering transport planes the second they got anywhere near their troops.

The Russian winter might stop the Germans, but it wasn't going to stop the women of Raskova's regiments.

Everyone must have been dreading the onset of another harsh winter—especially now that Marina's aviators had to work to keep the planes ready for combat every day. But aircrew and ground crew all *loved* their planes, and never resented the work it took to keep them in the air.

"When our crews were flying combat missions near our airdrome, we mechanics could recognize the sound of our guns and machine guns as a mother can tell the voice of her child," said Galina Drobovich, the chief aircraft mechanic for the 586th Regiment, talking about the fast and dangerous Yak fighters. Even though their pilots flew solo, the ground crew thought of the Yaks as their planes too. "We worried until our planes returned."

Nina Shebalina, Commander Aleksandr Gridnev's mechanic, was passionate about "her" plane. "During the war my attitude toward my aircraft was really like it was a living creature, my baby. I cared for it every day and night, and I had to go through lots of tears when I lost my plane. I saw it off and said goodbye to it when they went on a combat mission, and then I was impatiently awaiting their return. If it didn't come back it was a misery. . . . We all knew our own aircraft: you didn't have to see it, you just heard it and you knew."

An aircraft couldn't easily be replaced. When a pilot found herself in the sky in a machine that was damaged or out of fuel, rather than parachute to safety she'd do her best to glide back to earth so the plane could be landed in one piece.

Katya Polunina, the 586th's senior mechanic, and her team were soon forced to improvise once the harsh conditions of winter set in.

"There was no water, so we boiled snow; there was no antifreeze for the planes, so we drained [the radiators] in winter after each mission and drained the oil and heated it in barrels with a stove underneath," Katya said. "The barrels were on skis like a sleigh, to take to the planes."

When a plane landed away from the airfield after being shot down or running out of fuel in combat, the mechanics would tow the oil barrels to the downed plane themselves, sometimes hiking many kilometers as they dragged the oil through the snow.

But as the 586th's first winter of defensive combat began to bite down in November 1942, the young aircraft mechanics didn't have any of this rehearsed to a fine art.

How's this for a relaxing night: At three a.m. on November 7, 1942, Sofya Osipova and the rest of her group got woken up by their chief mechanic. A severe cold snap was in danger of turning the water in the planes' radiators to solid ice, which would break the radiators. In the middle of the night, Sofya and the others stumbled out of bed and began to defrost the planes by spraying them with hot water from a tank truck. They had to stand on the planes' wings to do it.

"We feel the water taps in the dark. They are covered with a thin coating of ice, so it is difficult to open them," Sofya said. "As we are moving step by step . . . along an icy crust, the wind keeps knocking us off the wings. . . . The wind grabs the heavy, iced[-]over [radiator] covers out of our hands. You threw one end upward and the other one flew back with the wind, knocking you off your feet. Three times I was knocked down from the wing to the ground."

The streaming hot water soaked everyone to the skin, and as soon as the water cooled down, everybody was wet and freezing. Sofya's hand froze to the propeller blade of the plane she was working on. By dawn, people's faces were covered with white spots of frostbite and their hands were bleeding.

But in the morning when the pilots came running out to their aircraft, none of the planes had been damaged by the sharp cold. The radiators had all been refilled and the engines were running smoothly and were ready for the next defensive flight mission.

• • •

The 586th stayed based in Anisovka, protecting Saratov, until February 1943. Not surprisingly, the vacation cabins the pilots had been living in all summer turned out to be drafty and freezing cold in the winter. The wooden walls weren't insulated. The only heat source was a brick stove that didn't warm up anything more than three steps away. In some of the thin-walled houses, it was so cold that water could freeze in a bucket before you'd finished washing. Or, if you tried to clean the floor, it would only dry near the fire—the rest of the floor became an icy skating rink. Wet clothes froze solid when you tried to dry them anywhere but right next to the fireplace—but when you dried them there, they sometimes ended up burned.

In the harsh Russian winter, sometimes the pilots moved into dugouts, because it was warmer underground!

The cold of the Russian winter was more than an endurance test. Sometimes it could be deadly.

On December 3, 1942, three pilots from the 586th took off in their solo Yak fighters into a snowstorm on a mission to escort a VIP away from the Stalingrad Front. The plane they were escorting, a transport aircraft with good navigation equipment, landed safely; but the three Yaks ended up crash-landing in the snow.

Zhenya Prokhorova, the aerobatic pilot who'd discovered the mice in her cockpit, was flying one of these planes. Blinded by dense snow and freezing fog, Zhenya wasn't able to see where she was landing, and one of her wings hit the ground. Her plane flipped and she was trapped in the dark and the cold.

The commander at the airfield where this happened, dealing with three crashed planes in a snowstorm, didn't send anyone out to check

Zhenya's aircraft until the next morning. There, the local ground crew discovered Zhenya's body trapped in her Yak. She didn't seem to have any injury at all. But she'd frozen to death overnight.

Another Russian winter was closing in, and it hadn't finished taking its toll.

MARINA IN THE WIND

For six months, the 586th Regiment had been defending strategic positions in their dangerous solo Yak fighters and the 588th Regiment had been harassing German troops with bombs dropped from their flimsy Po-2s. But because it had taken so long to deliver and master the powerful Pe-2 dive-bomber aircraft with its aircrew of three, the 587th Bomber Aviation Regiment still wasn't flying combat missions. This was the unit that Marina Raskova would be commanding herself—she, too, had had to learn to fly the complex Pe-2 before she could lead her flight crews into battle.

In December 1942, the women of the 587th finally completed their grueling training course and were assigned to fight on the Don Front, one of the areas of battle aggressively defending Stalingrad. Their mission was to bomb the German troops by day.

But winter had set in, and they struggled to get to their new base. First they had to wait for the weather to clear before they could leave Engels. Masha Dolina, who'd been flying in a men's regiment since the beginning of the war and had recently been recruited by Marina for the 587th because she was such an experienced combat pilot, had to cope with an engine failure and got separated from the others.

Then everybody got snowed in when they stopped to refuel—they had to dig the planes out and drain their radiators before they set off again. But they only had enough hot water for one squadron to leave. Marina stayed behind with the other squadron, entertaining them by playing the village school piano and reading them poetry.

By the time the weather cleared about a week later in mid-December, Marina got called away to Moscow—so her aviators had to continue without her. But two of the Pe-2s had engine trouble and stopped for repairs along the way. At the end of December, Marina decided to meet the stragglers and fly with them to the Don Front herself.

Again, dreadful weather set in. Yet again, the aviators had to land short of their new base. Their little group of three pilots, three navigators, three gunners, and one mechanic celebrated the new year in a village called Lopatino while they waited for the snow and wind to die down.

Marina was growing impatient and was anxious about getting to her regiment, so soon to be assigned to combat and still without their commander. There was a great deal of pressure on her, after more than a year of preparation, to finally prove herself as a woman who could lead a combat regiment.

At last, on January 4, 1943, they had a chance to try again. There was a break in the weather, and though it wasn't likely to last, Marina was a confident navigator and knew that she'd found her way through bad weather before. She'd have her own highly experienced chief navigator, Kirill Khil, along with her for support. She decided to risk it.

Marina led the way, taking off in a Pe-2 with three men: her gunner, Nikolai Erofeev; one of the mechanics, Vladimir Kruglov; and Kirill.

Determined that this time she was going to make it to their new base at last, Marina gave orders to the other two Pe-2 pilots, Galina Tenuyeva and Gubina Ljubov, not to break formation unless they had an engine failure.

But clouds closed in on them. Galina, flying after Marina, could hardly see the wings of her own aircraft—let alone the two other planes in the formation. Before long, the three Pe-2 pilots were flying blindly alone in deadly fog, hoping only that they could find a place to land.

Galina said, "I think Raskova . . . was looking for a place to land and trying to recognize the landscape. We would go into clouds and out, and in and out of them, and when we saw she was maneuvering, we dropped back a little in our formation and lost Raskova's aircraft in the clouds."

Galina's navigator gave a yell as she finally saw something—the ground right in front of them. Then their plane slammed into the earth on its belly. Galina's face smashed into the controls, and her navigator catapulted past her into the instrument panel.

But they both survived the landing.

Gubina, the other pilot in the formation, was also struggling to see where she was. By chance, she saw a dark patch looming in the murk ahead of them, and Gubina pulled up the nose of her plane to avoid hitting it. Then her plane, too, struck the ground on its belly. The thing she'd tried to avoid turned out to be a bush—a bush that saved her life and those of her crew. If she hadn't raised the plane's nose at the last second, she'd have flown straight into the ground.

All three planes crashed that day—including Marina Raskova's.

Marina's plane came down near Saratov, painfully close to the familiar airfield at Engels, just out of reach and invisible in the storm. Even with two experienced navigators on board, they couldn't find a place to land.

Marina flew blindly into the side of the Volga River's high bank. As the plane hit the ground, she was thrown forward against the gunsight. In the impact, the metal back of the pilot's seat beheaded her navigator, Kirill, who'd been standing behind her.

Nikolai and Vladimir survived the crash but froze to death before anyone was able to find them.

And Marina's head was split in two by the impact with the gunsight. She was killed instantly.

Why did Marina press on that day?

It may have been against her own better judgment. She may have been overthinking her role as commander of the not-yet-in-combat 587th Regiment, the last of her regiments to go to war. She may have been anxious to perform bravely and to prove herself both to her aviators and to her nation.

She may have been thinking of Stalin's Order 227. She may have been thinking of her own relationship with Josef Stalin, whatever it was, and how Order 227's command, "Not one step back," made it an act of treason to retreat in the face of danger.

Galina noticed that they flew over three airfields they could have landed at before the flight ended in disaster. She said, "[Marina Raskova] did not use the good judgment to land while the weather conditions were good enough to do it. She was anxious about her regiment and wanted to get there."

Marina had made the fatal mistake of continuing to fly into bad weather.

Everyone who had trained in the 122nd Air Group was devastated by the news.

Zoya Pozhidayeva and other pilots in her squadron of the 586th Fighter

Aviation Regiment were at an unfamiliar airfield when they heard. They were still stuck at the base where Zhenya Prokhorova froze to death after her crash in thick fog. How heartbreaking, in addition to Zhenya, to learn now of the death of their beloved Marina Raskova!

Zhenya Rudneva, navigator and storyteller, recorded in her diary the moment that the 588th Night Bomber Aviation Regiment found out:

"In the morning, when the squadrons formed up, we heard the terrible news. Rakobolskaya came out and said: 'Raskova is dead.' We all let out a sigh; all stood at attention and silently bared our heads. My mind was in a turmoil. I told myself mentally: 'It must have been a printing error; this couldn't have happened.' Our Major Raskova! Even now, when I think of it, I still can't believe it."

Masha Dolina, who'd been slowly struggling between snowstorms to make her own way to the 587th's new air base with her navigator and gunner, had stopped to refuel. That was when she heard the news. One of the local pilots told her that her commander had been killed, and she reacted with complete disbelief. "That's not something you should joke about!" she yelled. By the time someone showed her the newspaper announcement, she was already shaking.

Like Masha, most of the aviators of the 587th Regiment didn't find out about Marina's death until January 9, five days after the crash. "Our commissar gathered us together in a big dugout and told us what had happened," said the regimental navigator, Valya Kravchenko—the one who'd last year scrounged cabbages on the train ride to Engels. "We just cried."

Marina Raskova was given the Soviet Union's first state funeral of the war, with Moscow city and Soviet state officials in attendance, a thundering salute of guns, and an air force flyover. As a final honor, Marina's ashes were placed in the Kremlin wall next to Polina Osipenko's, the woman who'd been Valentina Grizodubova's copilot on the *Rodina* flight.

The news of Marina's death was reported throughout the nation and around the world. Many American newspapers carried the story, praising the brave commanding woman who'd flown for the Soviet Union, allied with the United States against the Nazis. Marina was such an international celebrity that her obituary and photograph even made front-page news in some American papers.

The grieving aviators of the 587th had lost their commander just as they were about to receive their first combat assignments.

And the question on everyone's mind was "What will now happen to our regiment?"

The women were worried that without Marina's driving force behind them, they would be disbanded. The war had already been going on for a year and a half while they were training—they were supposed to be the Soviet Union's only women's dive-bombing regiment, and they still hadn't dropped a single bomb. Maybe their planes would be taken away to beef up an existing men's regiment, and they'd be back to square one looking for a way to volunteer.

But that didn't happen. Zhenya Timofeyeva, the deputy commander of the 587th, was out in the subzero wind clearing snow from the Pe-2s when she was called back to her new and unfamiliar headquarters to receive a transmitted message.

An officer told her she'd been temporarily put in charge of the regiment. Now she was going to have to lead them in their first bombing mission.

Zhenya was stunned and reluctant—but she knew all too well that an order was an order. She was also worried that if she *did* refuse, her superiors would be encouraged to close down the 587th as a regiment.

She told the officer, "Yes, Sir! Am taking over the Regiment!"

. . .

The 587th now shared an airfield with the 10th Leningrad Bomber Aviation Regiment. The men of the 10th Leningrad turned out to be friendly and sympathetic, and were assigned to help train the 587th in battle techniques in their challenging, powerful Pe-2 dive-bombers. The two regiments flew together until the end of the war, starting with the 587th's very first combat mission on January 28, 1943. That day, Zhenya Timofeyeva and her navigator, Valya Kravchenko, flew in formation along with another 587th Pe-2 and seven Pe-2s from the 10th Leningrad. They were supposed to bomb enemy defenses northeast of Stalingrad, near an important tractor factory.

"When we took off at dawn, a frosty mist shrouded the ground. Below, settlements flashed and trucks moved along roads," said Zhenya. "Finally, the ruins of Stalingrad appeared—a dark line of demolished buildings stretching endlessly along the Volga. Then came the first explosions of antiaircraft artillery shells."

The German troops had started firing at the Soviet planes overhead.

When the leading plane suddenly made a steep descent, Zhenya swooped after him. The other pilot's sharp thinking probably stopped the exploding German shells from hitting Zhenya's plane.

Zhenya and Valya watched to see when their leader's bomb bay doors opened, to give them a clue when to drop their own bombs.

Back at their base, during the report they had to make about how the mission went, they joked with the 10th Leningrad pilots, calling them "brothers" or "old men."

Zhenya spoke of them warmly. "Together we fought, together rejoiced in each other's successes, and together mourned our fallen comrades."

On January 30, only three weeks after they learned of Marina Raskova's death, the 587th flew an independent combat mission for the first time. But they were ready for it. Beneath them, the blackened ruins of Stalingrad were softened by a fresh fall of snow, and around them the Soviet air and ground forces were flattening the last German troops outside the city.

The German commander surrendered on January 31—despite orders cabled from Hitler to fight to the death. On February 2, 1943, the six-month-long battle for the city of Stalingrad came to an end. The USSR had scored its first real triumph of the war—and Hitler had received his first serious defeat.

The German forces hadn't been halted in their furious bid for military supremacy over the USSR, but the front was no longer advancing. At last, the spirits of the Soviet people began to lift a little.

But Hitler wasn't anywhere near done with them. He had his generals get to work on a springtime plan for crushing the Red Army near the city of Kursk, and hoped to get to Moscow that way. The new plan had a new name: Operation Citadel.

The fight to defend the Motherland was far from finished.

VALENTIN MARKOV

The new quarters for the flight crews of the 587th were in a village about three kilometers (two miles) away from their base. Each morning they'd trek to the airfield with one woman breaking snow up to her waist for the rest of the line.

At the snow-covered airfield were three dugouts, a runway, and a taxiway. Here, the 587th took off for their initial aggressive combat missions in their powerful Pe-2 dive-bombers; back on the ground, every aircrew of three and all the rest of the regiment waited anxiously to find out who their new commander would be.

They were still in mourning for their beloved Marina. "We liked her very much," Katya Fedotova said. Katya was one of the four flying friends whom Marina had assigned so they could stay together. "Liked her as our commander, older friend, and a person. And suddenly she was gone. We cried unashamedly. We were so anxious to know who [was] going to replace her!"

Zhenya Timofeyeva, who'd taken temporary command of the 587th Regiment on January 15, turned it over to its new commander on the last day of the Battle of Stalingrad, February 2, 1943.

His name was Valentin Markov.

At the age of thirty-three, Valentin was already an experienced combat pilot and commander. When he received his new assignment, he had just recovered from hospitalization after being injured in battle, and he wasn't happy when he learned that he'd be leading a women's regiment.

The women of the 587th were equally disgusted. Valya Kravchenko commented, "We women wouldn't even hear of a man coming to command our regiment!" and added, "Behind his back we called him 'bayonet.' He was so strict and straight."

There was apprehension and prejudice on both sides when Valentin Markov took up his new post. But the young women of the 587th and their new commander were going to surprise each other.

When Valentin and his navigator, Nikolai Nikitin, first arrived at the 587th's base near Stalingrad, they watched the Pe-2s dive-bombers coming and going from the frozen airfield. Valentin had to admit that the women pilots could handle their planes.

However, when he inspected the aircraft up close, he wasn't impressed with the grease on some of the machine guns. He gave one of the armorers a lecture about the importance of good maintenance. To his horror, the young woman looked as if she were about to burst into tears. Valentin had no idea how to cope with a crying female—he quickly backed off.

Then he called all the women of the 587th together so he could make a speech. His new regiment stood lined up in the snow before him while he pointed out someone's dirty boots and a hole in someone else's jacket.

"I am your new commander," Valentin told them. "I warn you, I am going to expect a lot from you. Don't count on any allowances from me because you are women."

He didn't have a chance of making a good impression.

It didn't do Valentin any favors that the young women he was talking to were still stunned with grief over the loss of their beloved Marina Raskova. But also, they didn't like how he was talking down to them. They weren't a group of naive schoolgirls—they were a regiment of well-trained aviators, and some of them had already flown in combat under enemy fire.

"At first, we gave him a hard time," said pilot Katya Fedotova. They resented being told to clean what they considered to be spotlessly clean aircraft cockpits; they burst into tears if someone got left out of an aircrew assignment.

But whether or not Valentin wanted to be there leading the 587th, and whether or not they wanted him there, he wasn't going to shirk his responsibility as a commander. Valentin Markov came up with a rigorous training program for his pilots. Even though they were already flying combat missions, he made them drill in high-altitude flying and precision dive-bombing.

Also, he wasn't insensitive. He realized he had to raise the young women's spirits—he couldn't let their grief affect their work. His showed his clear commitment to them by flying with them on many of their combat missions, which quickly gained their respect and admiration.

And he let them take pride in their accomplishments. He established a tradition that after a successful mission, each squadron would fly home together at a low height in an air-show formation. That way, Valentin said, "those on the ground would know that everybody was coming home with a victory."

Valentin Markov gave the 587th firm guidance and a positive outlook. And despite the terrible circumstances in which they first flew to war, under Valentin's command the regiment grew proud and united. Eventually they came to love their commander. After they'd been flying with Valentin for a while, they stopped calling him "bayonet" behind his back. Instead, they, too, gave him the fond nickname Batya, Russian for "Dad"—even though he was only about ten years older than most of them.

"We survived the war because of our regimental commander," said tail gunner Tonya Khokhlova. "All through the flights he was addressing his navigator, asking, 'How are the girls?'" When Valya Kravchenko navigated for Valentin, she'd grow absorbed in her map and suddenly hear him ask, "Where is Melashvili? Where is Spitsina, Yegorova, Matyukhina, Kirillova, Fedotova?" Valentin would make Valya look around for the rest of his squadron while he flew, often thinking harder about his flight crews than about the enemy targets.

Once, when one of Katya Fedotova's engines began to run rough as she flew in formation after Valentin Markov on a combat mission, he made everybody else slow down so that Katya's faulty aircraft could keep up with the other planes.

"So it was because Markov always tried to take care and see that we were protected that we made it back," Katya concluded.

The 587th Bomber Aviation Regiment, too, was now back on its feet, facing into a fresh wind.

EXHAUSTION AND HONOR FOR THE NIGHT BOMBERS

As soon as darkness fell each night, the night bombers began their harassment duties in their open-cockpit Po-2s, flying out to the front lines and relentlessly dumping exlosives on the Germans troops. As the war dragged on, the Soviets found these repeated night attacks also affected the morale of the German soldiers. The constant bombardment wore on their nerves, made dents in their weapons and food supplies, and deprived them of sleep.

Throughout the war, hundreds of Soviet night bomber regiments moved to follow the front line, as it skirted swamps or rough terrain, or bulged in one direction or another when there was a local victory. Soldiers fighting at the front had to live with constant uncertainty about where they'd be the next day. They built new airstrips as they needed them and lived with the local population or even in hastily dug trenches in the ground sheltered by tarpaulin sheets. They excelled at their job of making sure the enemy didn't get a wink of sleep, but that meant that they didn't get much sleep either.

Flying in the dark is a constant strain even if you don't have people shooting at you from the ground. The Po-2 pilots flew using visual flight references only—they couldn't navigate or even fly level if they couldn't see the horizon. The German antiaircraft searchlights, which completely ruined your night vision, were a horror to the bomber pilots. They put you as much at risk of crashing as of being blasted out of the sky.

"If a[n enemy antiaircraft] searchlight caught our planes in its beam, we couldn't see anything—we were blinded," said navigator Polina Gelman. "[Then] the pilot flew with her head very low in the cockpit because she could see nothing outside, and when we managed to get out of the beam we were still blinded for a few moments."

The night bombers took off in a line three minutes after each other— just like a factory production line. The targets weren't much more than fifteen minutes away. A plane would fly to its target and come back, land, refuel, and reload with fresh bombs. Then you were ready for the next mission. With thirty aircraft flying in the regiment, it was possible to keep a steady stream of bombers headed over the enemy lines all night long.

Zhenya Rudneva spent the night of December 14, 1942, flying seven missions as Dina Nikulina's navigator. Her diary entry the next day makes her teamwork with Dina—whom Zhenya adored—sound like a kind of dark comedy duo. "My pilot had a stupid navigator and I had a mindless pilot. . . . By her fifth sortie, Dina felt very tired and kept falling asleep."

Sometimes pilot and navigator both fell asleep in flight. Navigators in the 588th usually had piloting skills as well; Larisa Rozanova said, "We even had a kind of agreement between the pilot and the navigator that one of us would sleep going to the target and the other returning to the airfield."

According to Irina Rakobolskaya, the chief of staff and Yevdokia

Bershanskaya's second-in-command, "The pilots were so tired they never even came out of the cockpit. In the winter [people] even brought hot tea to the aircraft."

The ground crews worked just as hard as the flight crews. All night long, the chief engineer, Klavdiya Ilushina, and the other technicians checked every single aircraft as it came and went. All night long, mechanics refueled the planes and checked the oil and water levels as quickly as possible. They filled cans from the fuel trucks and carried them by hand to the aircraft. All night long, armorers loaded bombs by the faint beams of flashlights. If the batteries failed, or when it was too dangerous to let a light show, they'd have to feel their way in the dark to fix the heavy bombs in place beneath the Po-2s' wings.

Nina Karasyova was nineteen when she started loading weapons. The bombs the Po-2s carried could weigh from 25 to 100 kilograms (55 to 220 pounds), and they had to be lifted into place manually. In a single night, Nina might sometimes have to lift over three tons of explosives.

There weren't any machines that could do this work, so three women at a time worked together to lift the bombs. Nina said, "We worked in mud, frost, sleet, and water. . . . We had to work barehanded so that we could feel what we were doing. . . . We worked all night, then had a two-to-three-hour rest and returned to the planes in the morning to examine the bomb racks under the aircraft."

And just the way the lack of sleep was a constant battle for the aircrew, so it was for the ground crew. When the nighttime bombing missions were over, the technicians could snatch about two hours of sleep. Then they had to repair and test the same planes during the day so they'd be ready for the next night.

The mechanics and armorers felt a fierce sense of competition with nearby men's night bomber regiments doing the same job, and the women wanted to prove they were just as capable as the men. So they put their heads together and came up with a system to help make their work more efficient.

Instead of the usual Soviet routine of assigning a team to wait for and do all the work on one particular aircraft, they reorganized their teams so that one person did the same job for every aircraft. That job might be meeting each plane and guiding it to be refueled in the dark, or holding its wing before takeoff. Someone else would be working steadily at filling fuel cans, and someone else would carry them out to the planes. The armorers operated in teams of three as they loaded bombs.

This way, instead of every mechanic and armorer having to wait for their own plane to turn up, people could work efficiently on whatever needed to be done all night long. They got so good at it they could turn a plane around in five minutes. Soon the pilots and navigators of the 588th were flying a dozen bombing missions or more in a single night, far more than the men in the other Po-2 regiments.

Irina Rakobolskaya, the regiment's chief of staff, was so proud of this new system that she convinced her chief engineer, Sonya Ozerkova, to write a report suggesting that other regiments try it out. Not surprisingly, Sonya was reluctant. She was the one who'd been arrested and nearly shot just because she'd got stuck on the German side of the front lines. But Irina was persistent, and finally Sonya sent in her report.

The result? Sonya was scolded for violating the air force *Technical Maintenance Manual*.

For a long time Sonya was angry with Irina for getting her in trouble. But it didn't stop the 588th from working in teams. They kept on using their new, efficient system; they just didn't make the mistake again of telling anyone they were doing it. Sometimes the best way to get around Soviet regulations was to quietly ignore them.

In February 1943, the 588th Night Bomber Aviation Regiment was awarded a prestigious honor. They were given the special title "Guards"—the mark of an elite military unit. It was the reward for their success in combat that Marina had wished for them in her speech on the day they'd said goodbye to her.

The 588th's new name became the 46th Guards Night Bomber Aviation Regiment. There were four other regiments of Po-2s in their division, all staffed by men, but only the women of the 588th were honored by becoming a Guards regiment. They felt it was because their maintenance system allowed them to fly nearly twice as many missions each night as other Po-2 regiments, and they were extremely proud of themselves for outflying the men!

After they became the 46th Guards, they were allowed to form a third flight squadron and a training squadron. The training squadron was another unique innovation for this regiment, a bright idea credited to their commander, Yevdokia Bershanskaya. It meant that the 46th Guards could replace their own staff and aircrew, so they didn't have to get reinforcements from outside the regiment when they suffered combat losses (although they still received untrained new recruits).

Coming on top of the victory at Stalingrad, the honor of being made a Guards regiment must have been a fine boost for the night bombers' morale. But it didn't make their work any easier, and it didn't make the horrors of war any easier to accept.

Pilots, unlike ground troops, don't always experience the close-up destructive work they cause on the ground. It wasn't until February 1943 that Irina "Ira" Sebrova and her navigator, Natasha Meklin, saw their first dead German, when they nearly tripped over the corpse of a soldier that was lying in the snow on the side of the road between the airfield and the village where they were staying.

The pale, waxlike body was wearing nothing but a pair of blue underpants, and his blond hair was frozen to the ground.

It was impossible not to pity the young man, and impossible not to imagine how easily they could end up just like him—fighting and fighting until they were killed.

The 46th Guards were now stationed only about forty kilometers (twenty-five miles) from the front lines. As the snow began to melt, the ground around their base became so thick with mud and slush that supply trucks couldn't get through to them. To make matters worse, one night after a bombing mission, their aircraft got stuck at their intermediate airfield without food and low on fuel.

Resourceful as always, the young women collected the remaining fuel from each of their twenty aircraft and distributed it between eight lucky planes. After pushing and dragging the planes through mud and slush—"almost carrying them in our hands," said Larisa Rozanova—the young women got the eight Po-2s onto a makeshift runway made of logs. Then pilots, flying without navigators so the rear cockpit could hold the supplies they picked up, took off for a round trip of about 400 kilometers (250 miles) to a town called Kropotkin. There, they would be able to collect flour, sugar, and other provisions, as well as explosives and fuel.

The Po-2s didn't usually fly in daylight because their slow speed made them easy for enemy aircraft to chase and shoot down. So to make this trip safely, they had to fly at treetop level—that way they were camouflaged against the ground.

The hunger, the slush, the lack of sleep, the constant tension, the grime, the grief, and the cold were all exhausting. Larisa Rozanova was one of the pilots who flew to Kropotkin to pick up the supplies. Having eaten nothing but corn for three days, Larisa made three flights back and forth to Kropotkin in daylight, covering 1,200 kilometers (750 miles). Heavy cans full of fuel for the planes were attached to her wings and stacked up in the rear cockpit, weighing down the little Po-2 so that skimming the treetops was even more hazardous.

Then, when dark fell and the temperature dropped below freezing, everybody got ready to fly bombing missions. Larisa wasn't going to be the one who backed out because she was tired. She set out with navigator Vera Belik, who'd be able to help her with the flying if she needed to.

"The moment we took off I was almost snoozing away," said Larisa.

It was cloudy as well as dark, and Larisa couldn't keep her eyes open. She and the aircraft were both nodding, to Vera's alarm.

Still half asleep as she approached the target, Larisa couldn't figure out what she was looking at. She exclaimed, "Vera, fighters are attacking us; do you see them?"

"What fighters? You are dreaming! Do wake up!" Vera told her.

But Larisa kept mistaking the antiaircraft searchlights on the ground for the headlights of enemy fighter planes. She made the aircraft turn and dive violently, trying to avoid an unseen danger that didn't exist. The terrified Vera screamed her friend's nickname over the intercom to wake her up: "Speed, speed, Lorka!"

Vera's yelling finally cleared Larisa's head a little.

"I glanced at the instruments," Larisa said. "There were circles before my eyes; I couldn't discern any digits. I shut my eyelids until they hurt, rubbed them with my hand, opened them again, and still couldn't see anything. But Vera kept screaming: 'Speed, speed! Adjust speed!'"

Then Larisa put the Po-2 into a dive that was so fast and steep it made the plane vibrate. She was so disoriented she couldn't tell the ground from the sky.

"Larisa, wake up, what are you doing? There are no fighters; these are the searchlights!" said Vera. Larisa wouldn't let her take over the control stick—Vera had to fight her for it. At last, only 200 meters (about 650 feet) from the ground, Vera managed to straighten out the plane.

By now Larisa's teeth were chattering and her hands and feet were shaking so badly that at first Vera thought she must be wounded.

"You shouldn't have flown tonight," Vera scolded her.

Vera flew the Po-2 back to their base. When they landed, they discovered that their plane was so full of bullet holes that they couldn't fly another mission that night.

"Between us we had to fly three hundred missions every night," said pilot Nina Raspopova—thirty aircraft flying ten missions each. "But one night we were a single mission short and I was told to do one final flight. As we crossed the front line, I saw the Germans sitting close to each other, miserably looking up at the sky. Nobody fired a shot. Tanya, my navigator, grabbed the megaphone and shouted insults at them in German. I was so exhausted I didn't care if they shot me or not or if I lived or died."

Even though the pilots didn't have to fly during the day, the huge strain of the nightly combat missions affected their ability to relax. Irina Rakobolskaya said that sometimes the pilots wouldn't sleep for days, "afraid of having nightmares during which they struggled with searchlights."

"When we returned from our missions at dawn, I couldn't fall asleep," said Mariya Smirnova. "I tossed in bed and had anxiety attacks. We slept two to four hours each day throughout the four years of the war."

But just as fog didn't stop them from flying and an official reprimand didn't stop them from using their own maintenance system, exhaustion and anxiety attacks didn't stop them from fighting.

TWO AGAINST FORTY-TWO

Like the night bombers, the pilots of the 586th Regiment in their dangerous solo Yak fighters were growing hardened in combat too.

In February 1943 they were assigned to defend and protect railroad junctions and bridges near a city called Voronezh. Less than two weeks before, Soviet forces had won a fierce battle to free the city from German occupation. Now, "Operation Star" was planned to free the cities of Kharkov (the Russian name for Kharkiv), in Ukraine, and Kursk, in Russia, 450 kilometers (280 miles) southwest of Moscow. Part of this effort meant that first the invaders would have to be pushed back from Voronezh. For the next seven months, under Aleksandr Gridnev's command, the young women and men of the 586th would experience the most intense fighting of their entire war.

Sofya Osipova was one of nine mechanics who went to the new airfield at Voronezh ahead of the rest of the regiment. Their job was to get the living quarters ready, and to make sure the pilots could land when they arrived in their Yaks.

Sofya said that when she and her companions got there, "We found nothing all around but ruins." They camped out in a single building that was still standing among the remains of a burned-out factory complex.

The pilots turned up at this wasteland the next day and had to land in slushy snow. "The first machine touched down and a fountain shot up into the air," said Sofya. Once they'd landed, the planes couldn't get off the runway because they couldn't taxi—their wheels just sank into the slush. The propellers were in danger of hitting the ground. So the mechanics had to jump up on the tails of the aircraft to keep the planes' noses raised.

Sofya had to do this again and again as each plane arrived. The work was freezing, soaking, and exhausting. "I am lying on the tail. The wind forcefully presses me to the fin and penetrates my body, spattering snow on me. I can hardly breathe. The tail keeps rising and falling down. . . .

"When you climbed down from the tail, for a few minutes you were disoriented. Your ears, mouth, and nose were filled with wet snow. Your clothes were soaking wet, like a laundry which had not been wrung out. But you had to meet the next plane."

Of course the German forces had to deal with the exact same conditions. "General Mud and General Cold are helping the Russian side," said journalist Vasily Grossman at the time.

By now there was a drastic shortage of planes in the Soviet Air Force. For the fighter pilots of the 586th, this meant that every single one of their aircraft was constantly in use. As soon as one pilot returned from a mission, the ground crew quickly reloaded its guns, refueled it, patched up any damage, and another pilot would take off in it.

As a result, during the first month at Voronezh there was no relief for anyone working on the ground. Fourteen young women were in charge of keeping all the 586th's Yaks armed and flying.

"One machine is airborne, another is landing, and still another is being inspected and refuelled," Sofya said. "As soon as you finish, you run to help. . . . Quickly inspect and refuel the machine. It has had no time to cool down and again it takes off. Soaked, chilled, tired and, at times, hungry as well, but never downcast and always optimistic . . ."

TECHNICIANS OF THE 586TH FIGHTER AVIATION REGIMENT AT WORK ON A YAK

Later that spring, the regiment was lucky enough to be equipped with new Yak-7s, an upgraded version of their familiar Yak-1s. The Yak-7 was a simpler and more powerful aircraft. It was stable in the air and easy to handle, and thought of as one of the best Soviet fighter aircraft available.

The 586th Regiment was kept so busy that almost every single one of its aircraft was in the sky on the morning of March 19, 1943—with two exceptions. Pilots Tamara Pamyatnykh and Raisa "Raya" Surnachevskaya, aged twenty-three and twenty at the time, were reserved as "scramble fighters" in case an unexpected mission came up.

The pilots already in the air had all been sent together to turn back a huge raid the Germans were launching on a nearby town just south of Voronezh. When the 586th arrived in their Yaks, the enemy planes dropped their bombs in a snow-covered field instead of on their populated industrial target, and beat a hasty retreat. Nobody was hurt, no planes were damaged, and the regiment flew back to their home field, where the fuel trucks came driving out to meet them as they landed.

As the pilots climbed out of their planes, they were surprised to discover that Tamara and Raya had taken off while they were away. Inna Kalinovskaya, the ground staff officer in charge of keeping track of missions, explained what was going on: There was a large group of bombers

RADIO VERSUS RADAR

Marina Raskova made sure her fighter planes were equipped with radios, which let her pilots to talk to each other in the air. But they weren't using this equipment to track other aircraft. Radio had been around for most of the twentieth century by 1940, but what we call *radar*, using radio waves to look out for distant objects, was a very new technology in World War II.

Radio is a way of sending out a signal made of electromagnetic energy. The radio that picks up the signal doesn't have any way of knowing where it's coming from, unless the person who sent the signal tells them—which is what Marina was doing as the *Rodina*'s navigator.

But with radar equipment, it's possible to send out radio signals that bounce off another object and return to the sender—revealing heading to the railway station at Kastornaya, where huge numbers of Soviet troops were gathering as they prepared to join the battle to liberate the city of Kursk. Tamara and Raya were now the only fighter pilots in the air. But their radio messages were coming in clearly.

The ground staff was by now equipped with radar, and the deputy chief navigator, Nina Slovokhotova, was able to update Tamara and Raya by radio to tell them where to find the German attack planes.

Suddenly Tamara called back: "I see the enemy aircraft!"

"There are quite a few of them!" added Raya's voice over the radio.

Commander Aleksandr Gridnev was there to answer them himself. "Attack!" he told them.

Then the radio cut out. The regiment had lost contact with Tamara and Raya.

where that object is. This way, people can detect where a plane is even if it's not trying to contact them.

Early radar played a big role in preventing Germany's planned invasion of the United Kingdom in 1940, because British radar stations were able to find raiding Luftwaffe planes in the air before they reached their targets. Radar stopped the Germans from being able to launch sneak attacks. When British radio technicians on the ground spotted incoming swarms of German aircraft, they were able to tell their pilots where to find the enemy.

Soviet aircraft began to be fitted with radar equipment in 1942, but pilots and radio engineers weren't fully capable of using it until 1943.

DEPUTY CHIEF NAVIGATOR NINA SLOVOKHOTOVA AND PILOT ZULEIKA SEID-MAMEDOVA IN THE CONTROL ROOM FOR THE 586TH FIGHTER AVIATION REGIMENT

Aleksandr ran to his own plane, which he'd just jumped out of after the previous air raid. As soon as the planes were refueled, Aleksandr and three other fighters took off to support the two young women who were already in the air.

They reached Kastornaya. They flew over the busy railway station where the Soviet troops bound for Kursk were gathering, surrounded by a mess of smoking bomb craters in the dirty snow. But the only trace of an air battle the aviators could see below them was a fragment of a Soviet aircraft wing on the ground. Its red star marking was clearly visible.

Tamara and Raya didn't come back that night. No one in the 586th slept, hoping against hope that Tamara and Raya had somehow survived their battle.

When they'd taken off, Tamara and Raya had flown to Kastornaya looking for a single German spy plane to shoot down. They'd been unprepared to run into two full formations of German bombers. There were so many of the Luftwaffe planes that at first the young Soviet pilots thought the black dots in the southwestern sky must be birds.

But they were too high to be birds. They were enemy bombers, approaching a railway station filled with trains and soldiers.

Tamara and Raya had the advantage of height and the sun behind them, which would dazzle the enemy pilots if they looked in their direction. So the two young women in their Yak fighters, rapidly firing their guns, dived straight into the middle of the first group of German bombers.

Two of the aircraft they fired at fell in flames beneath them, and the bomber formation scattered.

But there was another group of planes in the sky ahead of them. Tamara and Raya each flew at this group from a different side, and Tamara managed to destroy another bomber.

"By that time my guns were empty, and I decided to ram one of their bombers with my aircraft," she said. "I came so close to the enemy that I could see the face of the pilot. . . . I was about to ram him when my plane was hit with gunfire, the wing separated from the aircraft, and I fell into a spin."

With her plane plunging through the air in flames, Tamara was thrown around so forcefully that at first she couldn't get her seat belt unfastened so she could use her parachute. She managed it at last, and with the cockpit canopy open she was thrown from the plane by accident. She was only 150 meters (about 500 feet) above the ground—terrifyingly low—when her parachute finally opened.

But lucky for Tamara, she hit the ground safely. She was bloody and battered, but she was alive. When she looked up at the sky, she saw Raya's plane circling around to make another attack on the bombers.

Tamara struggled to her feet. She knew she would have to make her way back to her regiment somehow, and the first thing she decided to do was find the nearest telegraph station to report that her plane had been destroyed. After walking for some time she saw, crossing a snow-covered field in her fur boots, Raya herself.

They ran to meet each other and hugged frantically. It felt to Tamara "that we had both been given birth again."

Raya explained that when she'd seen Tamara's plane falling in flames with its broken wing, she'd been so overwhelmed with rage and despair that she lost all sense of reason. She flew straight at the nearest German bomber and filled it with gunfire. She had the satisfaction of watching it dive earthward in black smoke before she realized that she, too, had been hit by gunfire.

Raya's plane had been damaged, but she could still control it. She managed to glide to earth and made a crash landing on a hillside, where local people greeted her armed with pitchforks, sticks, and rifles—they'd thought her falling plane might be a German fighter. They were relieved to see the red stars on the wings, but stared at Raya in amazement when she climbed out of it—a woman flying a fighter plane!

Raya and Tamara's meeting in the snowy field didn't happen by chance. Raya, like Tamara, was heading for the telegraph station to report that she'd been shot down. Both of them felt terrible about the damage to their planes. Tamara thought she should be punished because her plane had been destroyed. Raya's had forty-three bullet holes in it.

Back in Voronezh at the 586th's base, word finally came through at dawn the next morning: Raya and Tamara were both alive.

The commander of the front himself sent a telegram to the regiment, congratulating the two pilots on their fearlessness and airmanship: they had turned away forty-two enemy bombers, and shot down four of them.

Tamara and Raya were both awarded the Order of the Red Star. The battle was reported over the radio throughout the nation. The encounter received attention even outside the USSR; two weeks later the young women were both mentioned by name in American newspapers, the first time an official news release from Moscow gave special recognition to its women fighter pilots (though they were referred to as "junior airwomen"). The two valiant pilots of the 586th were sent gold watches through the Soviet minister of foreign affairs, said to be gifts from George VI, the king of England.

Tamara's plane had to be replaced; but the bullet holes in Raya's Yak were completely repaired, and soon she was able to take to the skies in it once more.

A NEW START FOR
THE 587th

Marina Raskova's other aviators were battling just as hard against the German invaders as the fighters in their Yaks. Her lasting legacy to the 587th Bomber Aviation Regiment was in choosing the challenging Pe-2 dive-bomber planes that they flew, and the 587th's commitment to those planes would have made her proud. Maybe some people thought the Pe-2s were "flying coffins" for their three crew members, but the 587th were making the most out of their Peshkas.

From April until July 1943 they flew their aggressive missions from a base in a village near Krasnodar, a city on the Kuban River. They were about 150 kilometers (90 miles) northeast of the Black Sea, where the Germans had been hammering the Soviet's navy and its Black Sea fleet. Few men were left in the war-torn Soviet villages—they were all at war, leaving the women to drive tractors, manage livestock, and raise crops. The local people seem to have been happy to host the women aviators.

Now Commander Valentin Markov flew with the 587th on many of their missions, leading the First Squadron with his navigator, Nikolai Nikitin. Zhenya Timofeyeva, as deputy commander, led the Second Squadron, with her navigator, Valya Kravchenko. Valya had come a long way from stealing cabbages!

In their bombing runs, the Pe-2s came under enemy fire from every possible direction: submachine guns fired by soldiers on the ground, anti-aircraft guns and ground artillery pointed at them in the sky—and of course, German aircraft attacking them. Each aircrew risked two or three of these bombing flights in a day.

But the regiment was given an injection of pride and spirit when, on May 4, 1943, they were awarded a new name. Now they became the 587th M. M. Raskova Bomber Aviation Regiment, in honor of their beloved Marina Raskova. They truly had become "Raskova's regiment."

The 587th was involved in six massive air battles while they were at Krasnodar, including, on a dismal and cloudy day in early June, probably their most dramatic engagement of the entire war.

On June 2, 1943, in back-to-back missions, Zhenya Timofeyeva led a formation of nine Pe-2 dive-bombers, each with its aircrew of pilot, navigator, and gunner, into combat toward the front line at the Kuban River.

Masha Dolina was at the head of one of the flights in the squadron. Masha flew with Galina "Galya" Dzhunkovskaya as her navigator, and with a male tail gunner and radio operator, Ivan Solenov. Masha always tried to get Galya to distract her in the air on the way to a mission, to take her mind off the hard and terrifying work that lay ahead. If Galya stopped talking—which was easy to do when she was busy juggling maps and pencils and the flight log—Masha would scold her.

"Why aren't you saying something? Tell me some kind of a story, or perhaps sing us a song. Only don't forget to turn off the radio."

That was so they wouldn't get in trouble if anyone with a radio receiver overheard them casually chatting to each other in the air!

PILOT MASHA DOLINA OF THE 587TH BOMBER AVIATION REGIMENT (LATER THE 125TH GUARDS) WITH A PE-2 DIVE-BOMBER

But all distraction was put aside as they approached the front line, flying low to avoid the clouds on this mission.

The fighting at the front that day was so ferocious that Masha thought it looked like "a continuous curtain of fire." The planes bounced and shuddered from the force of the explosions in the air around them. Masha followed Zhenya Timofeyeva steadily through the chaotic sky toward the target where they were supposed to drop their bombs.

Then one of Masha's twin engines began to hiccup. Her wingmen, Tonya Skoblikova and Masha Kirillova, following Masha in their flight of three planes as part of the full formation of nine aircraft, saw what was going on and matched their speed to cover for Masha's lagging plane.

They reached the target, everybody dropped their bombs, and the squadron soared around to fly home, still in tight formation after Zhenya.

But the clouds had now become so thick that the Pe-2s were flying lower than they'd planned. They got separated from the fighter planes of another regiment that were supposed to escort them and provide them with protection from enemy fighters. Zhenya's formation of nine Pe-2s was open to attack.

Suddenly the antiaircraft guns stopped firing—a sure sign that Luftwaffe planes were nearby. The German ground troops didn't want to hit their own aircraft.

Without delay, eight Luftwaffe fighters swooped down on Zhenya's formation of Pe-2s.

The German fighters tried to break up the Soviet formation. It would be much easier to pick on a single plane than on nine, whose pilots and navigators and tail gunners were all furiously firing their own guns and hurling grenades out of their cockpits.

But the nine pilots of the 587th stayed tight together. "We were all as if in a 'fist,'" said Klavdiya "Klava" Fomicheva.

One of Masha's engines was hit and caught fire. In the Pe-2 behind her, pilot Tonya Skoblikova blasted her machine guns at the German fighter planes to try to give Masha and her crew a chance to escape.

On the other side of the formation, pilot Klava Fomicheva also saw what was going on. She knew that if Masha left the formation, she'd be easy prey for the Luftwaffe fighters. And if Masha and her crew tried to parachute out of their burning plane, they would surely be killed by the enemy's guns as they fell. Their best chance of survival was to stay in ·formation as long as they could before they tried to land or abandon the plane—and to get back over the front lines into Soviet territory, if at all possible.

Now Tonya Skoblikova's Pe-2 let out a plume of white smoke as it, too, was hit by gunfire.

Behind their machine guns in Masha's Pe-2, her navigator, Galya, and their tail gunner, Ivan, had both run out of ammunition—but not before

Ivan had managed to shoot down one of the Luftwaffe planes himself.

As Masha's burning plane sank lower, one of the German fighters flew so close that Masha could see his grinning, freckled face. He raised one finger, then another.

What he meant was: Would Masha prefer him to shoot her down in one attack, or two?

At the time, Masha didn't understand what he was trying to ask her, and probably wouldn't have answered if she did. But apparently he decided on two attacks. He hit Masha's second engine and swooped away to line up for the next round.

Now both her Pe-2's engines were on fire. As the German pilot came in for a killing blow, Galya and Ivan, in desperation now that they were out of ammunition, threw lighted signal flares at him.

Amazingly, this scared him—he fled the air battle!

But now Masha's Pe-2 was flaming "like a torch." If she didn't get her plane back on the ground or jump out of it, she and her crew would all burn to death in an airborne inferno.

The moment Zhenya's formation of nine Pe-2s crossed into the safety of Soviet territory, Masha was the first to break away. Klava Fomicheva's navigator, Galina "Galya" Turabelidze, strained to keep her eyes on Masha's blazing plane so she would know where it went down.

Other damaged planes began to peel away from the formation as well. Both of Olga "Lelya" Sholokhova's engines were trailing smoke. Pilots Tonya Skoblikova and Katya Fedotova were able to waggle their wings in farewell as they flew off to find emergency landing places.

Klava Fomicheva and her crew flew in silence as they followed Zhenya Timofeyeva back to their base. Nobody felt like talking. Of the nine Pe-2s that had taken off on that mission, only five returned, and everyone was sure that Masha and her crew must be dead.

There was no way the squadron was going to be able to fly home in air-show formation as they usually did. For the first time since Valentin Markov had established the tradition, they landed without their low-level victory pass over the airfield.

Nobody felt like sleeping, either, and the survivors of the battle didn't go back to their quarters after they landed. They waited anxiously all night for a telephone call that might give them news of their missing aircrews. Everyone agreed that only Masha's plane had been on fire—surely the others had managed to crash-land safely somewhere?

Then, just after daylight broke, Katya Fedotova's Pe-2 came flying in and touched down confidently on the runway. Katya and her devoted air-crew, navigator Klara Dubkova and gunner Tonya Khokhlova, all jumped out safe and sound!

After the happy greetings with the other aircrew and the ground crew, Katya and Klara and Tonya explained what had happened to them after the battle. With bullet holes in their fuel tanks, they'd found a friendly Soviet airfield to land on. They'd repaired their plane themselves, sticking wooden plugs into the holes.

As everyone stood there on the field firing excited questions and exclamations at each other, another Pe-2 came in to land. It was Tonya Skoblikova's plane, and squeezed into it were Masha Dolina's crew as well—three in the main cockpit, with Masha lying on the floor, and three in the tail gunner's tiny cabin!

Masha, Galya, and Ivan were now able to fill the rest of the regiment in on the end of their own harrowing story.

When they left the formation in their burning plane, Masha ordered Galya and Ivan to use their parachutes.

Ivan told her, "Keep going, Commander; we are bound to make it. On the other hand, if we must perish, at least let's go together!"

Galya, standing behind Masha, pulled Masha's goggles down over her stinging eyes to protect them in the smoke-filled plane so that she'd be able to see to glide in to land. Masha brought down the Pe-2 on its belly in grass that was a meter high (a little over three feet). The pilot and navigator's cockpit was now ablaze; Masha and Galya's clothes caught fire, and so did the long grass around the plane.

Behind Masha and Galya in the tail gunner's cockpit, Ivan had been wounded in the leg. But after the landing he was able to crawl free of the aircraft, only to see that Masha and Galya were still trapped in the front cockpit of the burning Pe-2.

Ivan attacked the jammed canopy with a screwdriver and managed to pry it open. Galya's clothes were in flames as Ivan dragged Masha and Galya from the wreckage of their plane.

"When he pulled us from the cabin, we fell on the ground, and the grass around us was burning," said Masha. "We had to roll about to put the fire out around us and on us."

Fortunately they weren't hurt when their plane blew up—"a fountain of fire and smoke."

But the disastrous flight had a happy ending. Masha and her crew were picked up by friendly Soviet antiaircraft gunners, who drove them to a medical post. There, to their joy, they found Masha's friend Tonya Skoblikova and her aircrew! After Tonya had managed to land her plane safely, she and her crew had come to the same place to get their wounds treated.

Lelya Sholokhova and the rest of her aircrew turned up in an ambulance aircraft later that day.

All nine flight crews survived the June 2 battle, and while they'd been in the air they shot down four of the enemy fighters themselves. Their tight "fist" of a formation was so spectacularly successful that the air force commander used it as a strategic example for all Soviet bomber regiments. It even got the 587th a mention in the Fourth Air Army's official history.

And Ivan got a bonus of 1,000 rubles for shooting down a German plane—worth about $2,500 today!

Ivan, as the tail gunner in a Pe-2, had a job that was probably even more harrowing than the pilot's or the navigator's. The tail gunner's cockpit at the back of the plane stuck out and made an easy target for enemy fighters. The Pe-2's machine guns often jammed, and their bullets weren't always strong enough to penetrate the armor of Luftwaffe fighter aircraft. Most Pe-2 tail gunners were men, like Ivan Solenov, because it took so much strength to recharge the guns.

The athletic Tonya Khokhlova was one of a few women with enough upper body strength to do this dual job of tail gunner and radio operator for the 587th. Her pilot, Katya Fedotova, described Tonya as "quick and boisterous. She had a boyish haircut and grey, cunning eyes." Katya was one of the four friends who'd written a letter together begging Marina Raskova to help them get to the front; now she found new close friends in her Pe-2 aircrew, including Tonya and their navigator, Klara Dubkova.

Remember how a strong headwind can slow you down or help you take off, depending on how you use it?

Very occasionally, bad weather can come to your rescue. On one of Tonya's missions, she and her aircrew were saved "more thanks to the weather" than anything else.

They'd been hit by gunfire from a German fighter and, with an engine on fire, managed to escape the enemy plane by hiding in a storm cloud. Tonya put in a radio call to soldiers on the ground and told them that their Pe-2 was in trouble. Finally, after the enemy aircraft had flown away, Katya landed the damaged Pe-2 in a small field just inside Soviet territory over the front line.

Exactly as had happened to Masha and Galya on June 2, Katya and her navigator, Klara, couldn't get their cockpit open to get out of the crashed plane, and needed their tail gunner's help.

But Tonya, back in the tail gunner's compartment, was overcome by leaking fuel fumes.

"I was like a drunken person," she said. "There was a pounding noise, and four-letter words, and shouting to get out quick and help us!"

Tonya finally realized what was going on, and when she got herself out of her own cabin, her headed cleared enough that she managed to release her friends from the crashed plane.

In the meantime, the soldiers Tonya had been in touch with on the ground came hurrying to meet the stunned crew.

"What do you think they came with?" Tonya said. "Big, green leaves . . . full of strawberries! Probably they heard us talking and knew we were women, the gift sent to them from the sky. That was the first nice thing during the war—red strawberries, beautiful strawberries in green leaves!"

Fresh fruit was a wonderful and rare treat in wartime.

But more than that, the kindness of the surprise gift was the real treasure—a glimpse of ordinary humanity in the long, terrifying, and hellish slog of battle.

THE 46th GUARDS IN TAMAN, 1943

The 46th Guards Night Bomber Aviation Regiment, meanwhile, was also fighting fiercely in the spring of 1943.

In March, they moved their fleet of open-cockpit Po-2s to continue their harassment missions in the coastal area of the Taman Peninsula, which separates the Black Sea from the Sea of Azov east of the Kerch Strait. Here, there was a strongly fortified line of German troops, airfields, tanks, searchlights, headquarters, and machine gun and antiaircraft batteries. These embattlements squatted for 110 kilometers (about 70 miles) along riverbanks and inlets, marshes and mountains. The long fortification was known as the Blue Line and was part of Hitler's offensive as he tried to push through Crimea to take over the oil fields of the Caspian Sea.

The 46th Guards dropped bombs over the Blue Line for six months, right up to the point when the Red Army forced the Germans out of the Taman Peninsula in September 1943.

But they'd hardly been in Taman for a month before they suffered another horrifying loss.

Yevdokia "Dusya" Nosal was a calm, confident pilot who'd already flown more than 350 combat missions by this time. She had a good reason to want to fight the Nazis: in 1941, her baby was killed when a German bomb hit the maternity hospital where she'd just given birth.

On the night of April 23, 1943, Dusya was training a new navigator, Irina Kashirina. Dusya and Irina flew one successful harassment mission in their flimsy Po-2 by the helpful light of a moon three nights past full, returned to their base to refuel and reload their bombs, and then set out again. They dropped a second wingload of bombs over their target without any trouble.

But when they turned for home, Irina saw a flash in the sky ahead of them and realized that it was a German night fighter aircraft.

Irina didn't even have time to shout a warning to her pilot before suddenly the Po-2 turned and began to lose speed.

"Dusya! Dusya!" Irina yelled.

When Dusya didn't answer, Irina took over the dual controls.

"But the pedals were jammed," she said. "Then and there I understood that Dusya had been either seriously wounded or . . . No, I didn't want to think the unthinkable. I put the aircraft into a turn to fly back. Dusya kept sliding down into the cockpit, leaning against the control stick. I kept pulling her up by her collar."

Irina made it back to the airfield and managed to land the plane safely.

Only after she landed did she realize that indeed, the unthinkable had happened.

Dusya had been shot in the head by the Luftwaffe fighter plane. She probably died instantly.

The 46th Guards had to organize another funeral. They buried Dusya in the village of Pashkovskaya, now part of Krasnodar, giving her full military honors and covering her grave with flowers. Both her comrades and the local people laid wreaths for her.

DUSYA NOSAL'S FUNERAL

Soon afterward, Dusya was posthumously given the Gold Star of Hero of the Soviet Union, the first of the 46th Guards to be awarded this medal.

Anger is a powerful motivator.

Though grieving, the women of the 46th Guards didn't react to Dusya's death with fear or discouragement. They were *angry*. In the coming weeks, they flew their harassment bombing missions in Dusya Nosal's name and memory, even painting one of their Po-2 bombers with the inscription "To avenge Dusya."

On June 10, 1943, exactly a year after they'd flown their first combat mission, there was a special ceremony to celebrate the honor of being named the 46th Guards earlier that year.

Now the 46th received their special Guards' banner, and all took the Guards' oath: "I swear! While our eyes see, while our hearts beat and our hands move, to mercilessly annihilate the fascist invaders."

A PO-2 INSCRIBED "TO AVENGE DUSYA"

Then they sang together a new "Hymn of the Regiment" they'd written themselves, with words by their own infinitely creative chief navigator, Zhenya Rudneva, and music by Natasha Meklin, who'd just started flying her first combat missions as a pilot.

> Fight, girls, fighting friends,
> For the glory of the women's guard regiment.
> Fly forth
> With fire in your breast . . . !

THE HEAT OF BATTLE

Lilya Litvyak, Katya Budanova, Mariya Kuznetsova, and Raisa Belyaeva— the four pilots who'd transferred with their solo Yak fighters from the 586th to the men's 437th Fighter Aviation Regiment—didn't stay in the 437th very long. It was hard to provide maintenance for the Yaks there, since the rest of the regiment flew a different type of plane. So all four women transferred again, this time to the 9th Guards Fighter Aviation Regiment, a special unit for elite pilots, who were of course all men.

Not long afterward, they got an order telling them to return to the 586th.

Raisa and Mariya both did. But Lilya and Katya persuaded their commander in the 9th Guards to let them stay. They liked the excitement of flying on the front lines, and they probably felt that it would be hard to fit in comfortably with the women of the 586th again.

Because of yet another issue over aircraft types, Lilya and Katya soon transferred again so they could continue flying their familiar Yaks. Their new regiment, the 296th, was based on the same airfield as the 9th Guards, so they didn't have to move far. Lilya and Katya hadn't been with them long before the regiment was honored with the elite title of 73rd Guards Fighter Aviation Regiment in March 1943.

So many different regiment numbers! But the 73rd Guards is where they stayed. Their new commander, Nikolai Baranov, made them feel at home, even though they were the only two women in the regiment—he could see they were both fantastic combat pilots. Katya became Nikolai's wingman. Lilya became the wingman for another man, Alexei Solomatin.

Lilya's and Katya's female mechanics transferred with them. Their daily routine never got any easier. Inna Pasportnikova, Lilya's mechanic, said that the pilots slept in local homes in a nearby village, and "we mechanics slept at the airdrome near the aircraft in open trenches. When it became cold in the winter, we took the engine cover and put it over ourselves, and in the morning we would wake up with ice on our hair and faces."

Lilya soared from height to height as a combat pilot. She and Katya were both granted the special status of okhotnik, or "free hunter"—a fighter pilot who could use her initiative to go searching for enemy aircraft or ground forces to attack. Instead of being assigned missions, free hunters were allowed to go looking for trouble. Free hunting was a tactic the Soviet Air Force exploited in 1943 and assigned to experienced fighter pilots of exceptional talent.

This suited Lilya just fine: she liked to do as she pleased. She performed forbidden aerial stunts over the airfield when she returned from a mission and got away with it. She colored strips of parachute silk to use as scarves, and she carried a picture of roses on her Yak's instrument panel. When men were assigned to fly her plane, they'd sometimes find a bouquet Lilya had left in the cockpit. They'd utter a few bad words and toss it out before taking off!

On March 22, 1943, Lilya was involved in an air battle in which she and five other Yak fighters were outnumbered by the enemy two to one. She'd shot down one of the German planes when she suddenly felt a sharp pain in her leg. Before she could figure out what was going on, she found herself under attack by no less than six Luftwaffe fighter planes.

PILOT LILYA LITVYAK AND HER YAK FIGHTER

Ignoring the pain, Lilya flew straight into the middle of the German fighters. She knocked one of them out of the sky with her guns, and the rest scattered. Then, with her Yak full of bullet holes, Lilya flew back to her own airfield and managed to land.

She'd been shot in the leg—that was the pain she'd felt as the fight began. Safe on the ground, Lilya fainted before she'd even parked her plane.

Lilya's heroic fight and her battle wound turned her into a celebrity.

Komsomolskaya Pravda, the Communist Party's youth newspaper, published a feature about her. The Soviet Air Force magazine *Stalin's Falcons* ran a story titled "The Girl Avenger," calling Lilya "one of the Front's outstanding pilots." The youth magazine *Ogonyok* published an article about Lilya and Katya and their achievements, with a full list of the aircraft they'd shot down. A photograph of the two young women in flight helmets, grinning with pleasure, was splashed on the cover.

In the hospital, friends and even total strangers visited Lilya and brought her candy and other little presents. When she came back to her regiment she was limping, loaded with gifts, and extremely pleased with herself.

Lilya had to stay on the ground for six weeks recovering from her wound. Nikolai Baranov, her commander, sent her home on leave to her mother and younger brother in Moscow so she could recuperate. But being grounded made Lilya very restless. She missed her regiment and she missed the action of the front. Still limping, she made her own way back to the 73rd Guards early in May 1943.

Almost immediately after her return she shot down two more Luftwaffe fighter planes.

Not just for Lilya, but for all the pilots of Marina Raskova's regiments, the summer of 1943 was filled with flame and fury.

Back in Voronezh, Aleksandr Gridnev now flew with Valentina Lisitsina as his second-in-command in their fast Yak fighters, and he continued to prove himself as the right commander for the 586th Fighter Aviation Regiment.

On June 26, 1943, on one of their defensive missions to the city of Belgorod, not far from Kharkov—both cities were still under German control—Aleksandr and Valentina attacked a group of Luftwaffe bombers flying with a fighter escort. Valentina shot down one of the bombers and Aleksandr shot down one of the fighters. When two more Luftwaffe aircraft began to chase them, Aleksandr escaped into clouds while the two enemy fighter planes collided in flames. The air battle and the 586th's triumph of that day were reported in the national newspaper Pravda.

By the time they left Voronezh in August 1943, the 586th had helped to liberate Kharkov and had shot down ten German aircraft—and they weren't even fighting at the front.

They might not be at the front, but the 586th was still in easy reach of

German attackers. The Luftwaffe pilots figured out what time the 586th had dinner, and purposefully raided their airfield when they were eating. They flew low over the base's makeshift buildings and strafed the canteen with gunfire. The cook tried to run and hide in one of the defensive trenches but was killed in the attack.

If you think about the amount of harassment the Germans endured from the night bombers in their Po-2s, it's hardly surprising they resorted to shooting at the Soviet fighter pilots while they were trying to eat dinner.

The 586th Regiment didn't let this stop them from getting regular meals. Instead of serving dinner in the canteen, the ground staff brought food out onto the airfield. Now the pilots could sit and eat on the wings of their aircraft, ready to take off at any moment when the enemy turned up to interrupt their meal.

The fighting was so intense during the months at Voronezh that sometimes there wasn't even time to punish people when they disobeyed the rules.

Now that she was back in the 586th, the high-spirited stunt pilot Raisa Belyaeva was constantly getting in trouble for performing aerobatic loops or rolls in her plane, or flying upside down at low altitude after a combat mission. One day a visiting official saw one of her performances and ordered Aleksandr Gridnev, "She will be arrested for forty-five days for a violation of flight regulations." But before anyone had a chance to place her under arrest, Raisa took off for another mission.

As punishment for that, she was grounded, but she didn't let it stop her. The airfield was coming under fierce bombardment every night, and one night, when Aleksandr was sent to attack a German bomber, Raisa took off after him. Aleksandr didn't even realize who it was until he heard her voice over the radio—his wingman was supposed to be a male pilot from a different regiment.

Raisa managed to shoot down the bomber herself.

This time, instead of being arrested for disobedience, she was told she could be on active flight duty once again.

On July 19, 1943, Raisa failed to pull her Yak out of a dive over her own airfield. She was killed in the crash.

The whole regiment wept over their talented and personable friend. Aleksandr Gridnev cried too, in public, while giving the speech at Raisa's funeral.

Two of the men Lilya Litvyak flew with in the 73rd Guards were killed in the month after she started flying again. One was Nikolai Baranov, her sympathetic commander who flew with Katya Budanova as his wingman. The other was Alexei Solomatin, who flew with Lilya herself. Lilya was devastated. In a letter to her mother after his death, she called Alexei her "best friend."

Lilya took these losses hard, and her flying and fighting hardened along with her personality.

In May, she made a triumphant flight *on purpose* into enemy territory and back. There was an observation balloon tethered in a village occupied by the Germans so they could spot Soviet positions and tell their gunners where to fire. Whenever anyone flew at the balloon to try to shoot it down, the gunfire would get so hot that they'd have to give up.

Lilya had an idea for how to take care of it.

She flew over the front a long way from the balloon and traveled so far into German territory that she was able to circle around and sneak up on the balloon from behind—where the German gunners weren't at all expecting an attack. And she shot it down and came speeding home.

In June, she was promoted and became a flight commander.

In July, Lilya was injured again in a furious battle in which she and five other Yak pilots fought against thirty-six enemy planes—but she stayed in the air to shoot down a German bomber and a fighter anyway. As she was flying back in her damaged plane, which was trailing smoke, Luftwaffe fighters attacked her and Lilya received yet another wound. When she got back to her airfield with damage to both her shoulder and her leg, she let herself be given first aid but refused to go to the hospital.

Three days later, Katya Budanova was killed.

Katya died like a true Soviet fighter pilot, first filling an enemy fighter with bullets before using expert flight techniques to put out the flames that were engulfing her own plane. She crash-landed her Yak in one piece but was already dead when local farmers found her and buried her.

Lilya's way of grieving seems to have been to throw herself into battle. She, too, shot down a German fighter plane on the day of Katya's death, and she was back in the air the next day as well. This time, the fighting Lilya engaged in was so fierce, and her plane was shot up so badly, that she had to parachute to safety.

On July 28, 1943, Lilya sat in the cockpit of her Yak and dictated a letter to her mother while she waited to be given a combat mission. One of the ground staff wrote the letter for her, perching on the wing of Lilya's plane.

"I am completely absorbed in combat life. I can't seem to think of anything but the fighting," Lilya told her mother.

"I long . . . for a happy and peaceful life, after I've returned to you and told you about everything I had lived through and felt during the time when we were apart. Well, good-bye for now. Your Lily."

It was her last letter home.

On August 1, 1943, Lilya Litvyak flew mission after mission, each time coming back to base so she could refuel and rearm her Yak.

On her fourth flight of the day, Lilya and another pilot were returning from an escort mission when two German aircraft appeared from behind the clouds. The fighter planes started firing their guns, and more and more aircraft joined the fray, until there were nine Soviet fighter pilots battling forty Luftwaffe aircraft.

Lilya's Yak was hit by enemy fire, and another Soviet pilot, Ivan Borisenko, saw her dive into the clouds to try to escape.

No one ever saw her again.

Not long after Lilya's disappearance, a leaflet was handed out to Soviet troops, encouraging them to fight in memory of the "shining image of pilot Lily Litvyak, as a symbol of eternal, unfading youth, as a symbol of struggle and victory!"

Double ace Lilya Litvyak had destroyed eleven enemy planes by herself in less than a year, plus the observation balloon. Her commander wrote a recommendation for her to be posthumously honored as a Hero of the Soviet Union.

But Lilya and her aircraft had vanished. It was impossible to prove that she was dead, so by the Soviet Union's strict military regulations she couldn't be given the award.

It was absolutely Lilya's worst fear: to disappear, as her father had disappeared.

But that is what happened.

On September 16, 1943, a document was filed with the chief directorate of personnel officially listing Lilya Litvyak as "missing."

The Great Patriotic War had only just passed its halfway mark. It was nowhere near finished. But Lilya's part in it was over. The woman who was born on Aviation Day, the woman who was born to be in the air, had vanished in the air.

PART IV

THE GREAT PATRIOTIC WAR

THE THIRD AND FOURTH YEARS: 1943–1945

"OUR PLANES WERE BURNING LIKE CANDLES"

During that turbulent final week of July 1943, William Faulkner was on the other side of the world in Hollywood, California, feverishly pulling together the screenplay for the sweeping wartime movie *Battle Cry*. The film would never be made, but the world would never notice. The world was too busy tearing itself apart.

World War II really was a *world* war: it took place across oceans as well as continents. By the summer of 1943, the Atlantic was full of German submarines and British battleships. In the South Pacific, the United States Army Air Force and Navy were fighting a furious offensive against Japan. The Allies had forced the German troops from North Africa earlier that year, but in China there was an ongoing battle to drive out the invading Japanese. Indians and Australians were fighting for the British in the Pacific and the Far East; Canadians were fighting for them in the Mediterranean. In the air, Allied planes based in Great Britain were raining bombs on German cities and industrial sites, killing tens of thousands of civilians. And since May, the Allied nations had been hard at work planning a secret invasion of the western Atlantic coast of Europe to win it back from the Germans.

Stalin was counting heavily on this second front to stretch Germany's military to its breaking point and take pressure off the millions of Soviet soldiers who were throwing themselves at death day after day in the Soviet states on the Eastern Front.

The 46th Guards Night Bomber Aviation Regiment knew they were a small part of a much bigger machine, but their youth in the newly industrialized USSR had taught them how important a small part could be.

In their combat missions, the open-cockpit Po-2 biplanes flew toward that night's harassment target one by one, each three minutes behind the next.

NIGHT BOMBING WITHOUT PARACHUTES

The Po-2s were slow. And when a harassment plane was caught in the beams of antiaircraft searchlights and hit by a gunner shooting from the ground, or by an enemy fighter plane shooting from the air, if it caught fire the Po-2 could be entirely engulfed in flames in less than minute. Irina Rakobolskaya, the deputy commander for the 46th Guards, said that "a single incendiary bullet could turn it into a flaming torch." Ordinary people called the Po-2 a "kerosinka"—a kerosene lamp, because it went up in flames so fast.

Your only hope flying a Po-2 under enemy fire was to stay low, stay quiet, and stay unseen. For most of the war the Po-2s of the 46th Guards weren't even equipped with self-defense machine guns.

One by one, each aircrew dropped their bombs and then returned to their intermediate airfield to refuel. Like so many other Po-2 night bomber regiments on the front, their strategy was to keep the German troops awake all night. The Soviet night bombers were small and slow, but the exhausted Germans hated them. When the Po-2s were in the air, the Germans never had a single moment's rest.

On the night of July 31, 1943, the fifteen aircrews of a Po-2 squadron got ready for their nightly bombing run. Thirty young Soviet women walked out to their aircraft together in the dark. Only twenty-two of them would return.

After the navigators climbed in and the pilots started their engines, fifteen 46th Guards Po-2s set out in a line one after the other, exactly three

Yet for nearly three years, the entire 46th Guards flew their night bombing combat missions without parachutes.

"Our pilots thought the plane itself to be like a parachute and felt they did not need them," said Irina. "Over our own territory we could get down quite easily, and over the German lines we felt that it was much better to burn up than to be captured by the Germans."

In the summer of 1944, at last the 46th Guards were equipped with parachutes. But the change saved only one single life. In a horrible twist of fate, when Rufina Gasheva and Olga Sanifrova parachuted out of a damaged Po-2, they landed in a minefield. They survived the landing, but Olga was killed by a mine.

minutes apart. They were headed for the village of Krymskaya, where German troops were camped along the fortified Blue Line, Hitler's offensive front in Crimea.

Squadron commander Mariya Smirnova took off, followed by the other planes. Zhenya Krutova flew with her navigator, Lena Salikova. Exactly three minutes behind them flew Anya Vysotskaya and Galya Dokutovich, the navigator who'd spent six months in the hospital after being run over by a truck. Behind Anya and Galya came Valentina Polunina and Irina Kashirina, who'd had to land her plane after her pilot, Dusya Nosal, had been killed in the air three months earlier.

As a pilot, Anya was one of several rookies in the air that night. Zhenya Rudneva, the regiment's chief navigator, had assigned her adored friend Galya Dokutovich to fly with Anya so she could have an experienced navigator in the air with her. Natasha Meklin, a navigator who'd retrained as a pilot, was flying one of her first combat missions at the controls of her Po-2, with Lida Loshmanova as her navigator. And Larisa Rozanova was flying with Nadezhda "Nadya" Studilina, a new navigator who'd started the war as a gunner and had recently retrained. This was going to be one of Nadya's first missions in the air.

Behind Larisa and Nadya came Sasha Rogova and Zhenya Sukhorukova.

As usual, the target was only about fifteen minutes' flight time from the airfield. The searchlights were combing the sky and the antiaircraft guns were firing as usual as the Po-2s approached the enemy lines.

Then, unexpectedly, the antiaircraft guns fell eerily silent.

Mariya Smirnova, the squadron commander, noticed the silence and reasoned—correctly—that the only reason the antiaircraft guns would stop firing was because there must be German night fighter aircraft patrolling the sky.

Sure enough, from the dark sky came a yellow flare, a signal from the German plane to let the gunners on the ground know he was up there.

"We had not been attacked in this way before," Mariya said. "We had not developed tactics to counter the attack of fighter planes."

Mariya was a hardened combat pilot and knew how to avoid the antiaircraft searchlight beams. She cut the power to her engine as she approached her target, to give her the advantage of silence. She was ready to throw her plane into a sideslip if a searchlight caught her, a flight maneuver that allows you to dive very fast and steeply without spinning.

But Mariya managed to avoid the beams in the darkness.

Behind her, flying far back in the line of Po-2s, Larisa and Nadya were over the Kuban River and halfway to the target when Larisa saw four searchlights suddenly begin to comb the sky. Like Mariya, she couldn't hear the antiaircraft guns firing. Unlike Mariya, she didn't guess at first what this might mean, though she thought it was strange.

Then Larisa saw a white spot caught in the crossing of the searchlight beams—a distant Po-2.

Natasha and Lida also saw the plane that was trapped by the search-lights. They saw the blue light of tracer bullets as the German night fighter fired at the trapped plane—missed—and fired again.

The white spot suddenly became a bright red spot, and Larisa realized that it was one of the 46th's aircraft burning.

Zhenya Krutova and Lena Salikova were in that Po-2. As their plane fell, colored flashes exploded from it—they were the aircrew's signal flares exploding. The flares were kept where the aircrew could reach them, and their explosions told Larisa that the flames had already reached the cock-pits of the burning Po-2.

Zhenya Rudneva, in line behind Larisa, also saw Zhenya and Lena's burning plane. The pilot who was now plummeting in flames was another of Zhenya Rudneva's dear friends. She could hardly believe what she was watching. "My arms and legs shook; for the first time an aircraft burnt down before my eyes."

Still the antiaircraft guns were eerily silent.

As the flaming Po-2 touched the ground, the searchlights came back on and caught a second plane.

Larisa flew on toward those lights, horrified and terrified. "A bitter tickling in my throat, incapable of breathing. Goosebumps were jumping along my back, and I could hardly feel my feet—they were as if made of cotton-wool."

Then, near Anya Vysotskaya and Galya Dokutovich's plane now captured by the bright searchlights, Larisa and Nadya saw flashes coming from the sky.

They shouted together, "A fighter firing!"

The German night fighter plane was picking off the line of Po-2s as they lumbered slowly into the waiting beams of the searchlights.

Still Larisa headed for her target. But now she was aware of the powerful fighter plane in the sky above her, fully armed and more than four times faster than her flimsy Po-2. "I was so frightened I couldn't even think of escape," Larisa said. "I was to be over the target in two minutes."

"If only we had a machine gun!" Nadya yelled angrily. "We could at least give him a scare. Should I load my pistol?"

Larisa told her ominously, "Load it. But you're not likely to use it."

Now, suddenly, the antiaircraft guns began to fire.

The German guns on the ground hit the plane flown by Valentina Polunina. She and her navigator, Irina Kashirina—who'd that spring flown her dead pilot's plane home to land safely—were both doomed to burn to death.

When the third plane began to blaze, Larisa snapped out of her frozen terror. She knew that the German fighter plane could climb faster and more steeply than she could. So she descended lower than she was actually allowed to fly.

As Larisa glided toward the target, she could see the white cottages and the dark treetops of Krymskaya's orchards below her. She could also see one of the Po-2s on fire, spinning earthward through the air as its flares exploded.

"We realized that our friends were dying," she said.

When Larisa's navigator, Nadya, released their bombs, their plane was so low that they were shaken violently by the explosion. "I thought we would split into pieces," Larisa said.

Searchlights clawed at the sky all around them. As their Po-2 climbed away from the carnage below, Nadya yelled, "They caught another air crew!"

Larisa glanced back over her shoulder and saw one more of the line of Po-2s going down in flames. Sasha Rogova and Zhenya Sukhorukova were in that plane.

"Our planes were burning like candles," said pilot Serafima Amosova.

"The tracer bullets set [the] planes on fire; our planes were so vulnerable they were burning like sheets of paper," Mariya Smirnova said. "It is a horrible scene when a plane is burning. First it explodes; then it burns like a torch falling apart, and you can see particles of [plane], wings, tail, and human bodies scattered in the air."

As Larisa and Nadya recovered from the shock of their own bomb exploding beneath them, they found themselves swept by the headlight beam of the German fighter plane. They saw the flash and heard the sharp rattle of the aircraft's machine guns in the dark, and bullets raked the wings of their Po-2.

Larisa said, "The entire lower and upper starboard wing portions were pierced by the burst; you could see a straight black line formed by the shot-holes."

But Larisa had managed to avoid the antiaircraft searchlights, and the German pilot's aim in the dark wasn't accurate enough to destroy their plane.

Four pilots and four navigators of the 46th Guards perished in flames in the space of half an hour.

The Luftwaffe night fighter pilot who was in the air that night was Josef Kociok. His plane wasn't equipped with radar, which at that time was too bulky and expensive to fit in any aircraft, so he'd relied on the searchlights to locate the doomed planes that were his targets.

The events of July 31, 1943, were the worst blow and the most devastating loss that the 46th Guards Night Bomber Aviation Regiment suffered during the entire war.

At first, the shocked ground crew waiting back at the intermediate airfield had no way of knowing who'd been killed until the surviving aircraft returned. Then they had to figure it out by process of elimination.

The rest of that night's missions were canceled.

Zhenya Rudneva was utterly heartbroken by the death of the brave, eloquent, determined Galya Dokutovich, who'd suffered so much already and hadn't let it stop her from flying. Zhenya even blamed herself for having assigned Galya to Anya's plane. "I kept running up to every landing aircraft, but there was no Galya. My Galya failed to come back!" The words spilled from her like tears. "There was emptiness, emptiness in my heart!"

The regiment was living at that time in a school building furnished with folding wooden beds, and when the surviving aircrews returned to their bunks they were stricken to see eight beds still folded up.

"It was impossible not to cry," said Serafima, one of the surviving pilots. Most of the regiment was too upset to sleep.

Even so, the next night they still had to take off and fly back to the front in the dark as usual, numbed by tragedy and fear and exhaustion.

But this time they had protection. Soviet fighter pilots cleared the sky of German night fighters around them for several nights. The Luftwaffe night fighter pilot Josef Kociok himself was killed in air combat eight weeks later.

Zhenya Rudneva couldn't quite believe that her friends had died such sudden and horrific deaths. She confessed in her diary two weeks later, "Now that Galya is no more and will never return . . . It is too cruel to take. I carry her photograph with my Party membership card; I can't yet transfer it into the tiny white envelope in which I've already placed the snapshot of Zhenya—I've buried this friend of mine, too, and with such an aching heart. But with [Galya] I simply can't part."

I'll rest and get better after the war, Galya had written in her own diary when she'd come back to the regiment last winter. She'd never even had the chance to fully recover from her back injury.

Polina Gelman, another 46th Guards navigator who'd been Galya's best friend since they were in school together, wrote to Galya's family and promised them: "If no enemy bullet kills me and some day I have a daughter, I shall call her Galya and bring her up to be noble and wonderful like our Galya."

NIGHT WITCHES

Yevdokia Bershanskaya didn't always go by the book as the commander of the 46th Night Bomber Aviation Regiment, but she was good at her job. One of her original ideas was to make sure her regiment was always in training. That way, if people were transferred or killed in combat, there were always competent airwomen ready to fly the open-cockpit Po-2s on their nightly harassment missions.

After the disastrous events of the night of July 31, 1943, Yevdokia thought hard about how to avoid the tragedy being repeated. She decided that the 46th Guards should change the way they flew their bombing missions.

"Let's fly in two-plane elements," she suggested. "One aircrew should bomb the target and the other 'tackle' enemy antiaircraft weapons."

Now, instead of flying in a predictable line, the Po-2s of the 46th Guards would fly in pairs.

Polina Gelman explained the plan: "We flew two planes at a time to the target. The first attracted all the searchlights and antiaircraft guns, and the other would glide in over the target, with its engine idling so the Germans couldn't hear it, and bomb the target. With all the attention on the first plane, the second could make a successful attack."

In the dark, without lights, at a height of about 1,300 meters (over 4,000 feet), the pilot of the attacking aircraft would cut the engine. Then she would silently glide down to 600 meters (less than 2,000 feet).

After dropping her bombs she'd power the engine up again and climb away.

Nadezhda "Nadya" Popova and her navigator, Katya Ryabova, were the first crew to test the silent bombing glide. Squadron commander Marina Chechneva and her navigator, Olga Klyuyeva, flew with them to the target. Marina had flown other bombing missions with Nadya, and the two pilots were comfortable flying their Po-2s in formation. The plan was that Nadya and Katya would drop their bombs while Marina and Olga, flying two minutes ahead of them, would have the terrifying task of purposefully attracting enemy fire.

Commander Yevdokia Bershanskaya cleared her pilots for takeoff. She was as nervous as they were about the dangerous, untested strategy.

Olga guided Marina through the dark night to the target, an enemy crossing on the Terek River near Mozdok, in the Caucasus region. Now it was up to Marina to distract the enemy. She pushed the control column forward to lower the nose of her aircraft, and applied power to gain speed.

She said, "In a few seconds, we found ourselves under a veritable hail of antiaircraft fire. The searchlight beams went berserk in the sky. I flew in a weaving pattern . . . now to the left and now to the right. We couldn't let the enemy catch us with two intersected beams and, at the same time, regardless of the risk, we had to 'lead on' the searchlight operators as long as possible."

As Marina threw her little Po-2 from side to side among the searchlights and gunfire, Nadya and Katya glided silently behind her toward the target and dropped their bombs.

Then Nadya powered her engine to climb away from the explosions. Now she and Marina had to swap roles. With full power roaring, it was Nadya's turn to caper around in the searchlights while Marina climbed out of view, then idled her own engine to glide silently back to the target.

When she'd successfully glided to the right place, Marina's navigator, Olga, released their bombs.

They'd done it! Both Po-2 crews had dropped their bombs over their target, and neither aircrew had been caught by enemy gunfire.

When the triumphant flight crews returned, another pair headed out to try the new strategy that very same night, and were just as successful.

Later that month, chief of staff Irina Rakobolskaya ordered new planes for the regiment. In addition to losing four aircraft on that terrible night at the end of July, the Po-2s they'd been using for the past year were wearing out—each small plane had already flown about 450 missions. And the 46th Guards weren't going to let anything stop each flight crew from flying at least that many more.

Maybe it was the sweeping sound made by the Po-2s' canvas wings as they dived low over the German troops in the dark. When the 46th Guards were quietly idling their engines, maybe the cowering soldiers below imagined that the swooping wings sounded eerily like witch's broomsticks soaring through the dark sky.

Maybe it was because the voices of women calling to each other in the night above them were so unexpected.

Maybe it was because of their screams as their flimsy aircraft went up in flames.

Whatever the reason, the German troops at the front invented a name for the young women of the 46th Guards, who bombed them so relentlessly, three hundred times a night throughout the war.

The Germans called them *Nachthexen*—"night witches."

"Nobody knows the exact day when they started calling us night witches," said pilot Serafima Amosova. "We were fighting in the Caucasus near the city of Mozdok. . . . We were bombing the German positions almost every night, and none of us was ever shot down, so the Germans began saying these are night witches, because it seemed impossible to kill us or shoot us down."

According to a German prisoner, the radio broadcasts to the German troops at the front warned, "Attention, attention, the ladies are in the air, stay at your shelter." Nina Yegorova-Arefjeva, an armorer for the 46th Guards, said that "sometimes, when our planes were throttled back gliding in over the target, the Germans would cry out, 'Night witches!', and our crews could hear them."

Soviet soldiers were more sympathetic. They called the airwomen in their Po-2s "heavenly creatures"; male pilots called them "little sisters."

The women of the 46th Guards were liked and admired by the men who fought not far away from them. When male pilots flew over their air base and spotted the women's underthings hanging out to dry—a big clue that this was a women's regiment—they'd perform noisy aerobatics in celebration. This was not entirely appreciated by the pilots and navigators, who were trying to sleep during the day!

Raisa Zhitova-Yushina liked to encourage the Soviet ground troops when she flew over them in the dark. "When I was flying very low I would close the throttle and say, 'Hey brothers, how are you?' and they would light their torches."

PO-2 BIPLANES RETURNING TO THEIR AIR BASE AFTER A MISSION

• • •

The women who worked and flew as pilots in the Great Patriotic War fought as relentlessly as the rest of the Soviet forces did. But it's an error to believe that they were *fearless*. It's an error to believe that most soldiers are fearless. Fear is part of being a soldier, something that you live with and battle as long as you're fighting.

During the course of the war, squadron commander Marina Smirnova flew 935 night bomber missions for the 46th Guards. But she never got used to being afraid. "Before each mission and as we approached the target, I became a concentration of nerves and tension," she said. "My whole body was swept by fear of being killed."

"After bombing and having escaped the enemy's fire, I couldn't pull myself together for ten or fifteen minutes," said Nina Raspopova, another 46th Guards pilot. "I was shivering, my teeth were chattering, my feet and hands were shaking. . . . I didn't want to die. I dreamed of a small village house, a piece of rye bread, and a glass of clear river water."

234

Larisa Rozanova and Alexandra Popova agreed about the physical terror. Larisa said, "When you leave behind the area of the target, the sea of antiaircraft fire, and the searchlights, the next instant you start shivering—your feet and knees start jumping—and you cannot talk at all because you are wheezing in your throat. This was a normal reaction after each flight. In a few minutes you recover."

When Alexandra was given a cardiogram after the war, the examining doctor found that her heart was so scarred, it looked as though she'd had a heart attack.

Irina Rakobolskaya, the 46th's chief of staff, could tell how difficult the night's flying might be just by the way a nervous pilot smoked a cigarette between missions.

How did they ever make themselves go relentlessly back up into the air, night after night, day after day, for three years and more?

Tonya Khokhlova, one of the few women who was a tail gunner for the 587th Regiment, sheds a little light on how people manage this fear. She and her crew got stuck one day in a Pe-2 whose engine failed on take-off, and the pilot had to crash-land the plane with live bombs attached beneath the wings. Tonya said afterward, "Either you have no time to be frightened or you have to act very quickly, but somehow it's not a helpless fright. You have to act, you have to do something, you have to save your life—not only your life but the lives of your friends."

Even today, a pilot is trained to learn emergency flight procedures as a memorized sequence, so that if your engine fails, you have an automatic routine to help you ward off panic and land safely. But knowing you are responsible for another life can sometimes add that extra strength of spirit you might need to hold yourself together until the danger has passed—especially if it's someone you have grown to love.

EQUALITY IN THE AIR

While the Soviet women of Raskova's regiments were flying, fighting, and sometimes dying in battle over Voronezh, Taman, and Kursk, in the United States the efforts of the American women Jackie Cochran and Nancy Harkness Love finally came together. On August 5, 1943, the Women's Flying Training Detachment and the Women's Auxiliary Ferrying Squadron merged to become the Women Airforce Service Pilots, or WASP.

The WASP wasn't a military organization—at first the women who joined even had to invent and supply their own uniforms! They were paid less than men doing the same job and received no benefits or pension; if one of their pilots was killed in flight, her companions chipped in to pay for the funeral themselves.

But at last American women were able to fly in the service of their country, and over a thousand women completed the WASP training course and began ferrying military planes all over the United States and across Canada.

WASP pilots had to cope with appalling gender discrimination during the war, ranging from a temporary flight ban when they had their period to being told by radio controllers to stop talking because a plane was landing—when the woman pilot was in fact the person landing the plane!

There was even nasty and deliberate sabotage, presumed to be by American men: practical jokes such as sugar in a fuel tank, which could—and did—prove deadly. A 1944 Hollywood movie called *Ladies Courageous* portrayed the WASP fliers as hysterical airheads prone to flirtation and pilot error. "I was never so embarrassed in my life," said pilot Caro Bayley Bosca after watching the movie.

In the United Kingdom, the women who flew for the ATA struggled with similar discrimination issues. But at least no one tried to sabotage their planes, and in general they were treated with more gender equality than their American counterparts—possibly because the ATA included both men and women. By the end of the war there were no restrictions on the types of aircraft ATA women could fly. But perhaps best of all was that, in June 1943, the ATA became the first British government organization to give men and women equal pay—which meant their women pilots now earned twenty percent more than they had at the beginning of the war!

⇢ 31 ⇠
LOSS AND HONOR FOR
THE DIVE-BOMBERS

The 587th M. M. Raskova Bomber Aviation Regiment would spend the next year moving from base to base, but in the summer of 1943 their crews of three flew the powerful Pe-2 dive-bombers on aggressive missions in the Battle of Kursk in Ukraine. Early in July, the German army made a huge effort to take control of the front in this region. For the next two months, thousands upon thousands of armored tanks on both sides stormed at each other in the largest tank battle in history. The tanks were defended by nearly as many planes, and about two million soldiers were involved in the fighting—a larger number than the combined populations of present-day Philadelphia and Pittsburgh.

By the end of August, the Red Army had smashed the Germans at Kursk. So now the women and men of the 587th Bomber Aviation Regiment moved on to help take back the Smolensk region, where the Germans had held Soviet territory for the past two years.

The 587th suffered some terrible blows in Smolensk—not all of them in the air.

Ground crew weren't flying into battle on a daily basis the way the aircrew were. But they were close enough to the front lines that nobody's life was safe. One hot, hazy, dusty day when all the 587th's planes were in the air on their way to a new base, the mechanics and armorers were left behind to clean up their abandoned site before traveling by rail to catch up with the aircrew. When they'd finished their work, they set off marching along the road through fields of corn to the train station, singing as they went.

Suddenly, rifle shots broke out around them. The young women dropped to the ground. They didn't lie there cowering, though. They fired back into the cornfield with their own guns.

But when they dared to raise their heads from the dusty road and get up on their feet again, one of the armorers, Tonya Yudina, was dead.

They never found out who'd fired the deadly shots. But after that, the armorers scrawled "For our Tonya!" on the bombs they loaded on the 587th's Pe-2s.

Meanwhile, with every flight, the Pe-2 aircrews risked their lives with a determination that's unimaginable for most of us.

Where do you get the nerve to keep flying, when in a single year you've already survived being shot down twice? That's what happened to pilot Sasha Yegorova, with her navigator, Nina Karaseva, and their tail gunner, Aleksandr Kudriavtsev. In one of their crashes, Aleksandr dislocated his shoulder as Sasha glided their doomed Pe-2 down to rest in a swamp. But all three of the crew survived, managed to get out of their wrecked plane, and found their way back to their airfield. They were issued a new plane, and as soon as Aleksandr's shoulder was in working order, they were back in the sky.

When their Pe-2 was again hit by enemy gunfire in battle on September 2, 1943, Sasha found she couldn't control the plane to glide to earth for a crash landing. "For the third time, we were going down in a knocked-out machine, enveloped in black smoke and fiery tongues," said Nina, Sasha's navigator. "Our fuel tank, [airframe], and the starboard wing were burning."

Sasha ordered Nina and Aleksandr to parachute out of the uncontrollable aircraft. Aleksandr let himself out of the hatch in the gunner's rear cabin, but when Nina tried to open the canopy over the pilot and navigator's cockpit, the release catch broke off. She and Sasha had to crawl into the back of the plummeting plane and clamber out through the lower hatch, too.

Both young women managed to claw their way out while their Pe-2 was still in the air. They opened their parachutes, but they lost each other in the sky as they fell. In the distance Nina could see another parachute, but she didn't know which of her crewmates it was.

The wind carried Nina farther and farther west, over the front line and into enemy territory. Luftwaffe planes fired their guns at her and at the other parachute as they drifted defenselessly to the ground.

Sasha, the pilot, hit the ground hard and lost consciousness.

When she woke up it was raining, and she was lying in a ravine full of bomb craters. She got up and started to make her way toward the sound of the familiar Soviet guns. She dropped to the ground in fear when she saw a German soldier standing with his back to her.

Sasha began to crawl.

Worming her way on all fours through the bomb craters made the night seem to last forever. But by dawn, Sasha finally reached a group of Red Army soldiers. They helped her find a truck driver who could take her to a nearby airfield. And from there, Sasha was able to get a flight back to her own base.

Behind enemy lines, Sasha's navigator, Nina, and her tail gunner, Aleksandr, weren't so lucky.

Nina's pistol had fallen out of its holster while she'd been falling through the air. Now she was in the worst possible of situations: she was in enemy territory and had no way to defend herself, or even to kill herself.

She didn't have long to wonder about what to do. As she was looking for a place to hide, two German shoulders came running toward her with machine guns.

"Their eyes were wild-looking and their faces distorted," Nina said. The furious Germans ordered Nina to raise her hands. As she stood there with her hands up, they went through her pockets. It wasn't until Nina pushed one of their hands away from her chest and told them sharply, "Don't touch!" that they realized, with surprise, she was a woman.

It all happened so quickly that Nina could still see the distant fire of her own burning aircraft as the German soldiers led her away.

Later, Aleksandr was also captured. In the beginning of their imprisonment, he and Nina were together briefly, and Nina could see that the gunner was in bad shape: he had "a wound in one leg, a cut eyebrow, and hands covered with blood." But the two Soviet prisoners weren't allowed to talk to each other. They could only hope that their pilot, Sasha, hadn't met the same fate.

Nina and Aleksandr had been taken prisoner behind enemy lines by the Germans: the Soviet soldier's worst nightmare.

Sergeant Artur Gartner, a Luftwaffe pilot, said that most Germans were shocked to discover that there were Soviet women fighting against them in the air. When a German pilot shot down a Pe-2 dive-bomber and found that a woman had been flying it, his commanding officer told him: "Don't mention it to anyone. We don't shoot at women."

Not surprisingly, the Germans didn't have prisoner-of-war camps set up to accommodate women soldiers. So Nina had to endure something far more terrible: she was eventually sent to the women's section of the concentration camp at Buchenwald, Germany.

It would be years before the pilot, Sasha, found out what had happened to the rest of her crew. As the September days dragged on without word from them, the grieving regiment had to assume that Nina and Aleksandr had been killed in battle.

Yet another Pe-2 crew came to grief in September 1943 while bombing lines of German tanks near Smolensk.

Enemy shell explosions were jolting and rocking the planes as they flew toward their target, and suddenly, the Pe-2 flown by Klava Fomicheva lurched as its left fuel tank was pierced by one of the shells. But even though the plane was trailing a streaking white jet of leaking fuel, Klava and her tail gunner didn't try to parachute out: Klava kept on flying, because her navigator, Galya Turabelidze, had been hit in the head and couldn't jump out herself.

Klava managed to find an airfield where she thought she could land. But a group of Yak fighters was taxiing along the runway. With fuel fumes filling the cockpit and making it difficult to breathe, there was only one chance to land the plane. Klava tried to set down her Pe-2 on the ground next to the runway.

Unfortunately, as she was braking to a halt, one of her wheels hit a bomb crater and the aircraft flipped upside down. The wounded navigator, Galya, was thrown clear, but Klava was trapped in the burning plane.

The local aircraft maintenance team came to the rescue. They dashed to the crash site and used axes to chop a hole in the floor of the cockpit of the upside-down plane.

They managed to drag Klava out just before the aircraft exploded; but her tail gunner was killed.

Klava was in the hospital for five months recovering from third-degree burns.

There were so many deaths and injuries in the 587th at Smolensk that they had to bring in reinforcements.

Antonina Bondareva—the pilot who tucked her knitting behind her parachute—was one of these. She'd become hooked on flying when a biplane landed in her village while she was in seventh grade, and she joined the local gliding club as one of eighteen students—and one of only two girls.

Antonina's father, who worked in an ore extraction factory, aggressively disapproved of her flying. As she'd leave to go off to the gliding club, he'd say, "Don't come back, you may not come back, I won't let you in!" But her mother let her go, as long as she did all her household chores first.

Antonina graduated from the glider club at sixteen and began to learn to fly powered aircraft, in the typical Soviet training plane, the open-cockpit Po-2. She was only seventeen when she became an instructor.

Of course, Antonina wanted to volunteer immediately for Raskova's regiments when the war started. But like so many other young women, she wasn't allowed to leave the flight school where she was an instructor. Also—she had a toddler to take care of. In the morning she would lock the little girl in the room they shared, leaving her on her own with some porridge, and go to work to train new—male—cadets to fly.

By 1943 her husband had been killed at the front, and Antonina had 2,000 flying hours. She was finally sent to join the 587th Regiment. She left her little girl with her husband's family.

• • •

Yekaterina Chujkova joined the 587th in 1943 as a reinforcement for the armament mechanics. She'd been sixteen when war broke out, and living in Leningrad. She went from high school to digging trenches, then escorted other citizens to shelter during Leningrad's long siege of bombing and starvation.

For the first year of the Leningrad blockade, Yekaterina lived on not much more than a daily ration of soup made with boiled water and four slices of brown bread.

In January 1943, Soviet soldiers managed to get control of the railway in and out of Leningrad, allowing a little relief for the desperate citizens of the city. Yekaterina's sister worked at a factory that was evacuated from Leningrad to Moscow, and Yekaterina was able to go along.

When Yekaterina joined the 587th, she was so thin and starved that she could hardly move. But somehow, she managed to convince the recruiter that she'd be able to work. She trained on-site at the airfield were the regiment was currently stationed, arming bombs and attaching them to the Pe-2s. Each aircrew usually flew three combat missions in a day, and there was only an hour in between flights for the mechanics to refuel the aircraft and the armorers to reload the bombs and the ammunition in the planes' machine guns. Like the armorers of the 46th Guards, the armorers of the 587th Regiment handled over three tons of bombs in a day.

At night, the mechanics cleaned machine guns—or they had to take turns guarding the aircraft. Yekaterina didn't like guard duty. It was lonely and eerie, straining your eyes and ears in the dark as you watched for possible enemies. If Yekaterina heard a noise, she'd call out. Then, if no one answered, she said, "I'm sorry, but I'm going to shoot; excuse me, I'm going to shoot!"

The apology was little more than nerves and politeness, because

Yekaterina meant what she said. One night, a figure appeared who didn't answer her challenge. She fired her gun at the intruder, and the blow knocked him over. It turned out to be another Russian guard—he hadn't answered because he'd forgotten that night's password! Fortunately—for both of them—he wasn't hurt.

The 587th Bomber Aviation Regiment had been flying in combat for only about six months when they suffered their heavy casualties and reinforcements in the summer of 1943. But it doesn't seem to have damaged their morale. The Battle of Kursk was a huge operation, and they felt that they were making a difference. They were rewarded for it when in September they, too, were ceremoniously awarded the elite title of "Guards." Now they were officially the 125th M. M. Raskova Guards Bomber Aviation Regiment.

THE 125TH GUARDS WITH A PE-2 DIVE-BOMBER

This must surely have given them new resolve when they may have desperately needed it. Every honor was a cause for celebration.

"When we are awarded orders or medals in our army, we have a tradition: to drop our orders and medals into a crystal glass filled with vodka and to drink that glass of vodka to the bottom," said Yekaterina. "In the wartime we had to use empty food cans instead of the crystal."

Even the smallest of ceremonies helped to boost morale, and the honor of becoming Guards was no small achievement.

September 1943 also marked a significant milestone in the war: Germany's Axis partner Italy surrendered to the Allies.

But the nations of Europe that were occupied by the Germans were still fully under their military control. Millions of civilians were being coldly and methodically slaughtered in the German concentration camps. Now, as the third winter of the Great Patriotic War approached, the Soviet Union began the long and harsh process of pushing Germany's occupying army westward 2,000 kilometers (over 1,200 miles) back across Russia, Ukraine, and into eastern Europe out of Soviet territory. The Germans had stormed in like lightning in a single month in 1941: it took the Soviet Union *three and a half years* to push them out again.

For Marina Raskova's regiments, the next year and a half would keep them on the move as the ground and air forces of the USSR began that push. It was a slow but steady process, and for the airwomen there wouldn't be much variation in the routine of the next eighteen months—fueling and arming planes, dropping bombs, eating "blondie" porridge and herring, snatching a few hours' sleep, and starting all over again hour upon hour and day after day—all the way to Berlin, the capital of Germany and the heart of Hitler's Third Reich government.

And the bright autumn days of 1943 continued to hold tragedy for the 125th Guards, despite their proud new name.

On October 14 they lost three of their Pe-2s in a single battle. Some of the three-person aircrews managed to parachute to safety as the Pe-2s burned and crashed. But pilots Lyuba Gubina and Anya Yazovskaya were both killed, as well as navigator Lena Ponomareva.

The mourning regiment planted a little birch tree for the three young women over their grave. The tree's autumnal leaves trembled, reminding navigator Valya Kravchenko of "little yellow flames, in the rays of the setting sun."

The survivors were stunned. Grieving in their dugout that night, someone started to sing a folk song. Others soon joined in:

O black raven! O black raven!
Why do you hover overhead?
Fly away, I'm not your prey,
Black raven, I'm not dead!

→ · 3 2 · ←

OVER THE BLACK SEA

In October 1943, the 46th Guards received a new award for their many successful missions in their Po-2s. They were now named the 46th Taman Guards in honor of their spring and summer harassing the German troops in the Taman Peninsula.

That same month, Marina Chechneva flew her five hundredth mission in a Po-2—her five hundredth mission in a little more than a year of combat. It was a nerve-racking night of dense cloud and stormy weather, but when Marina got back to her airfield, a surprise was waiting for her. Commander Yevdokia Bershanskaya had planned a party to celebrate. The party food was a huge watermelon with the number 500 carved into the rind!

Marina wasn't the first in the regiment to have reached this milestone—squadron commander Mariya Smirnova, Natasha Meklin, and Katya Ryabova had also flown five hundred missions. Together, these three veterans lifted up the watermelon and grandly presented it to Marina.

"Take the 'crown,'" said Mariya. "We wish you still another one before the war ends."

Then everybody devoured the watermelon, wishing they were able to have parties more often.

The German army's blockade of the city of Leningrad, which had begun on September 8, 1941, finally ended in its defeat there on January 27, 1944. During those 872 days nearly a million people died in Leningrad—about one-third of the city's population. Most of them starved to death. Now, at last, the survivors were free.

Of course, hindsight tells us that the war would go on for nearly another year and a half after the end of the Leningrad blockade, but as the Red Army began to win significant victories over the invading Germans, people hoped that the war would soon be over. Some Soviet citizens, thinking positively, even dared to wonder if the NKVD and the Siberian prison camps wouldn't be needed anymore after the war. Maybe Stalin would give his government and the Motherland a fresh start once all this was over. This, too, helped to increase the morale of the people of the Soviet Union.

In the meantime, they now fought against Nazi fascism with renewed determination.

On March 8, 1944, International Women's Day and the anniversary of the Russian Revolution, the 46th Taman Guards Night Bomber Aviation Regiment received two important visitors: the commander of the Second Belorussian Front and the commander of the Fourth Air Army. As the regiment lined up to greet the VIPs, one of the visiting men had an idea.

Thinking he could do a good deed for these brave young women who'd been working and fighting so hard for nearly three years without a break, he commented that it might be helpful if ten or twenty men were sent to help load bombs onto aircraft for them, and assist them with other heavy work.

"We don't need any helpers, we're managing just fine on our own!" everyone answered quickly.

Of Marina Raskova's original three regiments, there were men now flying and working in both the 586th Regiment and the 125th Guards, and those units were now led by men. The 46th Taman Guards was the only Soviet regiment to remain entirely staffed by women throughout the war, and they were proud of it. They worked as hard as their male counterparts, and they were able to outfly all the other Po-2 bomber regiments for sheer numbers in their nightly missions. They didn't want to be given special treatment.

Olga Yerokhina, an armorer who'd worked in a men's regiment before Yevdokia Bershanskaya recruited her as a reinforcement for the 46th Guards, said that the physical work *was* easier when men did the heavy lifting.

"But," she continued, "from the point of view of human relationships, it was much better in the women's regiment."

In the spring of 1944, the 46th Guards helped to drive the Germans out of Crimea. They moved to a base in a resort area near the Kerch Strait, between the Black Sea and the Sea of Azov, with their little Po-2 biplanes lined up in a field along the cliffs above the sea.

Moving to a new airfield was often difficult and dangerous for the Soviet aviators. Once, when the 46th Guards arrived at a new base for the first time, they didn't immediately cover their Po-2s with the camouflage nets that hid them from enemy spy planes. While the women were eating breakfast, a group of German aircraft descended on the thirty wood-and-canvas Po-2s, firing their machine guns.

All the pilots leaped up from their food and ran to the parked planes.

They scrambled into the cockpits, took off, and scattered in every direction in the air—turning the Po-2s into difficult targets. The quick reaction saved the regiment's planes.

On another occasion, they were not so lucky. Klavdiya Ilushina, the regiment's chief engineer, was staying with a local family who'd made her a delicious Easter dinner that included eggs and cake. Klavdiya enjoyed this rare treat, and she went to bed hoping for a good night's sleep, too. Instead, she was shaken awake in the middle of the night by her hostess, who urged her, "You must get up, your airfield is being bombed, your aircraft are burning!"

Klavdiya and her companions threw on their clothes in the dark and ran to the airfield. But in her rush, Klavdiya accidentally put on the high heels she'd worn earlier when she'd dressed up for her host family's special meal! As she ran, one of her heels came off her shoe. At exactly the same instant, a German aircraft swooped over Klavdiya's head, so low she could see the pilot's face as he fired his machine guns at her.

Klavdiya threw herself flat on the ground as the German plane passed over.

He missed her in the dark. Klavdiya wasn't hurt. After the plane had passed, she got up and hurried on to the airfield in her broken shoes.

Some of the 46th's aircraft were already destroyed—and some were still on fire. Klavdiya climbed into one of the Po-2s that seemed to be okay, but as she was checking the cockpit for damage, the German fighter planes came back. She leaped out of the plane and lay on the ground under the Po-2's fabric wing—the regiment had been at this base for such a short time that they hadn't yet dug trenches to shelter people from air attacks.

Everybody lay on the ground waiting breathlessly for the gunfire to stop. There was nothing else that they could do.

At last the German attack planes flew away again, leaving the women of the 46th to repair the damage and help their friends who had been wounded.

In the Kerch area, the 46th Guards shared the sky with the male pilots of the Soviet Black Sea Fleet. When the women first arrived, the men greeted them with insincere politeness—and some sneering. "A broads' regiment . . . Well, well . . ."

But the men had set up a snug and spotless dugout for the pilots of the 46th Guards to sleep in. "There were snow-white sheets on the bunk beds and even fresh flowers stood in containers on tables," said Serafima Amosova. The young women wondered if the attention to detail was a subtle challenge. They'd been given a clean and pretty place to live, but did they deserve it? Could they earn their keep? Were they up to the grueling combat work that lay ahead?

Of course, they were up to the work even without the challenge.

Despite their lukewarm first impression of the Black Sea Fleet pilots, the women of the 46th Guards came to know and like these men, who struck at the German forces during the day while the 46th Guards struck at night. And the men quickly grew to appreciate them in turn. They even surprised navigator Tatyana Sumarokova on the morning of her birthday after her night's bombing missions, presenting her with a bottle of champagne and singing her a song they'd made up themselves!

One of the jobs that the 46th Guards had here, along with other Po-2 regiments, was to fly emergency supply runs for the Red Army troops. This required a different kind of skill and daring. Instead of dropping bombs from 600 meters (nearly 2,000 feet) above the ground, on a supply run a pilot had to swoop down as low as 50 meters (164 feet) and dump food, ammunition, and medical supplies in a schoolyard or vacant lot marked by the light of a bonfire.

Marina Chechneva would fly her plane so low on these missions that she was able to scream over the side at the waiting troops, "Take your 'presents,' brothers!" Her navigator would yell, "Greetings to you from the 46th Guards Women's Air Regiment!"

From the ground in the dark, they could hear the grateful shouts of thanks in return. Marina said, "The whistling of the wind and the noise of the incoming tide made it impossible to distinguish individual words. All the same, it was good to hear the voices."

On April 9, 1944, Chief Navigator Zhenya Rudneva decided to fly the night's mission over Kerch with Polina Prokofyeva. Polina was a new pilot on her very first bombing mission. Zhenya's friend Nadya Popova took off after them, and there were other Po-2s in the sky as usual. It wasn't always easy to tell who was who, especially when the guns started firing.

Pilot Kaleriya Rylskaya and navigator Nadya Studilina, also in the sky that night, became aware of another Po-2 flying a little above them. They could see the blue flame of the other aircraft's exhaust, and it cheered them up to know they weren't alone in the air.

They had trouble taking aim at their target because the sky was full of scraps of cloud, but they managed it at last. After they'd dropped their bombs, Kaleriya and Nadya headed for the open water of the Black Sea to avoid being shot at from the ground. As they flew back toward their own airfield, Nadya could see a fire blazing back on the land far below.

They landed safely, but their comrades who came to meet them on the ground were anxious. They'd all been able to see a Po-2 come down from the sky in flames, bright against the clouds.

"Who came back?" the ground crew called out as the Po-2 taxied in.

Both young women yelled the pilot's last name together: "Rylskaya!"

The Po-2 that Kaleriya and Nadya had seen flying above them hadn't come back. It turned out that the blaze Nadya Studilina had spotted as they'd flown away from their target was the burning wreck of the other Po-2.

Nadya Popova had seen it too. In fact, she'd seen the plane as it got caught in the searchlights and was hit.

It was the plane flown by Polina Prokofyeva and navigated by Zhenya Rudneva, the astronomy student who'd told so many stories and recited poetry to her adored and adoring friends, who'd written such enthusiastic letters home about flying.

This is silly, a complete paradox: after all, the war is going on, there is so much horror and spilled blood all around, yet I am convinced that for me this is the best time of my life.

"I saw their aircraft burning, and the flares they carried began exploding," said Nadya Popova. "The burning plane crashed while the searchlights continued to hold it in their lights."

Zhenya and Polina were both killed in the inferno. It had been Zhenya's 645th combat mission.

Irina Rakobolskaya, in her role as chief of staff, had been on the airfield as she always was, checking each of her aircrews as they took off and landed. She had watched in helpless anguish while the flaming plane slowly glided to earth, knowing that her friend Zhenya was burning to death in the air.

"Grief paralyzed me," Irina said. "I was blind and deaf. I could hardly pull myself together to keep on handling the combat of the regiment on the ground."

• • •

Zhenya Rudneva, astronomy student and poet and storyteller, was awarded the Gold Star of the Hero of the Soviet Union in December 1944. Many years later, in 1976, an asteroid was named "Rudneva" in her memory. Larisa Rozanova took her place as the chief navigator for the 46th Guards.

It's amazing how you can fear for your life, work until you are fainting with exhaustion, and still

CHIEF NAVIGATOR ZHENYA RUDNEVA OF THE 46TH GUARDS

find joy in simple things: flowers by your bed, a song on your birthday, a watermelon decorated with a significant number. Zhenya Rudneva was *so good* at this. And she'd shared that joy widely with her comrades.

But they all had that ability to some extent. Flying over the Black Sea at night, even on her way to a combat mission, Serafima Amosova was able to take an astonishing moment to appreciate the majesty of the darkened landscape:

"Below, quite near, the white crests of the waves flashed. After circling once above the airfield and gaining the necessary altitude, we headed in the assigned direction. We looked around. Everything was amazingly beautiful: to the right, the white 'battlements' of the mountains; beyond them the dark silhouette of the Caucasus Range, with its snow-covered peaks, made pinkish by the disappearing sun; below, the sparkling sea, black and with a bluish tint; and above, the dark sky, sprinkled with many stars."

CROSSING THE LINE

In the personal histories of the Soviet women who flew and worked on aircraft during the war, there are many stories of gender discrimination, but there's practically no mention of sexual aggression or assault. It's not obvious whether this is because it didn't happen, or because it simply wasn't something these women chose to talk about when they looked back on their wartime experiences. Women from other branches of the military rarely mention it either.

There certainly were problems, whether or not people volunteered to talk about them. In many cases, a male commander would try to pull rank to take advantage of an enlisted young woman. Harassment—indeed, flirting or having an affair or any kind of hanky-panky—was considered a disgrace to the Communist Party. The gravest issues seem to have occurred among the partisans, the guerrilla resistance fighters on the German-occupied side of the front lines. Beginning in 1943, the Komsomol even took steps to campaign against partisan sexual harassment and discrimination.

Olga Lisikova, who flew as a transport pilot in a men's regiment, was grabbed after a formal dinner by a general in the division where she'd just been transferred. She knew he'd overpower her if she struggled, and the really frightening thing was that she was sure no one dared to come to her rescue. She lied to him desperately, "I fly with my husband in my crew!"

The general was so surprised that he let Olga go. She rushed out to find her radio operator and mechanic and commanded one of them to pretend to be her husband—she'd completely made up the excuse just so she could get away from her attacker.

Olga was so shaken by this that she couldn't sleep that night.

"I couldn't believe any commander would behave like that," she said. "Were generals allowed to do anything that came to mind?" It was a huge relief to be able to fly away from the situation early the next morning.

Yelena Karakorskaya, the deputy engineer in special aircraft equipment for the 586th Fighter Aviation Regiment, experienced another incident. She tells of how a famous Russian pilot and a triple Hero of the Soviet Union, A. I. Pokryshkin, landed at the airfield to refuel his fighter plane. The 586th's commander, Aleksandr Gridnev, was away, and the deputy commander at the time, also a man, ordered Yelena and her group to fill the famous flier's aircraft with fuel.

Yelena replied that engineers weren't allowed to refuel planes—the mechanics were supposed to do it.

What happened next was suddenly, shockingly violent.

"[The deputy commander] grabbed me by the collar, and I pulled away," said Yelena. "His hand slipped down onto my breast, and I slapped him on his face instinctively. He pulled out his pistol and wanted to shoot me, but the girls hung on his arm and prevented it."

Instead of being shot, Yelena was imprisoned in the basement of the officers' guardhouse for ten days with the job of whitewashing the walls. When Aleksandr Gridnev returned, he released her. He gave her a day to recover—and the deputy commander was discharged from the regiment, although it's not obvious this was a direct result of the incident.

Stories like this one are rarely recorded. Far more common are examples of ridiculous misunderstandings made by male soldiers, or men treating the airwomen like children or inferiors. When a Soviet air army VIP, General Vorzheykin, visited the 125th Guards and inspected the regiment, he stopped by Katya Fedotova's plane and demanded of Commander Valentin Markov: "Why aren't the pilots in their cockpits by now?"

All the young women were already sitting in their planes, but they were so much shorter than men that the general couldn't see them from the ground. Katya had to unfasten her straps and climb up out of the cockpit to prove that she and her crew were ready for combat.

Tail gunner Tonya Khokhlova, of the 125th Guards, told how on one occasion some Soviet pilots flew low over their airfield and dropped an object out of their plane. When the commander sent someone to clear the airfield before an accident occurred, the thing turned out to be a big teddy bear.

It was from a men's regiment of fighter planes who'd been assigned to protect the Pe-2 bombers on their next mission. There was a note pinned to the bear that said: "Dear young girls, we just learned we are escorting you. Don't you get frightened; we'll do everything to defend you, fight for you with the last drop of our blood. Thank you!"

A cute present—but presumably the men didn't feel the need to drop reassuring teddy bears off at other men's air regiments just before a combat mission! However, the 125th Guards seem to have laughed it off, returning the joke by dropping homemade wooden dolls over men's airfields.

For us, looking back at these events and trying to understand them, there is a frustrating paradox at work here. The men who flew and worked with the women of Marina's regiments, more often than not, treated them as "little sisters." Their caring and reassuring attitude is genuine. At the same time, though, military women throughout the USSR were often viewed by their superior officers as fair game for sexual exploitation.

The women of Raskova's regiments seem to have generally escaped assault and unwanted attention. It's likely they were so segregated from ordinary fighting units and considered so special that the women of these regiments were, to a certain extent, untouchable.

ALLIED FORCES

The threat of assault from superior officers was certainly an unwelcome hazard to negotiate. But for the Soviet women aviators of the Great Patriotic War, it seems that the norm was cooperation and respect from their male counterparts of equal rank—the pilots who flew with them and the ground crews who worked with them.

Because so little is known about the men who flew the solo Yak fighters for the 586th Fighter Aviation Regiment, it's easy to forget that they were flying and sharing in daily life alongside the regiment's women. The 586th spent the fall of 1943 defending Kursk and then the Ukrainian city of Kiev, newly liberated from German occupation. But they didn't stay in the Kiev region long, moving on in February 1944 and again in March. For the next six months they were assigned to protect railway lines and other industrial targets near the border with Poland.

They still weren't seeing frontline action, but when a fighter pilot of the 586th was involved in an aerial battle, it could be fierce and grim. You could lose a friend as quickly as you made one—men as well as women.

On June 5, 1944, 586th pilot Klavdiya Pankratova flew alongside a new male pilot, Kolya Korolev, to hunt down a Luftwaffe spy plane. Kolya had been assigned to the 586th after being wounded while ramming a German aircraft. When the two pilots in their Yaks caught up with the Luftwaffe plane, they fired at it together, then turned around and fired at it again, until Klavdiya could see that one of its engines was aflame.

In and out of cloud the three planes flew, with the two pilots of the 586th teaming up after every pass, until they saw that their prey had crashed.

"We flew home wing tip to wing tip, like in an air show," Klavdiya said. "I saw Kolya's white-toothed smile and his thumbs-up sign. He was a good lad. He spent only one month with us; in the next air battle he received a fatal wound."

The day after Klavdiya and Kolya's shared victory, on June 6, 1944, the Allied nations finally launched their organized attack against the German occupation of western Europe. Ground, sea, and air troops from the United Kingdom, the United States, and Canada, supported by the French resistance, stormed onto the beaches of Normandy in France. This "D-Day" invasion was the beginning of the "second front" which Stalin and the USSR had been urging and hoping for. Now the German troops would have to fight on front lines in both the east and the west of Europe.

The "second front" had been a dream for so long that everybody in the USSR had started to make cynical jokes about it—but now it was really happening. The night after the Normandy Invasion, restaurants in Moscow were packed with excited people thrilled to have a reason to celebrate.

In the June weeks that followed, the Red Army launched a renewed attack on the Eastern Front. The 46th Guards Night Bomber Aviation

TARAN: AERIAL RAMMING

Aerial ramming—or, in Russian, *taran*—was a desperate tactic to be undertaken as a last resort. The idea was that if your plane ran out of ammunition, you could still destroy an enemy plane if you crashed into it on purpose. That's just what Kolya Korolev had done before his transfer to the 586th.

Ramming wasn't necessarily fatal. Unlike the kamikaze attacks flown by Japanese pilots, *taran* wasn't meant to be a suicide maneuver. But it was hugely dangerous and often did result in the pilot's death. The celebrated Russian aviator Pyotr Nesterov—who, incidentally, was the first person ever to fly an aerobatic loop, in 1913—also made the first known *taran* attack. On September 8, 1914, Nesterov rammed an Austrian plane flown by Franz Malina. Both pilots were killed—the very first pilots to die in World War I.

On the day Germany invaded the Soviet Union in 1941, at least eight unarmed fighter pilots rammed German aircraft.

As you can imagine, this desperate measure wasn't encouraged by the air force. But the government talked it up as a patriotic move, and

Regiment was part of the storm of bombing when the Soviet Air Force flew massive assaults on the German lines on the third anniversary of their entry into the war. Now the Soviets began to prepare to take back the eastern region of Belorussia from German occupation.

The combined Allied forces' Normandy Invasion in June 1944 is famous the world over. But a smaller group of Allies had been helping each other out on the Eastern Front in Russia for some time now. Late in 1943, an unusual early in the war pilots did it anyway when they had no other way to force down an enemy plane.

There is a technique to it, and it took an expert and daring pilot to pull off a *taran* attack—the idea was to try to hit the other plane's control surfaces, such as the tail.

Only one woman, the Soviet pilot Yekaterina Zelenko, is known to have performed a successful *taran* attack. She was a flight commander in the all-male 135th Bomber Aviation Regiment. She'd been wounded in a furious air battle and her navigator had been killed, and when she ran out of ammunition, she destroyed a German plane by ramming it with her own aircraft.

She'd done such a calculated job of using her aircraft as a battering ram that she was still able to use her flight controls afterward. But another enemy fighter shot her down and killed her.

Yekaterina Zelenko died early in the war, in September 1941. But it took so long to pull together evidence about what she'd done that she wasn't awarded a posthumous Hero of the Soviet Union and Gold Star until 1990, only a year before the collapse of the USSR.

section of the French Air Force, later known as the Normandie-Niemen Regiment, had joined the Soviet troops to defend them in the air. They stayed with the Soviets until the end of the war. They were the only Western force to fly on the Eastern Front, and they were stationed right by the 125th Guards Bomber Aviation Regiment.

For over a year, the male French pilots of the Normandie-Niemen Regiment, flying dangerous Soviet Yaks, frequently served as fighter escorts for the women of the 125th Guards in their powerful Pe-2 dive-bombers.

On their first few aggressive missions together, the French pilots didn't even realize that the pilots and navigators of the Pe-2s' crews of three were women.

Léon Cuffaut, one of the Normandie-Niemen pilots, was there for the first face-to-face encounter of the two regiments. It happened when a Pe-2 dive-bomber landed at Normandie-Niemen's airfield during a snowstorm in the winter of 1943–1944.

"Delighted, we watched the daredevil make an excellent landing in very poor visibility," said Léon.

He and the other French pilots were utterly amazed when the aircrew that climbed out of the plane turned out to be "young girls"—pilot Lelya Sholokhova and navigator Valya Volklova.

The women of the 125th Guards liked and appreciated the Frenchmen who flew for the Normandie-Niemen Regiment and protected them in the air. They even kept in touch and had a couple of reunions in Moscow after the war. Galina Brok, a navigator for the 125th Guards who flew with pilot Antonina Bondareva, found it reassuring when she sometimes heard the "broken Russian" of the French pilots coming over the radio.

"When there were friends in the sky, the attacking enemy fighters seemed less terrible," she said.

Perhaps the most joyful alliances from this time were those that ended in marriage—and quite a few of them did.

Yevdokia Bershanskaya, the commander of the 46th Guards, married the commander of a nearby men's regiment. Tamara Pamyatnykh, the 586th Regiment's squadron leader who helped chase off the forty-two Luftwaffe bombers, married a fighter pilot from a male Soviet regiment based close to hers in 1944; she even transferred to his regiment so they could be together. He was shot down and imprisoned in the Buchenwald concentration camp only a month later, and Tamara didn't see him again until the war was over. But she stayed in his regiment and flew there with the men until the end of the war.

Several women of the 125th Guards ended up married to men of the 124th Regiment stationed near them. Tonya Khokhlova, the tail gunner for the 125th, married her navigator Klara Dubkova's brother. After the war, Valentin Markov himself married one of the 125th Guards squadron navigators, Galya Dzhunkovskaya, the young woman who sang songs and told stories to her pilot, Masha Dolina, while they flew.

Antonina Lepilina, the armorer for Galya's aircraft, said that the regiment guessed these two had feelings for each other, even though "they didn't act in any way but properly, ever." But Antonina noticed a giveaway: after a battle "when the girls were brought back burned and injured, Valentin Markov himself carried Galya out of the plane."

There was, however, a bit of a double standard when it came to romance. The women of Raskova's regiments, with Soviet society reinforcing their heterosexual standards, felt that marriage was acceptable; but affairs were not. In the 46th Guards, the regiment was stunned when, near the end of the war, one of their pilots had a baby. The general of the air army that they flew with thought that the joke was on the enemy, and said that the new mother should be given a medal.

"She bombed the Germans while pregnant. What a hero!"

It wasn't a joke for the 46th Guards, though. Commander Yevdokia Bershanskaya and Chief of Staff Irina Rakobolskaya were scandalized. Irina called it a "nightmare" bringing "shame" on the whole regiment. This was the only Soviet regiment to be staffed entirely by women throughout the war, and they took pride in this segregation. On the whole, they felt that they should also keep themselves out of relationships with men during the war—going so far as to condemn even walking home with young men, as there "must be no affairs whatsoever."

Brotherhood and sisterhood in wartime was necessary and acceptable—for the Motherland. But sexual relationships were not.

❧· 3 5 ·❧

THE EDGE OF THE CLOUDS

Without a doubt, the most intense wartime relationships formed by any of Marina Raskova's aviators were the bonds formed by a flight crew in combat.

In the spring of 1944, as poor weather kept the challenging, powerful Pe-2 dive-bombers on the ground, there had been a lull in the aggressive fighting as the USSR prepared for their offense in Belorussia. The 125th M. M. Raskova Guards had spent the winter in a village practically destroyed by the Germans. Administrative staff, and some of the aircrew, lived in one of only two local houses that were still standing; everybody else lived in dugouts among a few scattered oak and birch trees that hadn't been blown up or used for firewood. The 125th had a chance to draw breath here. Their reinforcements settled in, some of the more senior pilots and navigators were promoted, and the three-person flight crews got changed around.

Navigator Galya Dzhunkovskaya, who used to sing to Masha Dolina in the air, now flew with Klava Fomicheva. Klava was the one whose plane had crashed the previous September and who'd spent five months in the hospital with third-degree burns. Now she was in command of the regiment's second squadron, and Galya was a little shy of her battle-hardened and serious pilot. There was no more singing—Klava found it distracting. "I don't like doing two things at the same time," she said.

But Galya liked her. Klava let Galya lean over her shoulder in the air and try out the flight controls as they flew toward their targets. And she noticed that Klava still carried a photograph of Marina Raskova in her map case.

As the Allied forces moved through western Europe following the D-Day invasion of Normandy, the Soviets moved on the Germans in Belorussia, bringing another wave of desperate combat for the 125th. Soon they were engaged in air battles just as fierce as those they'd fought the previous summer.

KLAVA FOMICHEVA OF THE 125TH GUARDS

On June 23, 1944, the 125th's commander, Valentin Markov, led a formation of Pe-2s, including Klava and Galya's plane, to bomb German positions in Belorussia. When Valentin's own navigator, Nikolai Nikitin, was wounded, it didn't stop either of them. Valentin and Nikolai didn't turn around until they'd dropped their bombs over the target. Then, when they'd flown back through the storm of antiaircraft fire and enemy fighter planes and were safely over Soviet territory again, Valentin let Klava take over to lead the flight home. He left the formation so he could rush his bleeding navigator to the hospital.

What Klava's commander didn't know was that her aircraft had also been hit. Her starboard engine had been pierced by a shell and her tail gunner, Grigoriy Grishko, had been killed. Klava herself was wounded in the leg, and before long, fire began to spread along the wing of their Pe-2 from the damaged engine.

Only minutes before, Galya had been checking with Grigoriy to make sure the camera hatch was open to record their bombing. He'd been cut off in the middle of a sentence.

"Was he killed?" Galya couldn't believe it. "Was he really killed?"

Klava didn't answer. She might have been trying to banish agonized thoughts of her previous tail gunner, who'd also been killed, less than a year ago. She didn't like doing two things at the same time. And now, as well as leading the flight formation and dealing with the pain in her wounded leg, she was switching off the Pe-2's burning engine.

It didn't help, though—soon the entire left wing was blazing and the plane began to fill with smoke.

Klava and Galya knew that the other pilots in the formation could see the flames streaking behind them. "They were mentally saying goodbye to us," Galya said.

But Klava and Galya didn't yet dare to abandon their flaming aircraft. They knew which way the wind was blowing. And they were still so close to German territory that they were afraid they'd be blown back over the front lines if they tried to use their parachutes.

They sped through the sky until the plane became so hot that their parachutes started to smolder. They had to bail out now or never. Galya grabbed the emergency canopy release and the top of the cockpit "flew off instantly, like a piece of paper."

But when Klava tried to tip the plane forward to eject them, the control surfaces were so badly burned that they didn't react. Instead, the Pe-2 went into a dive all by itself, and the increased gravity trapped Klava and Galya in the open cockpit.

They fought and struggled to get free of the plunging plane. Dangerously close to the ground, at a height of about 200 meters (about 650 feet), they finally managed to claw their way out and open their parachutes.

Klava's boots were dragged off in the air by the force of her fall. She landed barefoot and filthy with smoke and soot. But she was still alive. She and Galya were both still alive.

They were rescued on the ground by Soviet soldiers who'd seen the plane crash. This was the moment when they were brought by a flying ambulance back to their own airfield, and Valentin Markov lifted Galya out of the plane himself and carried her to safety.

About a month later, the members of the 125th were honored again for their determined gallantry: they were renamed the 125th M. M. Raskova Borisov Guards. Borisov was a town the 125th had liberated from the Germans in Belorussia. The regiment was so pleased that Masha Dolina and her navigator flew over the town and dropped a message on a banner made of towels sewn together. They sent their best wishes to the city, hoping the damaged buildings would soon be fixed, and that—in Masha's own words—the inhabitants would "flourish, continue peacetime jobs, and help people survive, while we continued our job at the front."

It was exhilarating to know that the tide of the war had turned, even though there was still a long way to go before the enemy was defeated. But as the German soldiers grew more frustrated and demoralized, they resorted to new and desperate measures against the relentless Soviet forces.

"Around this time, all kinds of booby-trapped trinkets were being scattered on our airfield," said Vera Tikhomirova, the 586th Regiment's deputy commander for political affairs. "Plastic toys, colored little balls, and fountain pens charged with explosives."

You didn't know where the next attack might come from. The 586th, whose Yak fighters were stationed in western Ukraine until September 1944, had a creepy and sobering experience between defensive flights during the hot summer. A group of young women got permission from Aleksandr Gridnev to swim in a nearby river—and the following day their legs and backs were covered with strange burns.

The Germans, it turned out, had poisoned the river shore with an yperite mixture—more commonly known as mustard gas. Mustard gas, which had been used in World War I by both opposing fighting forces, was so horrible that it had been banned from warfare in the 1925 Geneva Gas Protocol. The 586th added "the need to increase vigilance" to their Party staff meeting agenda.

Belorussia was still crawling with Nazi forces, who would clearly resort to the dirtiest and deadliest of attacks, and that's where the invigorated Red Army concentrated their efforts now.

That summer the young women of the 46th Taman Guards moved their open-cockpit Po-2s to fly harassment missions in Belorussia's deep forest, along the northern end of the front. As the Germans were pushed out of the occupied towns, the liberators discovered mass graves that told silently of the horrific holocaust suffered by Belorussia's Jewish inhabitants. Decomposing bodies hung from lampposts. Among the dead was the little boy of Zinaida Gorman, a staff member for the 46th Guards. When she was close enough to fly to her home village to check on it, she discovered that her parents and her child had been shot along with everyone else in the village.

Zinaida returned to her regiment, climbed from her plane, and sat on the grass sobbing. Every one of her fellow pilots, navigators, and mechanics gathered around her and swore to avenge her grief—not just for Zinaida and her child, but for all Soviet mothers.

The woodland of Belorussia was so thick that there was hardly any place to use as an airfield, so the 46th Guards had to take off and land in forest clearings. In these tight open spaces surrounded by trees, the only way to get enough momentum for a plane to lift off the ground was for the mechanics to use their own weight to hold down the wings while the pilot ran the engine up to full power. Then everyone let go at the same time and the Po-2, heavy with bombs, struggled up from the sandy soil to climb above the pine or birch trees.

The 46th Guards now "led a 'gypsy' life," said pilot Kaleriya Rylskaya, who'd been flying the night that Zhenya Rudneva was killed. "Each night we struck at new targets and each night we slept in a new place, under the wings of our aircraft. This was our work area, bedroom, and dining room."

A thoughtful mechanic would park a Po-2 so that there was a little rise under the plane's wing, which meant you wouldn't be lying in a puddle if you slept there when it rained. She'd hang a cloth cockpit cover on one side of the wing to shield her aircraft's pilot and navigator from the wind. "Then she would bustle around the engine," Kaleriya said, "quietly tapping her wrenches, so as not to disturb the sleeping crew."

As they lay on the grass trying to sleep one day, a ragged and haggard old woman came up to them, followed by a few staring children, and offered the resting aircrew a small basket of berries she'd picked in the forest.

"Please take revenge for me on the Germans," she told them. "They killed my husband, burned my village to the ground. I have no home, no family, nothing is left." She and the children were living with the partisan guerrilla fighters in the Belorussian forest.

"For the next few weeks, every night when I was flying, I saw her face and the faces of those children," Nadya Popova said.

There was misery everywhere, inescapable misery. Even in the air you couldn't escape it: the memory of the suffering faces of the young and the old.

For the rest of her life, pilot Yevgeniya Zhigulenko never forgot finding a small boy with a haunted, thin face and huge green eyes alone in a deserted village. His mother lay dying in a trench, and he begged Yevgeniya to fly to find his father at the front. She gave him all her emergency rations: chocolate and candy and sweetened condensed milk. But there was nothing else she could do for him—except remember. Years later, as a filmmaker, Yevgeniya made that child "a symbol of the great Russian tragedy of the millions of homeless, orphaned children."

In August 1944 the 46th Guards moved through Poland, where they would eventually take part in the battle for Warsaw. They spent the last part of that summer in the shady park of a Polish estate, falling asleep as the sun rose after the night's missions, lying under trees on mattresses improvised from kit bags stuffed with hay. While they were based here, Tanya Makarova and Vera Belik were shot down.

Vera was the navigator who'd been terrified when her previous pilot, Larisa Rozanova, kept falling asleep in the spring of 1943. Now Vera and Tanya, like so many of their companions, perished in the flames of a

"RUSSIA HAS NOTED WOMEN WAR FLYERS"—AND AMERICA ADMIRES THEM

The Soviet Union's "women flyers" had made appearances in the American media since the 1930s. When Marina Raskova began teaching at the Zhukhovsky Academy, American newspapers carried the story along with her photograph and the headline "Woman Becomes Soviet Air Ace." The flight of the *Rodina* was widely reported throughout the United States in 1938 and 1939. One Missouri paper, in a story aimed at women's interests, called Valentina Grizodubova a "buxom Amazon of the civil air force"—then transitioned effortlessly into fashion tips for "that problem child—the teen-age girl"!

Though it can't be said the American press always took the Soviet Union's women pilots seriously—or *any* women pilots—you can tell that Americans were fascinated by their achievements. Also, once the United States entered the war, there was a real surge of support for their ally, the Soviet Union. The *New York Times* ran a story by Ralph Parker in March 1942 about the different wartime jobs Russian women were able to do: "aviation instructor" is one of them. The same reporter wrote an expanded version in February 1943 and upgraded the aviator's job to flying "ambulance-planes"! In the same month, American radio fans could hear a dramatized version of the 588th Night Bombers' exploits through the weekly broadcast series *Treasury Star Parade*. Tamara Pamyatnykh and Raisa Surnachevskaya were mentioned by name as fighter pilots in an Associated Press news report in April 1943. In June 1943, an American ship was named after Marina Raskova.

As the war went on, the stories became more accurate. In December 1943, an Associated Press headline stated plainly, "Russia Has Noted Women War Flyers." The article mentions dive-bombers and night bombers, although the reporter didn't point out that the aviation regiment commanded by Yevdokia Bershanskaya was made up *entirely* of women.

All doubts were cleared up by 1944. In an article called "Those Russian Women" for *Survey Graphic* in February 1944, Rose Maurer described Soviet women in many combat roles, including that of bomber pilot—and she pointed out that unlike Americans, Soviet women could expect equal pay with men and didn't have to "fight against race discrimination."

Quentin Reynolds, an American journalist, interviewed Katya Budanova before her death. In a portrait of "Three Russian Women" for his book *The Curtain Rises,* published in 1944, he describes her incredible career as a fighter pilot at Stalingrad.

And in July 1944, *Aviation* magazine ran an in-depth story by Madelin Blitzstein called "How Women Flyers Fight Russia's Air War." This article includes pictures of Lilya Litvyak and Lera Khomyakova. Lera, in parachute and aviation googles, is smiling broadly, and the caption beneath the photo says that "she is now a fighter pilot" who had shot down a Luftwaffe bomber.

It's a little sad to think that by the time the thrilling stories of Katya, Lilya, and Lera reached an American audience, they'd all been dead for over a year.

burning aircraft. Their friends buried them under the maple trees of the estate.

No matter what suffering they witnessed and how much they suffered themselves, though, the one thing Marina's aviators could rely on to bring them strength and comfort was their dependence on each other. Friendship firmly bound the 46th Guards together, and their stretched nerves depended on it.

Every night the sky became for them a strange world of moonlit cloud, the ominous red light of aircraft flares, and too many aircraft for safe flight, all heading for the same target. Sometimes, just knowing that you weren't alone up there made all the difference.

The 46th Guards were constantly on the move in the fall of 1944, with the task of bombing roads as the Germans retreated near the port of Danzig (now Gdansk, in Poland).

On one of these missions Kaleriya Rylskaya and her navigator, Nadya Studilina—the navigator who'd flown as a rookie with Larisa Rozanova on the terrible night of July 31, 1943—found themselves in cloud beneath a full moon. They dropped their bombs and were glad to be able to make their way free of the eerie, dangerous sky. But partway back to their airfield, unexpectedly, their Po-2's engine failed.

Thinking they'd have to make an emergency landing in the forest, Kaleriya and Nadya glided down so low they barely managed to clear the frost-covered wires of electrical pylons—and then, to their relief, the Po-2's engine suddenly roared back into life.

As they flew beneath the bright, moonlit clouds, hoping their engine would hold out long enough to get them home, they were joined by two other Po-2s. The newcomers settled into a formation with them, escorting Kaleriya and Nadya in their struggling aircraft. The very company of planes from their own regiment cheered them up as they coaxed their unreliable Po-2 homeward.

It was broad daylight by the time they made it back to the intermediate airfield. When they got there, the field was almost empty—all the other aircraft had been cleared away until the next night. But two small figures stood waiting there for them, anxiously watching the skies for their return: their beloved regimental commander, Major Yevdokia Bershanskaya, and the squadron commander, Nadya Popova.

It was good to feel that there was always someone watching your back and waiting for you.

The same was true for the 125th Guards.

By December 1944, the three-person flight crews of the 125th Guards were aggressively using their powerful Pe-2 dive-bombers to attack troops that blocked routes to the Latvian port of Riga on the Baltic Sea, though the German forces were no longer in control of the city itself. The Germans had now been pushed back over the entire western border of the USSR.

Klava Fomicheva and her navigator, Galya Dzhunkovskaya, both of them long since recovered after parachuting from their burning plane that summer, flew one of these cold and dark missions over northerly Riga. They led a formation of nine Pe-2s, leading the first flight with two other Pe-2s as their wingmen. Though the December skies were cloudy, everyone felt a little safer when they flew over the airfield to pick up their escort and found thirty-six Soviet fighter aircraft joining them in the sky.

"Now we can relax," Galya told her pilot, smiling.

They sped on toward the fiery explosions over their target.

There, the sky was so dark with smoke that neither Klava nor Galya could see clear sky anywhere. Around them, shells of all different sizes exploded, flaming and colorful tracer bullets whizzed past, and antiaircraft guns fired from the ground and from ships stationed on the sea below.

The aircraft following Klava had an even tougher flight. Not only did they have to deal with the turbulent explosions, but they also had to try to stay in formation behind their leader as everyone's planes were buffeted about in the angry sky.

Klava and Galya reached their target and released their bombs, then tried to climb away to escape the battle. At 4500 meters (nearly 15,000 feet) the air grew so thin it was difficult to breathe. But they finally reached the edge of the clouds.

And there, Galya said, "I looked behind and saw that all were flying wing tip to wing tip. So Klava said: 'Just you look at them; they're flying like in an air show. Well done! Well done, indeed!' I had the urge to kiss my dear girlfriends, the airwomen of our squadron, for executing their mission so well."

Later that day, back at their makeshift base and burning their fingers eating potatoes baked over a campfire in a metal tray that started life as an ammunition box, Galya felt "that the fighter attack of an hour ago, the drop of high-explosive heavy bombs, and the cloud of shell explosions covering the sky—had never happened."

The 125th Guards paused in their bombing missions for one joyful, hopeful moment to celebrate the new year of 1945. There was a hot blaze in the iron stove, a festive tree smelling of pine needles, professional entertainers from Moscow, and an amateur talent show. One highlight was the very silly "Lost Navigator's Dance," which they'd invented themselves, sure to bring laughs. At the end of the evening, Galya and the other airwomen begged Klava to dance for them.

By now, Klava Fomicheva was twenty-seven years old. She was a squadron commander and a veteran; she'd been shot down and wounded twice and had spent six months in the hospital. But she was still flying. When her friends and comrades asked for a dance performance to celebrate the new year of 1945, she had to be coaxed, but she gave in at last.

"Smiling shyly and snapping her fingers rhythmically, she began circling the room," said Galya. "Dancing transformed her. She moved her shoulders somewhat coquettishly and her eyes and entire face were laughing and exuded joy."

This new year, they were sure, would bring about the end of the war.

❧ · 36 · ❧

FROM THE VOLGA TO BERLIN

It should be no surprise that now Josef Stalin was determined that his own Red Army was going to invade and capture Berlin, Hitler's capital city in Germany. Berlin was the ultimate prize of the war, and Stalin wanted to get there first, before the Germans gave up the battle or the Western Allies stormed into the city themselves. In a fresh and frenzied campaign in January 1945, six million Soviet soldiers surged along the Eastern Front against a scraggling and demoralized German force of about two million.

The Red Army sped forward as much as fifty miles a day, and Raskova's regiments flew with them. The 125th M. M. Raskova Guards would finish the war in Lithuania; the 586th Regiment would end up in Budapest, Hungary, and after the end of the war were even stationed in Vienna, Austria, for a time. The night bombers of the 46th Guards would fly all the way to Berlin itself.

While the troops of the USSR were relentlessly pushing the Germans back in the east, the Allied forces were doing the same thing in the west. But though the Nazi government of Hitler's Third Reich was clearly going to have to admit defeat pretty soon, they didn't give up easily. The German army continued to fight throughout the snowy winter of 1945 and into the spring.

The fighter pilots of the 586th Regiment didn't see much enemy action during the last six months of the war. They were stationed first in Romania and then in Hungary as the war drew to a close, defending railway junctions, bridges, and factories along the Danube River and around the Hungarian cities of Debrecen and Budapest.

But even with the end in sight, tragedy could still strike at any moment. Masha Batrokova, who'd already been decorated with the Order of the Red Star, was killed on a routine flight mission in the spring of 1945.

Galina Burdina learned how close she herself had come to being killed when she had a strange encounter with a Romanian pilot who surrendered to the Red Army with other Romanian troops.

He said that he'd been flying for the Germans over Kiev, a year or so earlier, and had seen Galina in flight, covering the 586th's commander Aleksandr Gridnev. He'd flown close enough to Galina in that air battle to be able to recognize her as a woman—and he'd chosen not to fire his guns at her *because* she was a woman.

Galina realized how lucky she'd been, all because of the other pilot's strange wartime chivalry.

"So he gave me back my life," she said.

The devoted trio of Katya Fedotova, Klara Dubkova, and Tonya Khokhlova was now considered one of the best aircrews in the 125th Guards, and they got permission to paint a swallow on their Pe-2 dive-bomber—a hopeful sign of both the spring and the victory they were counting on 1945 to bring them.

The 125th Guards operated in the German region of Prussia, flying aggressive missions along the southwest of the Baltic Sea from January to May 1945. Katya, Klara, and Tonya were shot down again as the front moved west. This time, Tonya herself managed to destroy an enemy plane with the machine guns in her tail gunner's turret in the back of their Pe-2. Tonya didn't even realize she'd done it until she heard the story from soldiers on the ground who'd seen the air battle, and the proof was in the automatic photographs that the plane took as its machine guns were firing.

Katya, the crew's pilot, once again managed to land her crippled plane in a forest clearing on the safe side of the front line. But a Pe-2 from another Soviet regiment was not so lucky. Under enemy fire, it crashed at the same time as Katya landed, and she and her horrified aircrew watched it burn.

Then, said Tonya, "Because there was no one else around, we had to pick up their remains: one arm, one leg, all smoked and roasted. I thought I would never look at any meat after that. Well, life is life. So we collected the remains of that crew, all three of them, torn apart. No heads, all apart. We gathered them together. There was a parachute intact, so we ripped the parachute apart, covered the remains, and buried them."

The fighting grew no less desperate at the end of the war, which meant that no one was safe—not even from their own regulations.

For example, someone in a position of authority decided the Pe-2s of the 125th Guards would be able to carry a heavier load of bombs if the planes carried less fuel. But of course this meant that the aircraft couldn't fly as far. It also meant they used fuel less efficiently because they were carrying more weight. Worst of all, it made a plane that was already difficult to take off even more difficult.

Waiting for their turn to leave on one of these missions in their overloaded Pe-2, Antonina Bondareva and Galina Brok watched aghast as, on the runway ahead of them, one of the aircrews from a men's squadron failed to get enough height to climb away safely. The plane crashed into a hangar and exploded.

"We were next in line to take off," said Galina. "You have to forbid yourself from thinking that your plane will end up the same way. You concentrate on a successful mission."

Even though it was Antonina flying the plane and not Galina, Galina could tell that their aircraft was too heavy to lift off safely. "We felt it dragging us back to earth," she said.

But somehow they made it into the air, flew to the assigned target, dropped their bombs, flew home, and landed safely.

"It was a victory," Galina said, "not over the German troops but over ourselves."

As for the night bombers of the 46th Taman Guards, in addition to harassing the retreating German army all night and every night, they and other Po-2 regiments had to again use their open-cockpit planes to drop supplies of cargo to stranded Soviet troops. In February 1945, when they were in western Prussia, once more the winter weather made the roads utterly impossible to travel on. The 46th Guards made supply flights in daylight as well as at night, in aircraft fitted with skis instead of wheels.

One night, the visibility was so poor that only a single Po-2 was able to complete the supply run—not because anyone was being prudent about continuing into bad weather anymore, but simply because none of the other pilots could figure out where they were heading, and had no navigators to guide them because the navigators' cockpits were full of supplies.

"I made the flight at a very low altitude, following the railroad tracks," said pilot Zoya Parfyonova, who managed to find the right place. "It was snowing very hard."

In the storm, flying so low she was afraid her wing might touch the ground if she turned, Zoya found herself over a German camp instead of the Soviet one she'd been heading for.

"German infantrymen began firing at me," Zoya said. "The airplane was hit all over like a sieve, and I was wounded in the leg."

In a shaking, damaged aircraft, Zoya made her escape and found the Soviet troops only three minutes away. She landed, unloaded her plane, and took off for home—but fainted from blood loss and crashed just as she was about to touch the ground again.

She survived the crash. It was her 701st combat mission—but only the first time she'd been wounded.

By March, the fields were so muddy that the Po-2s could not take off. Their wheels simply sank in the mud. One aircrew, lost in bad weather, landed in a field and couldn't leave until the next morning when the ground had frozen. They spent the night in a Polish village, too worried to sleep, and shared their "pilots' rations of vodka, biscuits, and milk" with the boys who guarded their plane during the night.

As the hard frosts grew less reliable, the planes continued to struggle to take off out of the mud. The fuel trucks couldn't move, either. So the airwomen of the 46th Guards improvised a way to get their planes into the air. They took down log fences and built a wooden platform 200 meters long and 30 meters wide (about 660 by 100 feet). Everybody helped refuel the planes by carrying cans from the trucks to the aircraft; the armorers had to carry the bombs out to the Po-2s by hand as well.

Finally, the ground crew would lift each loaded aircraft onto the platform. This gave it a short runway above the mud—almost like taking off from an aircraft carrier. When the plane returned from its mission, it would land in the mud, get pushed back to the platform, and the whole process would begin again.

"Our regiment made 300 combat missions from that field in those conditions," said Irina Rakobolskaya.

While the Po-2s of the 46th Guards were struggling in the mud and the Pe-2s of the 125th M. M. Raskova Borisov Guards were straining to get off the ground with their extra-heavy loads of bombs, the 125th's missing navigator, Nina Karaseva, was fighting a very different kind of war—and probably looking forward to victory even more than they were.

When she'd been captured by the Germans in September 1943, she'd been sent to an airmen's prisoner-of-war camp in Poland, where she spent seven months with other Soviet pilots—as well as a Frenchman from the Normandie-Niemen Regiment. But in May 1944, Nina was transferred to the women's concentration camp at Ravensbrück in Germany, and from there was sent to the Buchenwald concentration camp. Nina saw firsthand the undiluted evil of the Nazi killing machine. She had to live and endure its horror at Buchenwald for nearly a year.

On April 12, 1945, when the German guards fled from the Red Army as it approached the concentration camp, Nina and her fellow prisoners cut the lock off the gate and let themselves out.

Nina survived the war and lived to tell her own story. But she doesn't talk about what happened to her between unlocking the gates of Buchenwald and her later life as a civilian with a family. Every last Soviet citizen liberated from the German prison camps—even those at Auschwitz—was questioned as a possible spy. That's exactly what happened to Tamara Pamyatnykh's husband when he returned from Buchenwald. But both he and Nina were eventually able to return to civilian life.

Now that the Soviet Army was on the offensive, the terrifying Orders 270 and 227 didn't have to be enforced to the letter. But anyone who fell afoul of them was still put through the ordeal of inquisition as a traitor.

In many cases, whether you lived free or were sent to prison or were executed depended simply on whether the person who tried you was in the right mood.

As the Nazi concentration camps began to be liberated, the end of the war grew very near.

The 46th Guards made their way steadily through Germany until they were stationed north of Berlin, supporting the Red Army as it swept in for a final and brutal victory.

Even ordinary German homes seemed extravagantly comfortable to the Soviet soldiers. They were staggered by the wealth they saw in Prussia, and the 46th Guards were no exception. Irina Rakobolskaya spoke for her comrades when she voiced her amazement; so did the journalist Vasily Grossman.

"But why did [the Germans] come to us?" the Soviet soldiers all marveled. "What did they want?"

How could the people who owned such rich farms, such beautiful furniture and gardens, modern bathrooms, and electricity to run refrigerators have ever needed to come take over the Soviet Union's peasant huts?

Of course it made the Red Army soldiers even angrier at the Germans, but it also baffled them.

The last harassment missions were nerve-racking for the 46th Guards in their open-cockpit Po-2s.

"Everybody knew that the end of the war was near, and no one wanted to die," said navigator Polina Gelman, the woman who'd promised to name her daughter Galya.

But the commanders were eager for a big victory, and the 46th Guards were sent out on a bombing mission twice as far away as their usual targets took them. The engine of Polina's Po-2 overheated on the longer flight, and she and her pilot were now going to have to make a crash landing, only a week before the end of the war.

To make matters worse, because of thick fog, they couldn't see the ground. They hadn't found their target, and now that they didn't have any idea where they were, Polina and her pilot hesitated about dropping their bombs. "It could be on our own troops, on civilians, or on anyone," Polina said.

Knowing that now they might be flying a suicide mission, they decided to land with their bombs still attached to their plane.

They sank down to earth through the mist and landed on faith in a forest clearing—stopping a single meter (about three feet) away from the tree trunks. They were so thrilled to be safe and alive that both of them jumped out of the plane and started to dance.

One week later, Polina was supposed to fly yet another combat mission on May 8, 1945.

"Everything was ready," she said, "the bombs loaded and the crews on their way to the aircraft, when suddenly we saw the mechanics run up to our aircraft and do something. What they were doing was deactivating the bombs. The Germans had surrendered; the war was over. I burst out crying."

A PO-2 FLYING OVER THE BRANDENBURG GATE IN BERLIN, GERMANY

• • •

The 125th Guards Bomber Aviation Regiment was at Gruzdžiai, in Lithuania, when the war ended. At the end of a long day of aggressive flying, everyone was in bed and no one wanted to get up to answer the insistently ringing telephone. Finally, pilot Masha Kirillova couldn't stand the noise anymore and hauled herself to the phone.

When she heard the news she stood frozen, hugging the receiver against her chest.

Then she managed to tell the others, "The war has ended!"

Everyone leaped out of bed screaming with excitement.

"We just couldn't believe it," said navigator Galina Brok. "There were tears in our eyes; we greeted, hugged, and kissed each other; we laughed and we cried."

But hugging and kissing weren't enough. The 125th M. M. Raskova Borisov Guards needed to make some noise. They all ran into the street and started firing their pistols into the air in a victory salute.

The 586th Regiment lined up on their springtime-green airfield near Budapest on May 9, 1945.

Their Yaks were ready for a combat mission—but no assignment came. The war was over.

It was victory day at last. The young women of the 586th all sang together, as they'd done so many times before over the past four years.

> To the Homeland, happiness and friends!
> To those who fought bravely and fell . . .

One anonymous pilot's future husband proposed to her among the ruins of Berlin just after the war ended.

"I wanted to cry," she said. "To shout. To hit him! What do you mean, married? Now? In the midst of all this—married? In the midst of black soot and black bricks . . . . I almost hit him . . . I was about to . . . He had one cheek burned, purple, and I see: he understood everything, tears are running down that cheek. On the still-fresh scars . . . And I myself can't believe I'm saying to him: 'Yes, I'll marry you.'"

There was no way to separate the joy from tears. The war had brought too much grief to too many people.

PART V

AFTER THE WAR

ONE THOUSAND NIGHTS IN COMBAT

"After the war we had a lot of headaches, could not relax, and had very hard problems with our sleeping, because for nearly three years we turned over the day and night," said 46th Guards pilot Serafima Amosova. "I couldn't sleep for at least three months. . . . We had been fighting for one thousand nights—one thousand nights in combat."

Mariya Smirnova, who flew 935 harassment missions during the war, estimated that every one of the 46th's pilots made at least eight hundred combat flights.

In their three years on the front lines, the 46th Taman Guards Night Bomber Aviation Regiment flew more than twenty-four thousand combat missions in total. Most of their pilots and navigators flew around ten harassment missions every night of the entire war in their flimsy open-cockpit Po-2s. In the winter's long darknesses, during what they called their "maximum nights," they might make twelve to eighteen bombing runs in a single evening.

Twenty-four of these women were given the nation's highest military honor and became Heroes of the Soviet Union—including Polina Gelman, Natasha Meklin, Nadya Popova, Larisa Rozanova, Zhenya Rudneva, Mariya Smirnova, and Yevgeniya Zhigulenko.

Quality, not quantity, shines in the 1,134 combat missions flown by the three-person crews of the 125th M. M. Raskova Borisov Guards Bomber Aviation Regiment. In their Pe-2 dive-bombers, they dropped nearly a million tons of bombs. Five women in the regiment were awarded the honor of Hero of the Soviet Union—Masha Dolina, Galya Dzhunkovskaya, and Klava Fomicheva are the ones we'd recognize.

The 586th Fighter Aviation Regiment's statistics are more quietly triumphant. They made over nine thousand solo flights in their fast and dangerous Yak fighters—about half of those were combat missions, and 125 were air battles. Between them they shot down thirty-eight enemy aircraft, in addition to destroying targets on the ground and escorting dignitaries.

Considering their role was to defend and protect as they served in the rear guard and not on the front lines, it's sobering to realize that nearly a third of the women who flew with the 586th did not survive the war.

A frustrating epilogue to their story is that the 586th Regiment was never awarded the honorary and elite title of Guards. They were recommended for it—after their heroic service at Voronezh, they got special Guards uniforms ordered for them. According to their commander, Aleksandr Gridnev, the pilots of the 586th were photographed and filmed (even in battle!) in preparation for a press announcement that they were being honored with a Guards number. But the paperwork was never correctly submitted.

It's not obvious why this never happened. Aleksandr Gridnev actually blamed Tamara Kazarinova for somehow sabotaging plans for the 586th's Guards ceremony, perhaps in revenge for being dismissed as their commander. Aleksandr also suggested he was personally disliked by an important air force officer who ranked above him and who disapproved of the women fighters.

It's possible they weren't seen to be as important or as worthy as those who were fighting at the front. Despite their heroism, the 586th was never on the front lines, as were the two other regiments associated with Marina Raskova—the 586th's job was always to protect the Soviet forces at the rear.

It's ironic that the women's regiment consisting solely of fighter pilots—the most dramatic, boldest aviation role of which all the young women had desperately dreamed when they joined the 122nd Air Group— was the least united and least decorated of the three regiments formed under Marina Raskova.

One woman who'd flown with the 586th did become a Hero of the Soviet Union, though.

Twenty-five years after Lilya Litvyak disappeared in battle, in 1968, *Komsomolskaya Pravda* urged that she be given the honor posthumously.

But the Soviet Air Force Command insisted this couldn't be done unless there was proof that Lilya had died in battle. A stone monument in her memory, carved with a star for each Luftwaffe aircraft she'd shot down, was erected with a blank space on the memorial slab just in case one day there would be room to add "Hero of the Soviet Union."

Lilya vanished in 1943. It was more than forty years before a crashed plane and a body were found that were believed to be hers. Inna Pasportnikova, who'd been Lilya's mechanic when she flew with the 73rd Guards Fighter Aviation Regiment, spent three years searching with a metal detector for Lilya's plane. Her husband and grandchildren helped. So did the students in the school where Inna became a teacher after the war—Inna organized expeditions to hunt for wartime plane crashes. "We found thirty aircraft but not hers," Inna said.

In 1979, Inna discovered that an anonymous female pilot had long since been found and buried in a village called Dmitrievka in Ukraine—the body could no longer be identified, but the circumstances of the crash matched up, and there wasn't anyone else but Lilya who could have been flying in that place at that time.

Finally, in 1988, the report filed with the chief directorate of personnel on September 16, 1943, was officially changed to say that Lilya Litvyak had been "killed in action."

On May 5, 1990, nearly fifty years after Lilya's disappearance, Soviet Chairman Mikhail Gorbachev signed a decree honoring her as a Hero of the Soviet Union.

The award was presented to Lilya's brother, Yuri, who'd been waiting so long for his charismatic older sister's name, and his own, to be cleared.

Now it was official: the woman who was born on Aviation Day, born to be in the air, had died in the air.

In the harsh political winds of conflict that stormed across the globe in World War II, the USSR suffered the loss of more lives than the rest of the world combined. Cautious estimates begin at eighteen million casualties, but the number may even be as high as forty-five million. That's roughly equivalent to today's total population of New England, New York, and New Jersey all put together. About four million of those deaths were caused by starvation.

Just as it's difficult to count the Motherland's complete death toll, it's difficult to verify exactly how many Soviet airwomen were killed during the Great Patriotic War. The statistics vary wildly, from thirty to three hundred. Yevgeniya Zhigulenko, a 46th Guards pilot, said that one-third of her regiment was killed—did she mean just pilots? Or pilots, navigators, and ground crew? Reina Pennington, counting staff and ground crew as well as pilots and navigators (both male and female), estimates that twenty-nine women of the 46th Guards were killed, twenty-eight women of the 125th Guards, and ten of the 586th Regiment, including those sent to other regiments in 1942.

Whatever the final numbers may be, they are just numbers. Who can measure the loss to the world of a person as complex and energetic as Zhenya Rudneva at the age of twenty-two? Or as driven and charismatic as twenty-one-year-old Lilya Litvyak? Both were natural leaders, earning the respect of their companions and their superiors. Both died as followers, doing the work they were commanded to do. Neither had the chance at achievement that she deserved. They were caught in a wind too strong for them.

"Life is life." It isn't always fair.

Marina Raskova died young too, and probably through her own error. But throughout her life, she didn't just work with the wind: in a small way, she learned how to change it.

The women who survived their service in Raskova's regiments would eventually begin to change the wind themselves.

"DO NOT TALK ABOUT THE SERVICES YOU HAVE RENDERED"

Article 122 of the 1936 Constitution of the Soviet Union guaranteed that "Women in the USSR are accorded equal rights with men in all spheres of economic, state, cultural, social and political life."

The women who joined Marina Raskova's regiments knew this. The regimental engineer of the 46th Guards, Klavdiya Ilushina, insisted that they had "absolute equal opportunity with men." But the 1936 Constitution of the Soviet Union "guaranteed" a multitude of rights it didn't always deliver on, and a line on paper didn't suddenly make everyone's ideas shift from their old tracks.

A girl growing up in the USSR in the 1920s and 1930s could learn to fly, but she wasn't always encouraged to, and she wasn't expected to make a military career out of aviation. The women who did were persistent and exceptional. Soviet women "were frustrated by contradictory messages: become aviators, but not in the highest levels of the military," said Adrienne Marie Harris in her PhD thesis about women soldiers in the Soviet Union. Posters printed in the 1930s, encouraging young people to fly, were directed at both boys and girls. But after the war, posters from the 1950s showed only boys dreaming of flight.

The Soviet Union's head of state and a close colleague of Stalin's, Chairman Mikhail Kalinin, gave a speech in July 1945 addressed to the "Glorious Daughters of the Soviet People." These "glorious daughters" were a group of women who'd recently fought in the Red Army and Navy. It was only a few months after the end of the war, and Kalinin started out by congratulating them on their victory. Then he said, "In this unusual war, women not only supported the army by their work in the rear, but also fought with arms in hand."

He was drawing attention to the fact that the USSR was the only nation in World War II whose women engaged in combat—who were expected to kill just the way men killed as soldiers.

Kalinin pointed out right away that this isn't normal. It was a view generally shared by the women soldiers themselves. He then acknowledged that they were mostly now between twenty and twenty-three years old, that they'd left their families or schools as unfinished teens when the war began, and that they had no careers nor households of their own to return to. He told them that their wartime experiences would make them stronger and wiser, and that they could now apply these virtues to their civilian lives; and he promised that the Komsomol would help them find work—which it did.

But, Kalinin advised the young female veterans, "Do not give yourself airs in your future practical work. Do not talk about the services you have rendered, let others do it for you. That will be better."

When the enlisted women were demobilized, they had to sign a pledge promising they'd do just that—not say anything about what they'd done.

Stalin's government hadn't ever encouraged outspokenness among its citizens.

Now that the war was over, Stalin himself refused to allow women to continue in military service in the air force. His opinion was that women were "physiologically" unsuited for warfare. The Red Army closed down its women's units, and women were discouraged from continuing or pursuing careers in the military.

Many women who had flown during the war wanted to continue working in civil aviation but found that their years of combat had so shattered them in body and mind that they couldn't pass the required physical exam.

If anyone objected, they didn't say so—or didn't dare to say so.

And it doesn't look as though many people did object. The general Soviet sentiment, often shared by the women soldiers themselves, was that although women had done their part to drive out the invading enemy, their real role was to nurture, not to kill.

Women of the Soviet Union who were involved in the Great Patriotic War felt that they had been defending the Motherland—that fighting a war was an unnatural thing for a woman to do, but that defending her home for her children made complete and total sense. And if fighting a war is what she had to do to save her home and her children, then she'd do all it took to make that happen—including dropping bombs from an airplane or shooting other pilots out of the sky.

"Life is life," said Ludmila Popova, a navigator in the 125th Guards. "War is not a normal thing for any country, for any state, for any man, and especially for a woman."

Antonina Bondareva, the young widowed pilot in the 125th Guards who'd left her toddler with her husband's family, had to struggle after the war to get her sister-in-law to give back her now seven-year-old daughter.

"You can't have a daughter, since you abandoned her when she was little and went to war," the sister-in-law argued. She called Antonina cruel and said she had "no woman's soul."

But Antonina had suffered too, of course she'd suffered! She'd dreamed of her little girl, sometimes crying because she missed her so much. "Many of us left our children at home, I wasn't the only one," she argued. "We stayed women."

"The very nature of a woman rejects the idea of fighting," said Alexandra Akimova, a squadron navigator with the 46th Guards. "A woman is born to give birth to children, to nurture. Flying combat missions is against our nature; only the tragedy of our country made us join the army, to help our country, to help our people."

The chief of staff for the 586th, Alexandra Makunina, felt no different. "I myself could not have acted in any other way. . . . The very notion, the very sense of defending the Motherland, was the duty of all the men and all the women too."

Masha Dolina, the 125th Guards Bomber Aviation Regiment pilot who'd more than once landed her flaming Pe-2 and saved her crew, was awarded the nation's highest honor, becoming a Hero of the Soviet Union on August 18, 1945.

But even she insisted, "I want you to underline in red that it was the cherished dream of the girls to liberate the land, but none of us wanted to fight—to kill."

Most of the heroic women who fought in and survived the Great Patriotic War did exactly what Kalinin told them: they returned to civilian life after the war and went unrecognized for what they'd done.

46th Guards navigator Polina Gelman did have a daughter. She kept the promise she'd made and named her Galya.

Larisa Rozanova married and worked as an engineer; Natasha Meklin worked as a translator. Galya Dzhunkovskaya married her regimental commander, Valentin Markov; Yevdokia Bershanskaya married Andrey Molotov, the commander of a men's regiment who'd flown close to the 46th Guards during the war.

And they did remain silent about their services for a decade or so. But as they grew older, the political climate of the USSR changed. With the onset of the Cold War, Stalin's death in 1953, advances in space exploration, and the modern conveniences of the second half of the twentieth century, female veterans of World War II began to take pride in what they'd done.

They wanted to mark their service, and they wanted it to be remembered. In particular, women who'd been aviators, and women who'd worked as ground crew for Marina Raskova's regiments, began to preserve their history and to tell their own stories.

In a bittersweet twist, the first to do so was the inspirational astronomer and poet Zhenya Rudneva, of the 46th Guards. She had died in flames in 1944, but she'd written so much in her short life that in 1955 a collection of her letters and diaries was published under the title *For as Long as My Heart Is Beating*. After that, over thirty more memoirs were published by female aviators between 1957 and 1989.

Many of those who weren't natural writers gave interviews instead, and allowed their memories to be collected and published. The first significant collection was called *In the Sky above the Front* and was put together in 1962 by Marina Raskova's chief of staff from the 122nd Air Group, Militsa Kazarinova—the sister of Tamara Kazarinova, the first commander of the 586th. These memoirs were later added to and edited by other veterans. Raisa Aronova, of the 46th Guards, wrote an autobiographical book called *Night Witches*, published in 1980; in 1981, Yevgeniya Zhigulenko, who'd become a filmmaker, produced and directed a full-length feature film about the 46th Guards. *"Night Witches" in the Sky* paints a vivid and faithful portrait of the 46th Guards' experiences at the height of the war—from flaming death in the air to bunches of wildflowers in the cockpit.

But the young women who played the roles of the flight crew and ground crew of the 46th Guards were actresses, not pilots. In the years leading into World War II, and during the war, it was much more common for women to be involved in aviation than it is even now.

By 1941, nearly one-third of all Soviet pilots were female. But after the war, with Soviet women officially deemed "physiologically unsuitable for becoming military or even civilian pilots," the numbers dropped away drastically.

It's not as obvious why the numbers dropped throughout the rest of the world. Today, about 12 percent of all student pilots in the United States are women. Only 5 percent of commercial pilots worldwide are women.

The women who flew for the Women Airforce Service Pilots (WASP) in the United States weren't forced to sign a statement swearing they wouldn't talk about their experiences. But in a sense, their fate was even more humiliating. Unbelievable as this may sound, after the Allied invasion of Normandy in June 1944—a whole year before the war ended—the American government decided that the women pilots flying for the WASP had successfully completed their work and were no longer needed. No more pilots were to go through the WASP training program, and the organization was officially disbanded on December 20, 1944.

Because they'd never been connected to the military, the women who'd flown with the WASP got no pension or benefits of any kind. They weren't even given national recognition for their wartime service until 1977.

The British ATA continued ferrying aircraft until the spring of 1946, though they officially disbanded in November 1945. Like the WASP, they didn't receive any real recognition for their service, but at least this can't be blamed on gender discrimination—the men who flew for them didn't get any recognition either.

As for the British women, now that the war was over, the situation in the air was the same as it was in the United States and the Soviet Union. There were many more experienced pilots than there was air work to be done. Though a few ATA women managed to make careers in aviation, British flying jobs went almost exclusively to men. British Airways, the United Kingdom's national commercial passenger airline, didn't hire its first female pilot, Lynn Barton, until 1987. To put that in perspective— World War II ended eleven years before the first female pilot for British Airways was born.

When World War II was finally over, with women being told to return to their homes and an overabundance of male pilots to take up the civil aviation jobs available, few of the airwomen from Marina Raskova's regiments had the opportunity to continue careers in aviation.

There were exceptions. Mariya Akilina, from the 46th Guards, flew in the medical services and as a crop duster in civil aviation for twenty years after the war; Nadya Popova and Klava Fomicheva worked as flight instructors. Alexandra Krivonogova, from the 125th Guards, flew passenger planes for twenty-five years and then became an air traffic controller.

Several pilots from the 586th also became air traffic controllers. Galina Burdina flew as a civilian pilot for Aeroflot for fifteen years before joining air traffic control; her friend Tamara Pamyatnykh became an air traffic controller at a civilian airport.

The 125th Guards weren't officially disbanded until February 1947, nearly two years after the war ended. Though there was no longer any female air force unit for them to be part of, pilot Antonina Bondareva and two other women from the 125th continued to serve in a male regiment. But Antonina didn't make a career of flying—she quit in 1950.

Many years later, she said, "I often have dreams about aircraft—of flying. It is my favorite dream."

In today's world, financial constraints, gender bias, and lack of state support now make it almost impossible for Russian women to learn to fly. In Russia in 1998, there were no women flying in either military or commercial aviation. It took Svetlana Protasova eleven years of persistent struggle to become the first (and only) woman to pilot a MiG-29 for the Russian Air Force in 1999; by 2004 she was struggling to find opportunity to fly. Few Russian women who became pilots in the Soviet Union's state-sponsored clubs in the 1980s and early 1990s can afford to fly as private citizens now that the Soviet Union no longer exists. Without state sponsorship, aviation is available only to the wealthy.

"Among pilots, there are no gender stereotypes," said Anastasia Dagaeva in 2017, a Russian student pilot in civil aviation who writes for *Forbes Russia*. "But generally, aviation is still considered to be a man's world. If a woman tries to do it, people think it's strange, they think there's something wrong with her, or with the industry."

The good news is that in October 2017, the Russian Air Force accepted sixteen women into pilot training for the first time since World War II.

The wind is always changing.

"I have more than one hundred sisters," vowed Zoya Malkova, a mechanic for the 586th Fighter Aviation Regiment. "We regularly meet twice a year in front of the Bolshoi Theater on the second of May and the eighth of November."

Under Soviet rule, there was no formal annual commemoration for women veterans of the Great Patriotic War. So they designed their own.

The members of Marina Raskova's regiments would meet—and a dwindling few, now in their nineties, still do—in front of the Bolshoi Theater in Moscow, in May and in November. With no uniforms, they would dress formally in their finest and most feminine clothes, wearing makeup, hats, scarves, and jewelry. They would hold flowers. But also, with fierce and well-earned pride, they would display their medals.

VETERANS OF THE 46TH GUARDS ON THEIR REUNION DAY: FROM LEFT, RAISA ARONOVA, NATASHA MEKLIN, YEVGENIYA ZHIGULENKO, IRINA SEBROVA, AND DINA NIKULINA

Later, as they ate and drank together, and sang regimental songs, their reunion would also become a memorial service to their dead: an act of remembrance.

Anna Kirilina, an armament mechanic for the 125th Guards, sums up the huge depth of emotion that the war created for Raskova's regiments.

"The war made us not friends but relatives," she said. "It made us sisters—dear, dear creatures to each other. On the day of our reunion we say, I go to meet my sisters."

In every close-knit family group, there's always someone who comes up with exciting projects and encourages her siblings to leap into action. There wouldn't have been any women's aviation organizations during World War II if not for the driving forces of individual people. Marina Raskova led the way for the three women's flight regiments of the USSR. Jackie Cochran and Nancy Harkness Love built the units that merged to form the WASP. Pauline Gower fought to allow women to be admitted to the ATA. Each of these women, on her own, gauged the wind of her nation and used it to help her sister pilots get off the ground.

The winds of war, and of change, come and go. But no one should ever underestimate the ability of one single person, man or woman, to change the world.

The world still needs change. Yesterday's Marina Raskova was never as alone in the sky as today's Svetlana Protasova. But people like Marina show the rising generations that it is possible to make a difference—and that it is worth it.

If there is one thing to be learned from the thousand sisters of Raskova's regiments, it is that change is possible. It can begin with one person.

Go out and change the wind.

SOURCE NOTES

Complete bibliographic information can be found in the bibliography on page 359 for the sources listed here by author and page number.

EPIGRAPHS

VII Life is life, and war is war: Galina Tenuyeva-Lomanova in Noggle, 155.
VII War is war, and life is life: Antonina Bondareva-Spitsina in Noggle, 109.
VII If the women of the world united: Alexandra Akimova in Noggle, 94.

BATTLE CRY: A PROLOGUE

2 And moviemakers did their part: Wilde & Borsten, xii–xiii.
2 The novelist was already famous: Schneider, 236.
2 So working on *Battle Cry* was William Faulkner's way of contributing: Hamblin & Brodsky, xvi.
2 "Battle cry . . . rises from the throats of free men": Faulkner, 185.
2 William Faulkner was excited: Hamblin & Brodsky, xvii.
3 By the end of that hot July: *Los Angeles Times*, July 27, 1943, 1.
3 The weather didn't stop director Howard Hawks: Hamblin & Brodsky, xxxvi.
3 Meanwhile, William Faulkner rewrote the Russian sequence: ibid., xxxvii.
3 The Russian story for *Battle Cry: Asbury Park Press*, Feb. 3, 1943, 14.
4 The original writers show Tania: Atkins & Bacher, 19–57; Faulkner, 217–48.
4 On August 3, 1943, after more than a month: Hamblin & Brodsky, xxxvii.
5 One of these young pilots: Cottam 1998, 152; Pennington 2001, 140.
5 In less than a year she'd shot down: S. Gribanov in Cottam 1997, 311; Cottam 1998, 152; Pennington 2001, 141–42.
6 Sadly, the epic project never: Wilde & Borsten, xi.
7 By the end of August: Hamblin & Brodsky, xl.

CHAPTER I: THE EARLY LIFE AND TIMES OF MARINA RASKOVA, NAVIGATOR AND PILOT

13 Less than a year later: Cottam 1998, 17.

13 Russians at home grew angry: Fleming 2014, 133–35, 140–41.

13 Now, throughout Russia, young women felt: Stites, 299.

14 Maria Bochkareva, who'd married a soldier: Abraham, 125; Pennington 2003 Vol. 1, 60–61; Pennington 2001, 5; Stites, 298.

14 Before World War I was over: Stites, 298.

14 Nadezhda Degtereva: Pennington 2003 Vol. 2, 395.

15 Workers and intellectuals in Petrograd: Fleming 2014, 161–68, 175–77.

15 A Provisional Government: Cottam 1998, xviii.

16 Lenin's vision of a better future: Lenin, *April Theses*, 1917.

16 In the same year: see Fleming, 2014, for a detailed account of the fall of the Romanovs.

16 Marina started going to elementary school: Cottam 1998, 17.

16 The winds of change blew harshly: Cottam 1998, 17; Cottam 2000, 17.

17 She was just beginning further education: Strebe 2003, 42.

CHAPTER 2: LEARNING TO FLY IN A NATION THAT'S LEARNING TO FLY

18 There were droughts in 1920 and 1921: Overy, 4–5.

19 One of the ways the Soviet government: Krylova 2010, 22.

19 In this respect, the United States: Rury, 22–24.

19 But in the years between the two world wars: Krylova 2010, 49; Vinogradova 2015, 26.

19 As a high school student: Cottam 1998, 18; Strebe 2009, 16.

19 When Marina reached the age of fifteen: Cottam 1998, 18; Markova 1986, 9; Strebe 2009, 16.

20 Marina had dreamed of a musical career: Cottam 1998, 18; Merry, 14, 151; Strebe 2009, 16.

20 When Marina graduated: Cottam 1998, 18; Strebe 2003, 42.

20 Girls and boys growing up in the Soviet Union: Krylova 2004, 630–31.

20 In 1928, the Red Army's chief of staff: Anderson, 121: Overy, 6, 9.

20 And so, beginning in 1932, military training: Krylova 2010, 51–52; McNeal, 77.

21 In Germany, restrictions: Zegenhagen, 583–84.

21 But in the USSR, by 1935: Merry, 36, 105; Pennington 2001, 10.

21 Nevertheless, according to the Soviet Constitution of 1936: 1936 Constitution of the USSR; Merry, 49.

22 letting girls into after-school flying clubs: Krylova 2010, 53; Merry, 19.

22 Marina was about eighteen: M. A. Kazarinova in Cottam 1997, 19; Cottam 1998, 18; Strebe 2003, 43.

22 Their daughter, Tatyana: Cottam 1998, 18; Merry, 151; Pennington 2003 Vol. 2, 351.

22 She drafted drawings: M. A. Kazarinova in Cottam 1997, 19; Markova 1986, 12; Merry, 151.

22 Air navigation became the focus: Cottam 1998, 18.

23 Marina was able to manage: Cottam 1998, 19; Pennington 2003 Vol. 2, 351.

23 The 1920s and 1930s are often called: Strebe 2009, 21.

24 The United States and the United Kingdom: *Aircraft Year Book* 1938, 11–13.

24 Stalin and the Communist Party: Krylova 2010, 38; Markwick & Cardona 2012, 8.

24 Before the Russian Revolution, about 80 percent: Fleming 2014, 5.

24 After the revolution, they'd claimed land: Overy, 17.

25 The number of small farms: Gruliow & Lederer, 5.

25 There was resistance to them everywhere: Overy, 23.

25 In addition to the collectivization of farms: ibid., 17–18.

25 One of the major goals: Christine A. White in Noggle, 6.

25 In 1933, at the age of twenty-one: M. A. Kazarinova in Cottam 1997, 19–20; Cottam 1998, 19; Pennington 2003 Vol. 2, 351; Strebe 2003, 43.

26 She was the first woman: Christine A. White in Noggle, 6; Cottam 1998, 19.

27 Being the trailblazer for women: Cottam 2000, 19.

27 As well as teaching: M. A. Kazarinova in Cottam 1997, 20; Cottam 2000, 19; Strebe 2003, 43.

Sidebar: "Women Don't Belong in Airplanes"

26 "Unlike American officials . . . world's foremost experts": *Arizona Republic*, June 11, 1936, 18.

26 The 1929 women's National Air Race: Gibson, 43.

27 "Women don't belong in airplanes. That's a man's job": Anonymous flight instructor quoted by Edna Gardner White in Gibson, 73.

27 When an American female pilot was killed: Gibson, 55.

27 In 1927, when Charles Lindbergh: ibid., 42.

27 By 1935, out of 13,949 licensed pilots: *Aircraft Year Book* 1935, 183.

27 around 800 were women: Gibson, 44.

27 that statistic wasn't much higher: Maksel, February 6, 2015.

27 It's a sharp contrast: Cottam 1983, 1; Pennington 2001, 10; Strebe 2009, 22.

CHAPTER 3: MARINA NAVIGATES

28 Stalin was a complex, confusing man: Anderson, 83; Montefiore, 90–97, 99–101, 127, 149; Overy, 24–25.

29 Stalin called on the People's Commissariat: Anderson, 97; Overy, 21–22.

29 In the weeks following the murder: Overy, 24–25.

29 In 1936 he began a series of random arrests: Anderson, 83; Overy, 25.

29 People tried to hide their identities: Anderson, 84, 86.

30 A chilling example: Anna Popova in Noggle, 228–31.

30 "the vigilant hawks . . . life-term inmates": Anna Popova in Noggle, 229.

31 Marina completed her pilot's license: Gibson, 121, 122.

31 In the same year: Pennington 2003 Vol. 2, 351; Strebe 2003, 43; Vinogradova 2015, 26.

31 Marina was only twenty-three: Cottam 1998, 19.

31 Right after she got her pilot's license: Cottam 2000, 19; Strebe 2003, 44.

31 In June 1937, Stalin's minions: Anderson, 128; Montefiore, 198.

32 He was tried, found guilty: Anderson, 129, 403; Montefiore, 200–201; Overy 28–29.

32 Less than a week later: *Aircraft Year Book* 1938, 148; M. A. Kazarinova in Cottam 1997, 19; Strebe 2003, 44.

32 But in October 1937, Tupolev: Gunston, 279, 378.

32 Andrey Tupolev would spend: Overy, 224.

32 Marina was well placed: Cottam 2000, 19; Strebe 2003, 44.

33 Marina no doubt took advantage: Bailes, 55, 58.

33 Marina, following in Aleksandr's footsteps: M. A. Kazarinova in Cottam 1997, 20; Cottam 2000, 20; Strebe 2003, 44.

33 Valentina herself was a deputy: Cottam 1998, 3, 9.

33 If Marina really was: Vinogradova 2015, 30–31.

33 In July 1938, Marina Raskova broke yet: Cottam 2000, 20; Strebe 2003, 44.

CHAPTER 4: THE FLIGHT OF THE *RODINA*

35 Valentina Grizodubova, the pilot: Cottam 1998, 3–4; Merry, 166–67.

35 This time, Valentina wanted to fly: Cottam 1998, 21; Krylova 2010, 77–78.

36 The flight was supported: Pennington 2001, 14.

36 boasted that its air force: *Aircraft Year Book* 1938, 11; Bailes, 70.

37 Valentina, Polina, and Marina spent the summer: Cottam 1998, 4, 13, 20.

37 But the flight of the *Rodina* had to be delayed: Cottam 1998, 21; Cottam 2000, 20; *Pittsburgh Press*, June 20, 1943, 1; Strebe 2003, 45.

37 Stalin, not a man to pay much attention: Cottam 1998, 5, 21; Cottam 2000, 20; Pennington 2003 Vol. 1, 186.

37 Early in the morning on September 24, 1938: Cottam 1998, 13.

38 Half an hour after takeoff: Cottam 2000, 21.

38 The crew was flying blind: M. A. Kazarinova in Cottam 1997, 20; Markova 1986, 39–40.

38 It wasn't just cloudy, though: M. A. Kazarinova in Cottam 1997, 20; Cottam 1998, 5, 13; Cottam 2000, 21; *Daily Chronicle*, 4 Oct 1938, 7; Strebe 2003, 45.

39 Marina and Valentina had to write notes: Markova 1986, 38.

39 Valentina flew the *Rodina* higher: M. A. Kazarinova in Cottam 1997, 20.

39 She had to take off her fur gloves: Markova 1986, 40–41.

40 Polina took over the flight controls for six hours: Cottam 1998, 13.

40 As it grew light, the weather got better: M. A. Kazarinova in Cottam 1997, 20; Markova 1986, 47.

40 They'd been flying without stopping: Pennington 2001, 15.

40 Valentina guessed that the mechanics: Cottam 1998, 5; Cottam 2000, 45; Pennington 2001, 16; Strebe 2003, 45.

40 In those tense minutes: Markova 1986, 47.

41 The navigator's cabin was by itself: ibid.

41 So Marina made her first-ever parachute jump: M. A. Kazarinova in Cottam 1997, 21; Cottam 1998, 14, 22; Cottam 2000, 21; Strebe 2003, 45.

41 With just enough fuel: Merry, 15.

41 Although her parachute had tangled in a fir tree: Markova 1986, 50.

41 Alone by herself in the taiga: Brontman, 71; Merry, 15.

42 Marina had accidentally left her emergency kit: Vinogradova 2015, 28.

42 For ten days, she survived on wild cranberries: Merry, 15; Pennington 2001, 16.

42 As she wandered in hungry frustration: Markova 1986, 58–59.

42 To her horror, one evening: Brontman, 80; Cottam 2000, 21; Markova 1986, 59.

42 Meanwhile, fifty aircraft and thousands: Cottam 2000, 21; *Daily Chronicle*, October 4, 1938, 7; Pennington 2001, 16; Vinogradova 2015, 29.

43 In the meantime, they dropped supplies: *Chicago Tribune*, October 5, 1938, 23; Pennington 2001, 16.

43 During the rescue effort that followed: Cottam 1998, 5; Cottam 2000, 21; Strebe 2003, 45; Vinogradova 2015, 29.

43 It was years before this tragedy: Cottam 1998, 5; Pennington 2001, 16.

43 For, in just over a day: Cottam 1998, 23; Krylova 2010, 78–79; Merry, 16; Strebe 2003, 46.

43 The day after the crash site was located: Cottam 1998, 22; Strebe 2003, 45.

43 She and her crewmates hugged each other: Markova 1986, 62.

44 When Marina was able to speak: Harris 2008, 42.

44 When the triumphant fliers got back: Cottam 1998, 14, 23.

44 Apparently Stalin himself greeted them: Pennington 2001, 17.

44 Valentina held her two-year-old son: Lambert, *New York Times*, May 1, 1993; Merry, 80; Petrone, 60–61.

45 Marina and Polina were each presented: Cottam 1998, 23; Strebe 2003, 46.

CHAPTER 5: "A GENERATION NOT FROM THIS UNIVERSE"

46 Two days after the flight: Merry, 81.

46-47 When Polina died in a crash: Strebe 2003, 46.

47 In June 1935, eighteen-year-old Anna Mlynek: Krylova 2010, 50, quoting *Komsomolskaya Pravda* for June 3, 1935.

48 Stalin often managed to shrug off the blame: Anna Popova in Noggle, 230; Overy 24–25.

48 Another teen who suffered: Cottam 1997, 304; Cottam 1998, 149; Pennington 2003 Vol. 1, 261.

48 She made her first solo flight: S. Gribanov in Cottam 1997, 305.

48 She was seventeen and already training: Merry, 151.

49 Lilya cut out newspaper articles: S. Gribanov in Cottam 1997, 304; Pennington 2001, 19; Strebe 2003, 46.

49 In 1937, when Lilya was sixteen: Inna Pasportnikova in Noggle, 199; Pennington 2001, 141.

50 "I hated Stalin throughout my life . . . when the war started": Antonina Khokhlova-Dubkova in Noggle, 117.

50 "eight boys and myself . . . let him fight for himself!": ibid.

50 "I was not brave, I was lucky . . . shot on the spot": ibid., 118.

50 "We are a generation not from this universe": Irina Rakobolskaya quoted in Krylova 2010, 12.

50 But while in the past: Cottam 1998, 23; Markova 1986, 5; Merry, 152; Strebe 2003, 46.

50 Marina had seriously injured her legs: Cottam 1998, 23.

50 But she'd been rewarded with a pile of cash: Cottam 1998, 23; Merry, 23.

51 anybody who couldn't get hold of the physical book: Vinogradova 2015, 38.

CHAPTER 6: "NOW EUROPE IS MINE!"

52 To the Soviet Union . . . "Now Europe is mine!": Overy, 49.

53 As soon as the United Kingdom: Curtis, 318–19.

53 At first, these women were restricted: ibid., 312–17.

53 Thousands of miles across the Atlantic: Gibson, 98; Strebe 2009, 5.

54 By now, one in every three or four pilots: Cottam 1983, 1; Pennington 2001, 10.

54 For most Soviet citizens at home: LaFeber & Polenberg, 250.

55 Hoping to soothe Soviet anxiety: Overy, 62, 64.

55 then in April 1941 the USSR: LaFeber & Polenberg, 252.

55 Hitler had had enough: Saywell, 133.

55 For all Stalin's preparation: Beevor & Vinogradova in Grossman 2006, 3; Overy, 69–70.

CHAPTER 7: THE STORM OF WAR BREAKS

59 June 22, 1941, was a Sunday: Olga Yakovleva in Cottam 1997, 285.

59 All over the USSR: Beevor & Vinogradova in Grossman 2006, 3.

59 One shocking feature: Bailes, 78.

60 Imagine, if you can, three million armed soldiers: Beevor & Vinogradova in Grossman 2006, 3.

61 Early on, supplies became so short: Grossman, 7.

61 In desperation: Grossman, 13.

61 The Germans first stormed through the cities: Saywell, 133.

61 "A cow, howling bombs, fire, women . . . just for a moment": Vasily Grossman in Grossman, 9.

61 Traveling with the Red Army: Grossman, 23.

61 Ripe grain went unharvested: Grossman, 39.

61 Twenty-year-old Mariya "Masha" Dolina: Mariya Dolina in Noggle, 119.

62 "with our own hands, where we had lived so happily": ibid., 120.

62 "When I flew over that night . . . the air was on fire": ibid., 120.

62 As the Red Army mobilized: Overy, 80.

62 There weren't any air raid shelters in Moscow: M. A. Kazarinova in Cottam 1997, 16.

63 But because military enlistment: Krylova 2010, 59.

63 Most young Soviet women found themselves struggling: Olga Yakovleva in
Cottam 1997, 285.

63 All over the USSR: S. Gribanov in Cottam 1997, 305; Cottam 1998, 149; Merry,
168; Pennington 2003 Vol. 1, 261–62.

63 At the beginning of the war: Pennington 2001, 21.

63 The government didn't like the idea: Harris 2008, 223.

64 Polina Gelman, who'd taken up flying in ninth grade: Polina Gelman in Cottam
1997, 162; Polina Gelman in Noggle, 39.

64 "We were brought up to believe . . . into the army, too": Polina Gelman in Noggle, 39.

64 "But we are indeed capable . . . sleep in the snow": Zoya Malkova in Cottam 1997, 298.

64 The man told them: ibid.

64 In August 1941, Stalin issued a fearful rule: Overy, 80–81.

CHAPTER 8: "DEAR SISTERS! THE HOUR HAS COME . . ."

66 Marina, too, tried to sign up to fight: Krylova 2010, 88–89; Merry, 23.

66 Pilots and navigators: Pennington 2001, 22.

66 Marina approached Josef Stalin: Flerovsky, 28; Markwick & Cardona 2012, 84,
88; Pennington 2001, 25.

67 "You understand, future generations . . . sacrificing young girls": Stalin's words
as paraphrased by Yevgeniya Zhigulenko in Keyssar & Pozner 1990, 39–40.

67 "They are running away . . . steal airplanes to go": Marina Raskova's words as
paraphrased by Yevgeniya Zhigulenko in Keyssar & Pozner 1990, 39–40.

67 "There were several girls who had asked . . . They just couldn't wait": Yevgeniya
Zhigulenko in Keyssar & Pozner 1990, 39–40.

67 "the peoples of Europe and America . . . war against German fascism": Stalin n.d.
(1944?), 9.

68 But Stalin didn't mention: ibid., 5–9.

68 nearly a million Soviet women: Alexievich 2017, x; Cottam 1998, xx; Markwick
& Cardona 2012, 1, 150.

68 By luck or persistence, either women: Krylova 2010, 98.

68 Even Marina's aviation regiments: Pennington 2001, 22.

68 It took several months of persistence: Merry, 23–24; Christine A. White in Noggle, 7; Pennington 2001, 23.

68 At the end of the first week in September 1941: Merry, 24; Pennington 2001, 29; *Washington Court House Record-Herald*, September 20, 1941, 4.

68 "Dear sisters! The hour has come . . . the warriors for freedom": The text of this speech by Marina Raskova is quoted in Russian in Markova 1986, 67; the English translation is from Pennington 2001, 29.

68 The USSR was the first: Campbell, 319–20; Markwick & Cardona 2012, 84.

69 People often assume there was a shortage: Merry, 24; Pennington 2001, 57.

69 There were hundreds of Soviet flight regiments: Merry, 50; Pennington 2001, 234, note 90.

69 Her daughter, Tanya, was a girl to be proud of: Galina Chapligina-Nikitina in Noggle, 139.

69 But the formation of the women's air regiments was kept quiet: Markwick & Cardona 2012, 85, 88–89.

69 On October 8, 1941, the People's Commissariat: Krylova 2010, 124; Christine A. White in Noggle, 7; Pennington 2001, 31.

70 To give Marina the authority: Krylova 2010, 125.

70 An official order was made: M. A. Kazarinova in Cottam 1997, 17.

70 The German army was now closing in: Grossman, 52; Stolfi, 215, 222.

70 Museum staff were frantically packing up: Overy, 96.

70 German aircraft flew over: Evgenia Sergeevna Sapronova in Alexievich 2017, 25.

71 Yevgeniya Zhigulenko was a horse rider: Yevgeniya Zhigulenko in Noggle, 53.

71 When, not surprisingly, they didn't get an appointment: ibid., 54.

71 "Marina Raskova is forming . . . you may personally talk with her": officer as quoted by Yevgeniya Zhigulenko in Noggle, 54.

71 "spellbound" when they found themselves: Yevgeniya Zhigulenko in Noggle, 54.

71 All the information was spread: Merry, 51.

71 Irina Rakobolskaya, who grew up: The memories are those of Irina Rakobolskaya in Noggle, 26–27. The quotation "generation not from this universe" is Irina Rakobolskaya as quoted in Krylova 2010, 12.

72 Irina was on duty: Merry, 51.

72 No one who heard the summons could resist: Krylova 2010, 121; Merry, 41.

CHAPTER 9: THE 122ND AIR GROUP

73 For the young women who answered: Pennington 2001, 37.

73 carrying only a small bag: A. M. Bereznitskaya in Cottam 1997, 98.

73 The women from Moscow: Vinogradova 2015, 24.

73 Throughout the huge nation: M. A. Kazarinova in Cottam 1997, 16–17.

73 One of them, when Marina assigned her: A. M. Bereznitskaya in Cottam 1997, 99.

73 On October 14 the girls were given military uniforms: Merry, 64; Alexandra Makunina in Noggle, 166; Pennington 2001, 38.

74 "right down to the underwear": Raisa Aronova, quoted in Pennington 2001, 38, from Raisa Aronova 2nd ed., 24; also quoted in Strebe 2009, 23.

74 Even in 1943, when they received skirts: Pennington 2001, 234, note 79.

74 One woman remembered: Klavdiya Ilushina in Noggle, 51.

74 But it couldn't happen in Moscow: Grossman, 60.

75 Then, on October 16, 1941, a Moscow radio: Overy, 97.

75 During that single chaotic night: Pennington 2001, 39.

75 Aboard one of those trains: Markwick & Cardona 2012, 88.

75 Marina's recruits had to wait: Irina Sebrova in Noggle, 74; Pennington 2001 41, 234.

75 They didn't have any idea where: A. M. Bereznitskaya in Cottam 1997, 100; Merry, 50; Pennington 2001, 40.

76 Their train was made up: Pennington 2001, 41; Vinogradova 2015, 45.

76 At the station, in the freezing darkness: M. A. Kazarinova in Cottam 1997, 15, 17–18.

76 In total, nearly a thousand young women: Merry, 55.

76 There, they would train: M. A. Kazarinova in Cottam 1997, 21–22.

77 During the long trip, Marina went: Merry, 55; Pennington 2001, 40.

77 And the recruits started to make friends: Vinogradova 2015, 44–45, 50.

77 There wasn't a lot of food: Markwick & Cardona 2012, 92; Vinogradova 2015, 48.

77 "just like rabbits . . . made us take it all back": Valentina Kravchenko-Savitskaya, quoted in Pennington 2001, 41, from an interview by Reina Pennington on May 7, 1993; see also Pennington 2001, 235, note 97.

78 "Service personnel must cover . . . have turned into mops": M. A. Kazarinova in Cottam 1997, 18.

78 Militsa was no-nonsense: Pennington 2001, 36.

78 There were no lights showing: ibid., 41.

78 Militsa, who'd graduated from the Engels Flying School: M. A. Kazarinova in Cottam 1997, 22; see also Vinogradova 2015, 63.

78 Their hearts must have lifted: Markova 1986, 73.

78 The gymnasium of the Red Army Officers' House: Pennington 2001, 42; see also Vinogradova 2015, 63.

78 "Is this some kind of a boudoir? . . . the girls don't have them either!": Marina Raskova as quoted by M. A. Kazarinova in Cottam 1997, 22.

78 Now a military representative: Markova 1986, 74; Pennington 2001, 42.

Sidebar: Combat Boots

74 Klavdiya Terekhova said that in one drill: Klavdiya Terekhova-Kasatkina in Noggle, 191.

74 But the young recruits were forbidden: A. M. Bereznitskaya in Cottam 1997, 99; Klavdiya Terekhova-Kasatkina in Noggle, 191; Pennington 2001, 39.

75 Combat boots in women's sizes for British soldiers: Drury, August 30, 2012.

75 In 2015, after American women soldiers: Scarborough, May 14, 2015.

CHAPTER 10: "NOW I AM A WARRIOR"

80 Marina hadn't forgotten Militsa's comments: Merry, 56; Pennington 2001, 42; Strebe 2009, 24.

80 The haircuts drove home to everyone: Olga Yakovleva in Cottam 1997, 285; Nadezhda Popova in Noggle, 81.

80 At first, headstrong, talented Lilya: Klavdiya Terekhova-Kasatkina in Noggle, 192.

81 When the young women . . . Marina had to admit that it did: The story and quotations are from Inna Vladimirovna Pasportnikova in Pennington 2001, 46. They are quoted from a typescript in Pennington's collection headed "Moi Komandir," 1989. See Pennington 2001, 235, note 129.

81 But she couldn't let such an outrageous violation: Krylova 2010, 274–75; Inna Pasportnikova in Noggle, 195; Pennington 2001, 46.

81 Hanging on to their feminity: Saywell, 138.

82 Marina divided the young women: Pennington 2001, 37.

82 To avoid argument, Marina made the decision: Gibson, 122.

82 Marina gave these assignments: Polina Gelman in Noggle, 39; Yevgeniya Zhigulenko in Noggle, 54; Pennington 2001, 37.

82 Women with physical strength: Merry, 36.

82 They began lessons immediately: Gibson, 122.

83 "Our days were filled . . . in the frosty air: 'Sing!'": Inna Pasportnikova in Cottam 1997, 313.

83 Sometimes, to get people used to combat: Pennington 2001, 42.

83 On November 7, 1941, less than a month: Markova 1986, 78; Markwick & Cardona 2012, 92; Pennington 2001, 42.

83 "Let's vow once more . . . beloved homeland": Marina Raskova, quoted in Markova 1986, 79; English translation quoted in Pennington 2001, 43.

84 "Now I am a warrior . . . mastering a fearsome weapon": Zhenya Rudneva, quoted in Markwick & Cardona 2012, 93.

84 Less than a month later, on December 5, 1941: Hook, 73–74.

85 Meanwhile, another ferocious wind: Hook, 72–74; LaFeber & Polenberg, 251, 254.

86 on December 9, 1941, under an order of Stalin: Markwick & Cardona 2012, 93.

86 Marina chose Militsa Kazarinova's sister: Alexandra Makunina in Cottam 1997, 254–55.

86 Marina also assigned commanders: Pennington 2001, 48, 94.

87 Marina chose Yevdokia Bershanskaya: M. A. Kazarinova in Cottam 1997, 27; Krylova 2010, 135; Markwick & Cardona 2012, 91; Vinogradova 2015, 107.

87 But Marina wanted her to take charge: Natalya Meklin-Kravtsova in Cottam 1997, 159; Noggle, 18; Pennington 2001, 75.

87 Yevdokia's second-in-command: Krylova 2010, 12

87 Irina had gone to war: ibid., 97.

87-88 Now, when Marina Raskova told her: Irina Rakobolskaya in Noggle, 27.

Sidebar: Units of Measurement

84 In World War II, in the USSR: Von Hardesty & Grinberg, 371.

CHAPTER II: WINTER TRAINING

89 The winter of 1941–1942 was the coldest: Stolfi, 220.

89 They covered their faces with masks: Vinogradova 2015, 89.

90 Throughout that fearsome winter: Belyakov, 34; Merry, 56–57; Pennington 2001, 43.

90 Beginning in January 1942: Pennington 2001, 47.

90 Training in wartime meant that: M. A. Kazarinova in Cottam 1997, 25.

90-91 "It was early morning . . . hands freeze to the metal": Zoya Malkova in Cottam 1997, 298–99.

91 "Other girls join in . . . you found new strength": ibid., 299.

91 The young airwomen truly: Pennington 2001, 45.

91 She hummed along to Rimsky-Korsakov: Merry, 109, 152; Pennington 2001, 29, 45.

91 At the end of the day's training: M. A. Kazarinova in Cottam 1997, 26.

91-92 "The Dugout": Quoted by M. A. Kazarinova in Cottam 1997, 26-27. It was written by the poet Alexey Surkov and beloved throughout the Soviet Union during the war. The English translation is my own, based on several English versions.

92 And she had a sympathetic ear: Antonina Skoblikova in Cottam 1997, 66.

92 Some of the women: M. A. Kazarinova in Cottam 1997, 27; Markova 1986, 65.

93 The one thing Marina didn't make time for: Yekaterina Fedotova in Cottam 1997, 51; Pennington 2001, 44.

93 Years later, when other men: Alexievich 2017, 113; Pennington 2001, 28.

CHAPTER 12: GROUND CREW

95 Irina Favorskaya was a student: Irina Lunyova-Favorskaya in Noggle, 209–10.

95 "We had to fix instruments . . . girls laughed and made fun of me": Irina Lunyova-Favorskaya in Noggle, 210.

95 Zinaida Butkaryova came from: Zinaida Butkaryova-Yermolayeva in Noggle, 184–85; Klavdiya Terekhova-Kasatkina in Noggle, 191.

96 "When one of our aircraft . . . the pilot got down safely": Zinaida Butkaryova-Yermolayeva in Noggle, 186.

97 One, Khivaz Dospanova, was from a town in Kirghiz: Markwick & Cardona 2012, 90.

97 Only a third of one percent of Soviet women: ibid., 89.

97 Zoya Malkova, the aircraft mechanic: Zoya Malkova in Noggle, 218.

98 Life was harder for ground crew: Pennington 2001, 116.

99 The young women who'd been assigned as Komsomol: Vinogradova 2015, 90–91.

100 "After I was in closer contact . . . we all became like sisters": Klavdiya Ilushina in Noggle, 49.

Sidebar: Kitchen Duty: Another Form of Elitism

98 Valentina Petrochenkova was so inspired: Valentina Petrochenkova-Neminushaya in Noggle, 175.

98 "and only the instructors in the bushes could stop us!": ibid., 175–76.

98–99 When she'd finished her course . . . she was still sitting there: The story, and the dialogue quoted with the officer, are quoted in Valentina Petrochenkova-Neminushaya's account in Noggle, 176.

99 Finally she wore him down: ibid., 176–77.

CHAPTER 13: THE AIRCRAFT ARRIVE

101 Late in December 1941: Markova 1986, 84.

101 These battered Sukhoys: Pennington 2001, 51; Vinogradova 2015, 81.

101 Remember Vladimir Petlyakov: Gunston, 279.

102 These Pe-2s were the planes: Krylova 2010, 126; Pennington 2001, 52.

102 by the end of the war the 587th loved this aircraft: Mariya Dolina in Cottam 1997, 71; Yekaterina Fedotova in Cottam 1997, 116; Vinogradova 2015, 101.

102 The aircraft for the 588th Night Bomber Aviation Regiment: Pennington 2001, 48.

102 They were Polikarpov Po-2 biplanes: Pennington 2001, 31; Vinogradova 2015, 98.

102 They were already being used at the front: Irina Rakobolskaya in Cottam 1997, 150; Vinogradova 2015, 106.

103 "It sounded like a sewing machine . . . as long as the Po-2s approached": Artur Gartner in *Wasps and Witches*, 39:29 ff.

103 "We hated the German fascists . . . to be able to fire at them!": Polina Gelman in Noggle, 39.

103 As for the 586th Fighter Aviation Regiment: Pennington 2001, 50.

103 The male technicians at the factory: Levin, 29–30; Pennington 2001, 50.

104 Marina decided to introduce: Pennington 2001, 51.

104 "Our aerodrome kids were transformed . . . pulled themselves up": The quotation is I. S. Levin, 29–30, English translation by Pennington 2001, 51.

104 It wasn't long before the splendid Yak-1: M. A. Kazarinova in Cottam 1997, 23; Nina Slovokhotova in Cottam 1997, 261; Pennington 2001, 51; Vinogradova 2015, 96.

104 Those fighter planes only had room: Pennington 2001, 51.

105 "outside when the wind was blowing . . . would be a deep blue color": Galina Drobovich in Noggle, 190.

105 Soon the young fighter pilots: Olga Yakovleva in Cottam 1997, 286.

106 "The machine is splendid! . . . I learned how to turn": Lilya Litvyak, quoted by S. Gribanov in Cottam 1997, 305.

CHAPTER 14: NOT QUITE READY FOR WAR

107 Hardly any of Marina Raskova's pilots: Markwick & Cardona 2012, 94; Pennington 2001, 73.

107 "You see this? . . . I cannot see it!": Raisa Zhitova-Yushina in Noggle, 90.

108 On March 9, 1942, it was deadly for the 588th: Vinogradova 2015, 117–18.

108 "It was like flying through milk": Yevdokia Bershanskaya, quoted in Vinogradova 2015, 117.

108 Marina stayed up late: Markova 1986, 87; Pennington 2001, 48–49; Vinogradova 2015, 117–18.

109 "My darlings, my girls . . . you shouldn't be sobbing": Marina Raskova as quoted by Klavdiya Terekhova-Kasatkina in Noggle, 194.

109 "These are our first losses . . . Clench your hearts like a fist": Marina Raskova as quoted by Klavdiya Terekhova-Kasatkina in Alexievich 2017, 564.

109 The incident shook everyone: Serafima Amosova-Taranenko in Noggle, 44.

109 Because of the accident: Markwick & Cardona 2012, 94; Pennington 2001, 49.

109-110 "We are having remarkable summer-like flying . . . very confident and completely grown-up": Lilya Litvyak in a letter, quoted by S. Gribanov in Cottam 1997, 306.

110 But before they could go to war: Vinogradova 2015, 121–22.

110 But when the 586th's assignment came: Yekaterina Polunina in Noggle, 164.

110 Instead, they'd be protecting the strategic city: Vinogradova 2015, 127.

111 On April 16, 1942, the women: Pennington 2001, 108.

111 Skylarks sang in the fields around them: Vinogradova 2015, 168.

111 every night the air raid sirens wailed: Nina Slovokhotova in Cottam 1997, 259.

111 The 586th's main mission: Pennington 2001, 103, 105.

111 Sometimes they also had to deliver urgent messages: Tamara Pamyatnykh in Cottam 1997, 160; Klavdiya Pankratova in Cottam 1997, 282.

111 In addition to being disappointed: Vinogradova 2015, 127.

111 Marina had appointed Tamara Kazarinova: Alexandra Makunina in Cottam 1997, 254.

111 "fairly well . . . not bad": Alexandra Makunina in Cottam 1997, 255.

111 Tamara didn't often fly along: Pennington 2001, 107.

112 Soviet fighter pilots were alone: Merry, 104.

112 Three of the 586th's fighter pilots: Nina Potapova in Cottam 1997, 347.

112 Lilya Litvyak and Katya Budanova: Inna Pasportnikova in Cottam 1997, 314–15.

112 "So May has almost ended . . . thirsting for battle, especially me": Lilya Litvyak, quoted by S. Gribanov in Cottam 1997, 307.

113 There were now more than twenty-five nations: Hook, 77.

113 The Americans were fighting an air and sea war: ibid., 82.

113 As the snow began to melt in Russia: See Anderson, 2015, for a detailed account of the Leningrad blockade.

114 But Moscow was still free: Hook, 81.

114 In March, the Red Army began fighting in Crimea: ibid., 84.

114 Encouraged by the warm weather: Beevor & Vinogradova in Grossman 2006, 116–17; Overy, 157–58; Pennington 2001, 79; Vinogradova 2015, 161.

CHAPTER 15: THE 588TH: IN COMBAT AT LAST

117 The 588th was sent to help: Mariya Smirnova in Noggle, 31; Serafima Amosova-Taranenko in Noggle, 44; Markwick & Cardona 2012, 96; Pennington 2001, 76.

117 Marina Raskova's young aviators: Pennington 2001, 49.

117 Marina flew with the 588th: Irina Rakobolskaya in Cottam 1997, 151.

118 Ten minutes before the planes: Raisa Aronova in Cottam 1997, 250.

119 the surrounding orchards were foamy: Markova 1986, 91.

119 When the young women climbed out: Pennington 2001, 76, referring to Raisa Aronova 1980, 52–53.

119 Once again, the young women's morale: Pennington 2001, 78.

119 The pilot who checked out Mariya Smirnova: Mariya Smirnova in Noggle, 31.

119 Before Marina flew back: Markova 1986, 91.

120 "Standing shoulder to shoulder . . . opening up in our lives": Natalya Meklin-Kravtsova in Cottam 1997, 158.

120 On June 10, 1942, three Po-2s: Markwick & Cardona 2012, 96; Pennington 2001, 73, 78.

120 The 588th's commander, Yevdokia Bershanskaya: Natalya Meklin-Kravtsova in Cottam 1997, 159.

120 As they approached the target area: Serafima Amosova-Taranenko in Noggle, 45.

121 "When we landed . . . hugging and kissing us": Serafima Amosova-Taranenko in Noggle, 45.

121 But for Lyuba Olkhovskaya's squadron: Markwick & Cardona 2012, 96; Zoya Parfyonova in Noggle, 71; Pennington 2001, 78.

122 "We painted on . . . our planes . . . the Death of our Friends": Serafima Amosova-Taranenko in Noggle, 45.

122 Lyuba's squadron had to fly: Zoya Parfyonova in Noggle, 71.

122 Mariya Smirnova, the pilot: Mariya Smirnova in Noggle, 31.

122 For most of the summer: Pennington 2001, 77.

122 Yevdokia Bershanskaya turned out to be: Natalya Meklin-Kravtsova in Cottam 1997, 159; Pennington 2001, 75.

122 She tried to balance military discipline: Olga Yerokhina-Averjanova in Noggle, 58–59.

122 Tonya Rudakova, who was tiny: Irina Rakobolskaya in Cottam 1997, 156.

123 "Be careful": Natalya Meklin-Kravtsova quoting Yevdokia Bershanskaya in Cottam 1997, 160, 199.

123 That was enough to reassure: Irina Rakobolskaya in Cottam 1997, 155.

123 They used two airfields: Irina Rakobolskaya in Cottam 1997, 154; Serafima Amosova-Taranenko in Noggle, 45.

123 "You point your plane . . . how I hate them!": Zhenya Rudneva, quoted in Vinogradova 2015, 109.

124 The release catch wasn't entirely reliable: Irina Rakobolskaya in Noggle, 29.

124 "I am not in the least afraid . . . so wonderful to fly!": Zhenya Rudneva in Cottam 1997, 218.

124 Flying in the dark: Irina Rakobolskaya in Noggle, 30.

124 Another sobering accident: Polina Gelman in Cottam 1997, 163; Vinogradova 2015, 157–58.

124 The darkened nighttime airfields: Pennington 2001, 81.

125 "Soon we'll be expected to land . . . commander's cigarette": Irina Rakobolskaya in Cottam 1997, 155.

CHAPTER 16: DIVE-BOMBERS FOR THE 587TH

126 Back at Engels: Markova 1986, 94; Noggle, 99; Valentina Kravchenko-Savitskaya in Noggle, 101; Pennington 2001, 53, 54.

127 "flying coffin": Antonina Bondareva-Spitsina in *Wasps and Witches*, 36:13ff.

127 "the control stick was heavy . . . tail up for takeoff": Yekaterina Musatova-Fedotova in Noggle, 147.

127 Marina Raskova was less experienced: Merry 109; Pennington 2001, 44; Pennington 2003 Vol. 2, 353.

127 Katya was there to see: Yekaterina Fedotova in Cottam 1997, 51; Vinogradova 2015, 128–29.

127 "Never mind, girls . . . certainly is airworthy": Marina Raskova as quoted by Yekaterina Fedotova in Cottam 1997, 51.

128 According to pilot Yelena: Yelena Malyutina in Newman, December 6, 2016.

128 In the back of the aircraft: Noggle, 99.

128 Now Marina ran into: Pennington 2001, 52–53.

128 Tonya Khokhlova was one: Antonina Khokhlova-Dubkova in Noggle, 114.

128 "but in the air it was one, two, and it was recharged!": ibid.

128 It was difficult for the armorers: Dasha Chalaya in Cottam 1997, 95.

129 The Pe-2 dive-bomber contained five: Galina Volova in Cottam 1997, 93.

129 "unspectacular but difficult and important": ibid., 94.

129 "the guns became very dirty . . . small girls for such jobs?": Natalya Alfyorova in Noggle, 131.

CHAPTER 17: "NOT ONE STEP BACK"

130 Spirits were very low: Overy, 158.

130 Refugees fled frantically: Vinogradova 2015, 152.

130 Sonya Ozerkova, the chief engineer: Markwick & Cardona 2012, 92; Vinogradova 2015, 143–45.

131 So on July 28, 1942, the Soviet government: Grossman, 117; Hardesty & Grinberg, 115; Markwick & Cardona 2012, 96; Merry, 111; Overy, 158; Pennington 2001, 79.

132 Lilya Litvyak's greatest fear: Inna Pasportnikova in Noggle, 199.

132 "I remember a night . . . and it was burning": Polina Gelman quoted in Pennington 2001, 79.

132 From August to December 1942: Pennington 2001, 73, 79.

133 Some nights in the Caucasus: Marina Chechneva in Cottam 1997, 167.

133 The mechanics on the ground: Mariya Smirnova in Noggle, 36.

133 On a foggy night in England: Everitt & Middlebrook, cxxxvii, 243–44.

133 "Landing in thick fog . . . ground for a landing": Mariya Smirnova in Noggle, 36.

134 One night, returning from a mission: Yevgeniya Zhigulenko in Noggle, 55; Pennington 2001, 79.

134 "When they hit the ground . . . one after another": Olga Yerokhina-Averjanova in Noggle, 59.

134 The Germans destroyed most: Hardesty & Grinberg, 164; Overy, 181–84; Vinogradova 2015, 163–65.

135 "Stalingrad is in ashes . . . bombing of the dead city": Vasily Grossman in Grossman, 125–26.

135 The 586th Fighter Aviation Regiment: Pennington 2001, 108.

135 In August 1942, squadron commander: Tamara Pamyatnykh in Cottam 1997, 160.

135 "I was afraid . . . our first night landings": ibid.

CHAPTER 18: BATTLE OF THE SEXES

137 By the middle of 1942: Curtis, 108–10.

137 American women still didn't: Strebe 2009, 7–8.

138 Jackie was an ambitious: Gibson, 103, 107–8.

138 In the spring of 1942, Jackie: Curtis, 142–43, Strebe 2009, 6–7.

139 Tamara Kazarinova, the commander of the 586th: Pennington 2001, 108.

139 "who didn't know how to fly a fighter": Aleksandr Gridnev, quoted in Pennington 2001, 108, from an interview by Reina Pennington on May 12, 1993; see also Pennington 2001, 250, note 17.

139 In September 1942, Lilya: Mariya Kuznetsova in Noggle, 167.

139 Marina Raskova flew over: Vinogradova 2015, 170.

139 Lilya, Katya, Raisa, and Mariya: Mariya Kuznetsova in Noggle, 167; Pennington 2001, 108–9, 130; Vinogradova 2015, 170.

139 Anya Demchenko, the pilot: Belyakov, 37; Vinogradova 2015, 171.

140 When the pilots flew to the new airfield: Nina Shebalina in Noggle, 203; Vinogradova 2015, 172.

140 "Whyever me? . . . take the girls away from me!": Conversation between Arkady Kovacevich and his commander, as Arkady Kovacevich reports it in *Wasps and Witches*, 13:16 ff.

141 A camel named Pashka carried water: Vinogradova 2015, 205.

141 The regimental commander arranged: Mariya Kuznetsova in Noggle, 169.

141 "These two girls proved . . . depended on skill": ibid.

141 In September 1942, Lilya flew: Cottam 1998, 150; Pennington 2001, 133; Vinogradova 2015, 187–88.

142 Before they'd even had a chance: Pennington 2001, 132–33.

143 Three days after her arrival at Stalingrad: S. Gribanov in Cottam 1997, 308; Cottam 1998, 150; Pennington 2001, 109.

143 The story goes that the German: Cottam 1998, 150; Pennington 2001, 133; Vinogradova 2015, 190.

144 "The Germans don't fly here . . . 'they are afraid of us'": Lilya Litvyak in a letter, quoted by Yu. Shteyn in Cottam 1984, 226.

Sidebar: A Heroine Out of the Spotlight

142 Kseniia Sanchuk had been flying supply: Pennington 2001, 48.

142 Some people, some women included: ibid., 33, 233, note 49.

142 When the Great Patriotic War broke out: Krylova 2010, 258.

143 In doing so, she became the only: Cottam 1998, 5; Merry, 167.

143 The 101st Long Range Air Regiment: M. A. Kazarinova in Cottam 1997, 17; Cottam 1998, 6; Merry, 167; Pennington 2001, 70.

143 Valentina flew more than 1,850: Cottam 1998, 7; Pennington 2003, 1, 187.

CHAPTER 19: TROUBLE IN THE 586TH

145 The male pilots fighting on the Stalingrad Front: Vinogradova 2015, 167–68.

145 the fragrant fields of the Russian steppes: Grossman, 124, 134.

145 Shockingly, the first death: Vinogradova 2015, 147.

146 The 586th's first combat loss . . . "Jump!" . . . "I felt so terrible . . . the first loss of the regiment": This story and the quotations within it are told by Zoya Pozhidayeva in Noggle, 216.

146 On the night of September 24, 1942: Vinogradova 2015, 184.

146 Nina Slovokhotova, the 586th's chief of chemical: Nina Slovokhotova in Cottam 1997, 259.

147 "According to the Air-Warning . . . its own bombs!": Nina Slovokhotova quoting a messenger in Cottam 1997, 259–60.

147 "You darling, you've just shot down a Heinkel!": Yekaterina Polunina, quoted in Vinogradova 2015, 184.

147 "Near the bridge . . . their unopened parachutes": Nina Slovokhotova in Cottam 1997, 261.

148 As well as being Lera's very first: Pennington 2001, 108–9; Vinogradova 2015, 185.

148 The regiment even got a splashy: Meos, 1019; Pennington 2001, 61, 110.

148 But Lera was one of the pilots Tamara: Pennington 2001, 110; Vinogradova 2015, 185–86.

148 Tamara had only been in charge: Merry, 73; Pennington 2001, 106–7.

149 It's even possible that some: Aleksandr Gridnev, quoted in Pennington 2001, 108, 118–19.

149 For a few days, she was replaced: Merry, 73; Pennington 2001, 111.

149 Aleksandr Gridnev had troubles: Pennington 2001, 112, 113; see also 252, note 37.

149 "Forever": Aleksandr Gridnev, quoted in Pennington 2001, 113; see also 252, note 38.

150 Aleksandr Gridnev took his role: Pennington 2001, 113.

150 In the fall of 1942, the two squadrons: Yekaterina Polunina in Noggle, 163–64; Pennington 2001, 105.

150 Aleksandr Gridnev got to work right away: Pennington 2001, 115.

150 A couple months after Alexandr Gridnev: ibid., 119.

CHAPTER 20: "LIFE IS LIFE"

151 Leningrad, Russia's old capital: See Anderson, 2015, for a detailed account of the Leningrad blockade.

152 Everyone's food was rationed: Merry, 93, 110.

152 Zinaida Butkaryova, the parachute packer: Zinaida Butkaryova-Yermolayeva in Noggle, 186; Vinogradova 2015, 191.

152 "Our ration was a soldier's . . . their own rations": Zinaida Butkaryova-Yermolayeva in Noggle, 186.

152 "When they sent us the American . . . canned milk": Aleksandr Gridnev quoted in Pennington 2001, 119, from an interview by Reina Pennington on May 12, 1993; see also Pennington 2001, 252, note 53.

152 Throughout the war, ground personnel: Zinaida Butkaryova-Yermolayeva in Noggle, 186.

153 The only heat: Anna Kirilina in Noggle, 124.

153 Water trickled into the dugouts: Yevgeniya Gurulyeva-Smirnova in Noggle, 110.

153 "When . . . there was so much water . . . back to sleep": Valentina Kovalyova-Sergeicheva in Noggle, 173–74.

153 There was never enough soap: Olga Yerokhina-Averjanova in Noggle, 60.

153 About once a week a truck: Antonina Pugachova-Makarova in Noggle, 127.

153 And in the 586th, every couple of weeks: Zinaida Butkaryova-Yermolayeva in Noggle, 186.

153 But the women had to share: Irina Emelianova as quoted in Pennington 2001, 116.

153-154 "It was in an open airfield . . . I didn't ever have breakfast!": Yelena Kulkova-Malutina in Noggle, 130.

154 The steppes, the flat grassland: Merry, 104–5; Pennington 2001, 115–16.

155 In wartime, being forced to wear: Yekaterina Chujkova in Noggle, 145; Pennington 2001, 102.

155 Two armorers from the 588th Regiment: Irina Rakobolskaya in Noggle, 29; Vinogradova 2015, 203–4.

155 Hanging on to femininity: Markwick & Cardona 2012, 101.

156 Under so much physical stress: Anonymous pilot quoted in Alexievich 2017, xvii; Alexandra Semyonovna Popova in Alexievich 2017, 195; Maria Nesterovna Kuzmenko in Alexievich 2017, 199.

156 "We wanted to make . . . in spite of the uniform": Nina Shebalina in Noggle, 204.

156 "We were sick and tired . . . my slippers in uniform!": Mariya Kaloshina in Noggle, 151.

156 Another young woman in the 587th: Marta Meriuts in Noggle, 136.

156 One pilot in the 586th got in trouble: Valentina Kovalyova-Sergeicheva in Noggle, 174.

156 The young women of Marina Raskova's regiments: Krylova 2010, 27–72.

156 "We dreamed of our grooms . . . happy, peaceful life": Yevgeniya Zhigulenko in Noggle, 56.

156 "after a night of combat we never forgot to curl our hair": Yevgeniya Zhigulenko in Noggle, 56.

157 "After the war you'll wear . . . going to win the war": Marina Raskova quoted by Valentina Kravchenko in Strebe 2009, 25; originally from *The Night Witches: Soviet Air Women in World War II*, documentary film produced and directed by Sissi Hüetlin and Elizabeth McKay, 1994.

157 But some of the young women felt: Yevgeniya Zhigulenko in Noggle, 56.

157 "bride's fair": attributed to Galya Dokutovich, in Markwick & Cardona 2012, 101.

157 "You've gone out of your minds!": attributed to an anonymous mechanic in Markwick & Cardona 2012, 101.

157 "the most beautiful girls in the world . . . And he is right": Zhenya Rudneva, referring to a speech by Konstantin Andreyevich Vershinin in a letter to her parents dated October 17, 1942, quoted in Markwick & Cardona 2012, 101 and 266, note 81; see also Zhenya Rudneva in Cottam 1997, 221.

157 Lilya Litvyak's friend: Krylova 2010, 281–82; Vinogradova 2015, 214.

158 Zhenya Rudneva makes it clear: Zhenya Rudneva in Cottam 1997, 216–36; Markwick & Cardona 2012, 104–5; Vinogradova 2015, 266.

158 Zhenya was also passionately in love: Cottam 1998, 96; Krylova 2010, 286–87.

158 There was one pretty, feminine thing: Krylova 2010, 269, 270, 272.

159 At about this time in the war: ibid., 272–73.

160 Antonina Bondareva, worked on a piece: Antonina Bondareva-Spitsina in Noggle, 109.

160 "Everybody embroidered the Pe-2 on their pillows": Yekaterina Chujkova in Noggle, 145. Mariya Kaloshina makes a similar but more general statement about embroidery in Noggle, 151.

160 In the 588th, people embroidered their foot cloths: Irina Rakobolskaya in Noggle, 28.

160 Most of the pilots and technicians: Zhenya Rudneva in Cottam 1997, 233; Irina Rakobolskaya in Noggle, 30; Harris 2010, 647.

160 All the women liked to keep track: Lina Yeliseyeva in Cottam 1997, 138.

160 Klava Serebryakova, always had her mandolin: Tatyana Sumarokova in Cottam 1997, 239.

160 The 586th held talent shows: Vera Tikhomirova in Cottam 1997, 353.

160-161 Their mechanics took a record player: Zoya Malkova in Noggle, 218.

161 Sonya Tishurova, organized a group: Alexandra Makunina in Noggle, 166.

161 When an airwoman for the 587th gave a concert: Galina Tenuyeva-Lomanova in Noggle, 155.

161 The armorers for the 587th sang: Yekaterina Chujkova in Noggle, 143.

161 the "USSR Honorable Singer . . . the regiment would join me": Nina Yermakova in Noggle, 171.

161 "You heard them singing . . . amateur talent performances": Lina Yeliseyeva in Cottam 1997, 138.

161 The 587th performed in hospitals: ibid., 137.

161 "When weather caused the cancellation . . . permission to fly": Irina Rakobolskaya in Noggle, 29.

162 The pilots and navigators of the 587th kept: Markova 1983, 105.

162 In November 1942, the commander: Pennington 2001, 79; Vinogradova 2015, 201.

162 "This is silly . . . the best time of my life": Zhenya Rudneva in Cottam 1997, 220.

162 And Galya Dokutovich, the navigator: Polina Gelman in Cottam 1997, 163.

162 "I am back . . . better after the war": Galina Dokutovich, from a diary entry quoted by Polina Gelman in Cottam 1997, 164.

CHAPTER 21: WINTER COMES EARLY

163 By December 1942, as another harsh: Overy, 183–84; Vinogradova 2015, 211–12.

164 "When our crews . . . We worried until our planes returned": Galina Drobovich in Noggle, 190.

164 "During the war . . . you just heard it and you knew": Nina Shebalina in Noggle, 204.

164 When a pilot found herself: Mariya Kuznetsova in Noggle, 168.

164 "There was no water . . . to take to the planes": Yekaterina Polunina in Noggle, 164.

165 "We feel the water taps . . . from the wing to the ground": This story and the quotation are as told by Sofya Osipova in Cottam 1997, 275–76.

166 the vacation cabins the pilots had been living in: Irina Emelianova as quoted in Pennington 2001, 116.

166 On December 3, 1942, three pilots: Zoya Pozhidayeva in Noggle, 216; Pennington 2001, 118.

CHAPTER 22: MARINA IN THE WIND

168 In December 1942, the women of the 587th: Valentina Kravchenko-Savitskaya in Noggle, 101; Pennington 2001, 54–55.

168 Masha Dolina, who'd been flying: Vinogradova 2015, 235.

169 Then everybody got snowed in: Cottam 1998, 26; Galina Tenuyeva-Lomanova in Noggle, 152–53.

169 At last, on January 4, 1943: Cottam 1998, 26; Gibson, 123.

170 Galina, flying after Marina, could hardly see: Merry, 152; Galina Tenuyeva-Lomanova in Noggle, 153.

170 Before long, the three Pe-2 pilots were flying: Vinogradova 2015, 235.

170 "I think Raskova . . . aircraft in the clouds": Galina Tenuyeva-Lomanova in Noggle, 153.

170 Galina's navigator gave a yell: Merry, 152; Galina Tenuyeva-Lomanova in Noggle, 153.

170 Marina flew blindly into the side: Galina Tenuyeva-Lomanova in Noggle, 153; Pennington 2001, 93; Vinogradova 2015, 236.

171 "[Marina Raskova] did not use . . . wanted to get there": Galina Tenuyeva-Lomanova in Noggle, 153.

171 Zoya Pozhidayeva and other pilots: Zoya Pozhidayeva in Noggle, 216.

172 "In the morning, when the squadrons . . . I still can't believe it": Zhenya Rudneva in Cottam 1997, 223.

172 "That's not something you should joke about!": Masha Dolina, quoted in Vinogradova 2015, 235.

172 "Our commissar gathered us . . . We just cried": Valentina Kravchenko-Savitskaya, quoted in Pennington 2001, 94, from an interview by Reina Pennington on May 7, 1993; see also Pennington 2001, 247, note 23.

172 Marina Raskova was given the Soviet Union's: Gibson, 123; Vinogradova 2015, 238.

173 The news of Marina's death: *Pittsburgh Press*, January 9, 1943, 1.

173 "What will now happen to our regiment?": Yevgeniya Timofeyeva in Cottam 1997, 41.

173 The women were worried: Yevgeniya Timofeyeva in Cottam 1997, 41; Pennington 2001, 94.

173 "Yes, Sir! Am taking over the Regiment!": Yevgeniya Timofeyeva in Cottam 1997, 41.

174 The 587th now shared an airfield: ibid., 42.

174 The two regiments flew together: Pennington 2001, 95.

174 "When we took off . . . antiaircraft artillery shells": Yevgeniya Timofeyeva in Cottam 1997, 43.

174 The German troops had started firing: Yevgeniya Timofeyeva in Cottam 1997, 43; Pennington 2001, 95.

174 "Together we fought . . . fallen comrades": Yevgeniya Timofeyeva in Cottam 1997, 45.

174 On January 30, only three weeks after: Yevgeniya Timofeyeva in Cottam 1997, 45; Pennington 2001, 95.

175 The German commander surrendered: Hook, 108–9; Overy, 184; Vinogradova 2015, 241.

175 But Hitler wasn't anywhere near done: Overy, 198.

CHAPTER 23: VALENTIN MARKOV

176 The new quarters for the flight crews: Yekaterina Fedotova in Cottam 1997, 51.

176 "We liked her very much . . . going to replace her!": ibid., 51.

176 Zhenya Timofeyeva, who'd taken temporary: Yevgeniya Timofeyeva in Cottam 1997, 45; Pennington 2001, 95.

177 His name was Valentin Markov: Valentin Markov in Cottam 1997, 47; Merry, 106; Valentin Markov in Noggle, 102; Pennington 2001, 95–96; Vinogradova 2015, 242.

177 "We women wouldn't even hear . . . so strict and straight": Valentina Kravchenko-Savitskaya in Noggle, 102, 103.

177 When Valentin and his navigator: Valentin Markov in Cottam 1997, 47.

177 His new regiment stood lined up in the snow: Vinogradova 2015, 243.

177 "I am your new commander . . . because you are women": Valentin Markov in Cottam 1997, 47.

177 He didn't have a chance: Yekaterina Fedotova in Cottam 1997, 52; Pennington 2001, 96.

178 "At first, we gave him a hard time": Yekaterina Fedotova in Cottam 1997, 53.

178 "those on the ground would know . . . victory": Valentin Markov in Cottam 1997, 48; Merry, 107.

178 Valentin Markov gave the 587th firm guidance: Valentina Kravchenko-Savitskaya in Noggle, 106; Pennington 2001, 97.

179 "We survived the war . . . 'How are the girls?'": Antonina Khokhlova-Dubkova in Noggle, 115.

179 "Where is Melashvili? . . . Kirillova, Fedotova?": Yekaterina Fedotova in Cottam 1997, 53.

179 Valentin would make Valya look around: Valentina Kravchenko-Savitskaya in Noggle, 106.

179 "So it was because Markov . . . we made it back": Yekaterina Musatova-Fedotova in Noggle, 149.

CHAPTER 24: EXHAUSTION AND HONOR FOR THE NIGHT BOMBERS

180 Soldiers fighting at the front: Pennington 2001, 73.

181 "If a[n enemy antiaircraft] searchlight caught . . . blinded for a few moments": Polina Gelman in Noggle, 40.

181 "My pilot had a stupid navigator . . . kept falling asleep": Zhenya Rudneva diary entry for December 15, 1942, in Cottam 1997, 222.

181 Sometimes pilot and navigator both fell asleep: Irina Rakobolskaya in Cottam 1997, 156.

181 "We even had a kind of agreement . . . returning to the airfield": Larisa Rozanova-Litvinova in Noggle, 68.

182 "The pilots were so tired . . . hot tea to the aircraft": Irina Rakobolskaya quoted in Pennington 2001, 80, from an interview by Reina Pennington on May 10, 1993; see also 244, note 38. Irina Rakobolskaya also makes reference to "a glass of hot tea" between flights in Cottam 1997, 154.

182 All night long, the chief engineer, Klavdiya: Klavdiya Ilushina in Noggle, 50.

182 All night long, armorers loaded bombs: Olga Yerokhina-Averjanova in Noggle, 59.

182 Nina Karasyova was nineteen: Markwick & Cardona 2012, 98.

182 "We worked in mud, frost, sleet . . . under the aircraft": Nina Karasyova-Buzina in Noggle, 86.

182 When the nighttime bombing missions: Klavdiya Ilushina in Noggle, 50.

183 The mechanics and armorers felt a fierce: Irina Rakobolskaya in Cottam 1997, 152; Irina Rakobolskaya quoted in Pennington 2001, 80.

183 Instead of the usual Soviet routine: Irina Rakobolskaya in Cottam 1997, 153; Markwick & Cardona 2012, 97; Irina Rakobolskaya quoted in Pennington 2001, 80, 82.

183 Irina Rakobolskaya, the regiment's chief of staff, was so proud: Irina Rakobolskaya in Cottam 1997, 154; Pennington 2001, 83.

184 In February 1943, the 588th Night Bomber: Merry, 125; Pennington 2001, 83.

184 After they became the 46th Guards: Larisa Rozanova-Litvinova in Noggle, 70; Pennington 2001, 75.

185 It wasn't until February 1943 that Irina: Vinogradova 2015, 251–52.

185 "almost carrying them in our hands": Larisa Rozanova-Litvinova in Noggle, 67.

185 the young women got the eight Po-2s: Larisa Rozanova-Litvinova in Cottam 1997, 211; Larisa Rozanova-Litvinova in Noggle, 67.

186 "The moment we took off I was almost snoozing away": Larisa Rozanova-Litvinova in Noggle, 68.

186 It was cloudy as well as dark: Larisa Rozanova-Litvinova in Cottam 1997, 211.

186 "Vera, fighters are attacking us; do you see them? . . . Speed, speed, Lorka!": The dialogue as quoted between Vera Belik and Larisa Rozanova-Litvinova is part of Larisa Rozanova-Litvinova's story in Cottam 1997, 212.

186-187 "I glanced at the instruments . . . 'Adjust speed!'": Larisa Rozanova-Litvinova in Cottam 1997, 212.

187 "Larisa, wake up . . . searchights!": Vera Belik quoted by Larisa Rozanova-Litvinova in Noggle, 68.

187 At last, only 200 meters: Larisa Rozanova-Litvinova in Cottam 1997, 212.

187 "You shouldn't have flown tonight": Vera Belik as quoted by Larisa Rozanova-Litvinova in Cottam 1997, 213.

187 Vera flew the Po-2 back: Larisa Rozanova-Litvinova in Cottam 1997, 213.

187 "Between us we had to fly . . . or if I lived or died": Nina Raspopova in *Wasps and Witches*, 39:43 ff.

187 "afraid of having nightmares . . . searchlights": Irina Rakobolskaya in Cottam 1997, 156.

187-188 "When we returned . . . four years of the war": Mariya Smirnova in Noggle, 32.

CHAPTER 25: TWO AGAINST FORTY-TWO

189 In February 1943 they were assigned to defend: Pennington 2001, 105, 118.

189-190 Sofya Osipova was one of nine . . . "We found nothing all around but ruins": Sofya Osipova in Cottam 1997, 277.

190 "The first machine touched down . . . you had to meet the next plane": ibid., 277.

190 "General Mud and General Cold are helping the Russian side": Vasily Grossman in Grossman, 223.

190 As soon as one pilot returned: Nina Shebalina in Noggle, 203.

191 "One machine is airborne . . . always optimistic . . .": Sofya Osipova in Cottam 1997, 277.

191 Later that spring, the regiment was lucky: Pennington 2001, 130.

191 almost every single one of its aircraft: Glancey, December 15, 2001; Agniya Polyantseva in Cottam 1997, 263.

191 Pilots Tamara Pamyatnykh and Raisa: Tamara Pamyatnykh in Noggle, 160; Raisa Surnachevskaya in Noggle, 187.

192 The pilots already in the air: Agniya Polyantseva in Cottam 1997, 263; Nina Slovokhotova in Noggle, 179.

193 "I see the enemy aircraft!": Tamara Pamyatnykh quoted by Agniya Polyantseva in Cottam 1997, 263.

193 "There are quite a few of them!": Raisa Surnachevskaya quoted by Agniya

Polyantseva in Cottam 1997, 263.

193 "Attack!": Aleksandr Gridnev, quoted in Pennington 2001, 104.

193 Then the radio cut out: Agniya Polyantseva in Cottam 1997, 263.

194 They reached Kastornaya: Glancey, December 15, 2001.

194 surrounded by a mess of smoking bomb craters: Raisa Surnachevskaya in Noggle, 187.

194 But the only trace of an air battle: Agniya Polyantseva in Cottam 1997, 263.

194 When they'd taken off, Tamara and Raya: Raisa Surnachevskaya in Noggle, 187.

195 So the two young women in their Yak: Agniya Polyantseva in Cottam 1997, 264–65.

195 "By that time my guns were empty . . . I fell into a spin": Tamara Pamyatnykh in Noggle, 160.

195 With her plane plunging: ibid., 160–61.

196 "that we had both been given birth again": ibid., 161.

196 Raya explained that when: Glancey, December 15, 2001; Raisa Surnachevskaya in Noggle, 188–89.

196 Raya and Tamara's meeting: Agniya Polyantseva in Cottam 1997, 265; Glancey, December 15, 2001; Raisa Surnachevskaya in Noggle, 188, 189.

196 Raya's had forty-three bullet holes in it: Raisa Surnachevskaya in Noggle, 189.

196 Back in Voronezh at the 586th's base: Tamara Pamyatnykh in Noggle, 161; Nina Slovokhotova in Noggle, 179; Pennington 2001, 105.

197 two weeks later . . . "junior airwomen": *Wilmington Morning News*, April 5, 1943, 11.

197 The two valiant pilots: Tamara Pamyatnykh in Noggle, 161; Nina Slovokhotova in Noggle, 179; Pennington 2001, 105.

197 the bullet holes in Raya's Yak: Raisa Surnachevskaya in Noggle, 189.

Sidebar: Radio versus Radar

193 Soviet aircraft began to be fitted: Nina Slovokhotova in Noggle, 178.

CHAPTER 26: A NEW START FOR THE 587TH

198 From April until July 1943 they flew: Yekaterina Fedotova in Cottam 1997, 114; Pennington 2001, 99.

198 Few men were left: Grossman, 119–20.

198 Now Commander Valentin Markov: Valentin Markov in Noggle, 103, 104.

199 on May 4, 1943, they were awarded: Pennington 2001, 99.

199 The 587th was involved in six: ibid.

199 Masha Dolina was at the head: Mariya Dolina in Cottam 1997, 71.

199 "Why aren't you saying . . . turn off the radio": Mariya Dolina quoted by Galina Dzhunkovskaya in Cottam 1997, 119; the same story appears as quoted by Galina Dzhunkovskaya in Markova 1983, 65. Markova is Dzhunkovskaya's married name, under which she published her own books.

200 "a continuous curtain of fire": Mariya Dolina in Cottam 1997, 71.

200 The planes bounced and shuddered: ibid., 72.

200 But the clouds had now become so thick: Markova 1983, 79; Pennington 2001, 99.

201 Suddenly the antiaircraft guns stopped . . . "We were all as if in a 'fist'": The story and the quotation attributed to Klavdiya Fomicheva are as told by Galina Dzhunkovskaya in Markova, 1983, 77.

201 One of Masha's engines was hit: Mariya Dolina in Cottam 1997, 72; Mariya Dolina in Noggle, 121.

201 On the other side of the formation: Markova 1983, 80.

201 Now Tonya Skoblikova's Pe-2: Mariya Dolina in Cottam 1997, 72.

201 Behind their machine guns: Mariya Dolina in Noggle, 121.

202 As Masha's burning plane sank lower: Mariya Dolina in Cottam 1997, 72; Mariya Dolina in Noggle, 121.

202 "like a torch": Mariya Dolina in Cottam 1997, 72.

202 The moment Zhenya's formation: Markova 1983, 81.

202 Klava Fomicheva and her crew: Yekaterina Migunova in Cottam 1997, 60–61; Markova 1983, 81.

203 There was no way the squadron: Markova 1983, 81; Mariya Dolina in Noggle, 120.

203 Nobody felt like sleeping: Markova 1983, 82.

203 Then, just after daylight broke: Antonina Skoblikova in Cottam 1997, 67.

203 When they left the formation: Mariya Dolina in Cottam 1997, 72.

204 "Keep going, Commander . . . let's go together!": Ivan Solenov quoted by Mariya Dolina in Cottam 1997, 73.

204 Galya, standing behind Masha: Mariya Dolina in Cottam, 73; Mariya Dolina in Noggle, 121.

204 Ivan attacked the jammed canopy: Mariya Dolina in Cottam 1997, 73; Vinogradova 2015, 277.

204 "When he pulled us . . . fire out around us and on us": Mariya Dolina in Noggle, 121.

204 "a fountain of fire and smoke": Mariya Dolina in Cottam 1997, 73.

204 Masha and her crew were picked up: ibid.

204 Lelya Sholokhova and the rest: Yekaterina Migunova in Cottam 1997, 63.

204 All nine flight crews survived: Mariya Dolina in Cottam 1997, 71; Yekaterina Migunova in Cottam 1997, 64; Cottam 1998, 141; Mariya Dolina in Noggle, 120; Pennington 2001, 99.

205 And Ivan got a bonus: Mariya Dolina in Noggle, 121.

205 "quick and boisterous . . . grey, cunning eyes": Yekaterina Fedotova in Cottam 1997, 112.

205 "more thanks to the weather": Antonina Khokhlova-Dubkova in Noggle, 114.

206 "I was like a drunken person . . . quick and help us!": ibid., 114–15.

206 "What do you think . . . strawberries in green leaves!": ibid., 115.

CHAPTER 27: THE 46TH GUARDS IN TAMAN, 1943

207 In March, they moved their fleet: Kaleriya Rylskaya-Tsiss in Cottam 1997, 184.

207 Here, there was a strongly fortified line: Mariya Smirnova in Noggle, 33; Vinogradova 2015, 273.

207 The 46th Guards dropped bombs: Pennington 2001, 73.

207 Yevdokia "Dusya" Nosal was a calm: Nina Ulyanenko in Cottam 1997, 176–77; Cottam 1998, 73.

208 On the night of April 23, 1943, Dusya: Cottam 1998, 74.

208 "Dusya! Dusya! . . . pulling her up by her collar": Irina Kashirina quoted by Nina Ulyanenko in Cottam 1997, 177.

208 Irina made it back to the airfield: Nina Ulyanenko in Cottam 1997, 177; Zhenya Rudneva in Cottam 1997, 226; Polina Gelman in Noggle, 37; Pennington 2001, 84.

208 The 46th Guards had to organize: Nina Ulyanenko in Cottam 1997, 177–78.

209 Soon afterward, Dusya was posthumously: Nina Ulyanenko in Cottam 1997, 178; Polina Gelman in Noggle, 37; Pennington 2001, 84.

209 "To avenge Dusya": Milanetti, 79.

209 "I swear! While our eyes . . . annihilate the fascist invaders.": The "Guards' Oath" as quoted in Markwick & Cardona 2012, 99.

210 "Fight, girls, fighting friends . . . fire in your breast . . .": "Hymn of the Regiment" by Zhenya Rudneva, as quoted in Markwick & Cardona 2012, 99.

CHAPTER 28: THE HEAT OF BATTLE

211 It was hard to provide maintenance: Vinogradova 2015, 192.

211 Raisa and Mariya both did: Cottam 1998, 150–51; Pennington 2001, 109.

211 Because of yet another issue: Cottam 1998, 150; Pennington 2001, 134–35.

212 Lilya and Katya hadn't been: Pennington 2001, 137.

212 But the 73rd Guards is where they stayed: Merry, 168; Pennington 2001, 135, 136.

212 "we mechanics slept . . . ice on our hair and faces": Inna Pasportnikova in Noggle, 196.

212 Lilya soared from height to height: Cottam 1998, 152; Merry, 168; Von Hardesty & Grinberg, 149.

212 She performed forbidden aerial stunts: Inna Pasportnikova in Noggle, 198; Pennington 2001, 137.

212 She colored strips of parachute silk: Krylova 2010, 275; Inna Pasportnikova in Noggle, 196.

212 When men were assigned: Pennington 2001, 136.

212 On March 22, 1943, Lilya was involved: S. Gribanov in Cottam 1997, 303, 304; Pennington 2001, 137.

213 Lilya's heroic fight and her battle: Pennington 2001, 61; Vinogradova 2015, 257–58.

214 Lilya had to stay on the ground: S. Gribanov in Cottam 1997, 309; Pennington 2001, 137; Vinogradova 2015, 259.

214 Back in Voronezh, Aleksandr Gridnev: Pennington 2001, 119.

215 The Luftwaffe pilots figured out: Mariya Kuznetsova in Noggle, 168.

215 "She will be arrested . . . violation of flight regulations": Alexander Osipenko quoted by Aleksandr Gridnev in Pennington 2001, 120.

215 As punishment for that, she was grounded: Olga Yamshchikova in Cottam, 326; Pennington 2001, 120–21.

216 Two of the men Lilya Litvyak flew with: S. Gribanov in Cottam 1997, 308.

216 In a letter to her mother . . . her "best friend": Pennington 2001, 138–39.

216 In May, she made a triumphant flight: S. Gribanov in Cottam 1997, 310; Pennington 2001, 139–40.

217 Lilya's way of grieving seems: S. Gribanov in Cottam 1997, 311; Cottam 1998, 152; Pennington 2001, 140.

217 "I am completely absorbed . . . anything but the fighting": A letter from Lilya Litvyak to her mother quoted by Inna Vladimirovna Pasportnikova in

Pennington 2001, 141, from a typescript in Pennington's collection headed "Moi Komandir," 1989. See note 72 in Pennington 2001, 257.

217 "I long . . . for a happy . . . Your Lily": A letter from Lilya Litvyak to her mother quoted by S. Gribanov in Cottam 1997, 311.

217 On August 1, 1943, Lilya Litvyak flew: S. Gribanov in Cottam 1997, 311; Cottam 1998, 152; Pennington 2001, 141.

217 On her fourth flight of the day: Inna Pasportnikova in Noggle, 198.

218 The fighter planes started firing: S. Gribanov in Cottam 1997, 311.

218 Lilya's Yak was hit by enemy fire: Merry, 169; Inna Pasportnikova in Noggle, 196, 198.

218 "shining image . . . struggle and victory!": Leaflet produced by the Political Administration of the Southern Front, quoted in Cottam 1998, 153.

218 Double ace Lilya Litvyak: Cottam 1998, 152; Pennington 2001, 142.

218 But Lilya and her aircraft had vanished: Inna Pasportnikova in Noggle, 199; Pennington 2001, 141.

218 On September 16, 1943, a document: Cottam 1998, 153.

CHAPTER 29: "OUR PLANES WERE BURNING LIKE CANDLES"

221 By the summer of 1943: Hook, 117, 123–24.

223 One by one, each aircrew dropped their bombs: Mariya Smirnova in Noggle, 31.

224 On the night of July 31, 1943, the fifteen: Larisa Rozanova-Litvinova in Cottam 1997, 213, 214; Vinogradova 2015, 300.

224 Squadron commander Mariya: Mariya Smirnova in Noggle, 34.

224 Zhenya Krutova flew with her navigator: Larisa Rozanova-Litvinova in Cottam 1997, 213.

224 Behind Anya and Galya: Mariya Smirnova in Noggle, 34; Vinogradova 2015, 300.

224 As a pilot, Anya was one of several: Larisa Rozanova-Litvinova in Cottam 1997, 213.

224 a new navigator who'd started the war: Larisa Rozanova-Litvinova in Noggle, 65.

224 Behind Larisa and Nadya came: Larisa Rozanova-Litvinova in Cottam 1997, 215.

224 As usual, the target was only: Larisa Rozanova-Litvinova in Noggle, 65.

224 Then, unexpectedly, the antiaircraft guns: Serafima Amosova-Taranenko in Noggle, 46.

224 Mariya Smirnova, the squadron commander: Mariya Smirnova in Cottam 1997, 33.

225 Sure enough, from the dark sky came: Vinogradova 2015, 301.

225 "We had not been attacked . . . fighter planes": Mariya Smirnova in Noggle, 33.

225 Mariya was a hardened combat pilot: ibid.

225 Behind her, flying far back: Zhenya Rudneva in Cottam 1997, 229; Larisa Rozanova-Litvinova in Noggle, 65.

225 Larisa and Nadya were over the Kuban: Larisa Rozanova-Litvinova in Cottam 1997, 213.

225 Then Larisa saw a white spot caught: Larisa Rozanova-Litvinova in Noggle, 65.

225 Natasha and Lida also saw: Vinogradova 2015, 301.

225 The white spot suddenly became: Larisa Rozanova-Litvinova; in Cottam 1997, 213; Larisa Rozanova-Litvinova in Noggle, 65.

225 Zhenya Krutova and Lena Salikova were in: Larisa Rozanova-Litvinova in Cottam, 213.

226 "My arms and legs shook . . . before my eyes": Zhenya Rudneva in Cottam 1997, 229.

226 "A bitter tickling . . . made of cotton-wool": Larisa Rozanova-Litvinova in Noggle, 65.

226 "A fighter firing!": Larisa Rozanova-Litvinova in Cottam 1997, 213.

226 "I was so frightened . . . target in two minutes": Larisa Rozanova-Litvinova in Noggle, 66.

226 "If only we had a machine gun . . . load my pistol?": Nadezhda Studilina quoted by Larisa Rozanova-Litvinova in Cottam 1997, 214.

226 "Load it. But you're not likely to use it": Larisa Rozanova-Litvinova in Cottam 1997, 214.

226 The German guns on the ground: Zhenya Rudneva in Cottam 1997, 229.

227 When the third plane began to blaze: Larisa Rozanova-Litvinova in Cottam 1997, 214.

227 "We realized that our friends were dying": Larisa Rozanova-Litvinova in Noggle, 66.

227 "I thought we would split into pieces": ibid.

227 "They caught another air crew!": Nadezhda Studilina quoted by Larisa Rozanova-Litvinova in Cottam 1997, 214.

227 Larisa glanced back over her shoulder: Larisa Rozanova-Litvinova in Cottam

1997, 215; Larisa Rozanova-Litvinova in Noggle, 66.

227 "Our planes were burning like candles": Serafima Amosova-Taranenko in Noggle, 46.

227 "The tracer bullets . . . scattered in the air": Mariya Smirnova in Noggle, 34.

228 "The entire lower and upper . . . by the shot-holes": Larisa Rozanova-Litvinova in Cottam 1997, 215.

228 But Larisa had managed to avoid: ibid.

228 Four pilots and four navigators of the 46th Guards: Milanetti, 86, 89; Vinogradova 2015, 302.

228 The events of July 31, 1943, were: Larisa Rozanova-Litvinova in Noggle, 67; Pennington 2001, 85.

228 Zhenya Rudneva was utterly heartbroken: Vinogradova 2015, 301.

228 "I kept running up . . . emptiness in my heart!": Zhenya Rudneva in Cottam 1997, 229.

228 "It was impossible not to cry": Serafima Amosova-Taranenko in Noggle, 46.

229 Even so, the next night: Mariya Smirnova in Noggle, 34.

229 Soviet fighter pilots cleared the sky: Larisa Rozanova-Litvinova in Noggle, 67; Pennington 2001, 85.

229 The Luftwaffe night fighter pilot: Milanetti, 89.

229 "Now that Galya is no more . . . I simply can't part": Zhenya Rudneva in Cottam 1997, 230–31.

229 *I'll rest and get better after the war*: Galina Dokutovich diary entry of December 20, 1942, quoted by Polina Gelman in Cottam 1997, 164.

229 "If no enemy bullet kills me . . . wonderful like our Galya": Polina Gelman quoted in Vinogradova 2015, 303. The quotation is from a letter written by Polina Gelman and published as part of *The Heart and the Wings* by Galina Dokutovich, translated from the Belorussian by Veronika Gorbyleva and Olga Vashkova; see Vinogradova 2015, 330, note 497, and 331 under "Dokutovich."

Sidebar: Night Bombing without Parachutes

222 "a single incendiary bullet could turn it into a flaming torch": Irina Rakobolskaya in Cottam 1997, 151.

222 Ordinary people called the Po-2 a "kerosinka": Beevor & Vinogradova in Grossman 2006, 133.

222 For most of the war: Pennington 2001, 75.

223 "Our pilots thought the plane . . . captured by the Germans": Irina
Rakobolskaya in Noggle, 27.

223 In the summer of 1944, at last: Noggle, 19.

223 But the change saved only one: Pennington 2001, 87.

CHAPTER 30: NIGHT WITCHES

230 One of her original ideas: Pennington 2001, 75.

230 "Let's fly in two-plane elements . . . antiaircraft weapons": Yevdokia
Bershanskaya quoted by Marina Chechneva in Cottam 1997, 167.

230-231 "We flew two planes . . . make a successful attack": Polina Gelman in
Noggle, 40.

231 In the dark, without lights: Irina Rakobolskaya in Noggle, 30.

231 Nadya Popova and her navigator, Katya: Marina Chechneva in Cottam 1997, 167.

231 "In a few seconds, we found . . . operators as long as possible": ibid.,
167–68.

231 As Marina threw her little Po-2: ibid., 168.

232 Later that month, chief of staff Irina: Markwick & Cardona 2012, 97.

232 Maybe it was because of their screams: This was suggested to me in a personal
discussion with Vladimir Ivanovich, a retired Soviet Air Force officer serving as
a docent at the Central Air Force Museum in Monino, Moscow Oblast, Russia,
on November 15, 2016.

233 "Nobody knows the exact day . . . shoot us down": Serafima Amosova-
Taranenko in Noggle, 46.

233 "Attention, attention . . . stay at your shelter": Anonymous German prisoner
quoted by Serafima Amosova-Taranenko in Noggle, 46.

233 "sometimes, when our planes . . . could hear them": Nina Yegorova-Arefjeva in
Noggle, 64.

233 Soviet soldiers were more sympathetic: Irina Rakobolskaya in Cottam 1997, 152.

233 When male pilots flew over their air base: Raisa Zhitova-Yushina in Noggle, 90.

233 "When I was flying very low . . . light their torches": Raisa Zhitova-Yushina in
Noggle, 90.

234 "Before each mission . . . fear of being killed": Mariya Smirnova in Noggle, 32.

234 "After bombing . . . glass of clear river water": Nina Raspopova in Noggle, 26.

235 "When you leave behind . . . you recover": Larisa Rozanova-Litvinova in Noggle,
68.

235 When Alexandra was given a cardiogram: Alexandra Semyonovna Popova in Alexievich 2017, 194.

235 Irina Rakobolskaya, the 46th's chief of staff: Irina Rakobolskaya in Cottam 1997, 156.

235 "Either you have no time . . . lives of your friends": Antonina Khokhlova-Dubkova in Noggle, 116.

Sidebar: Equality in the Air

236 On August 5, 1943, the Women's Flying: Strebe 2009, 8.

236 The WASP wasn't a military organization: Merry, 65.

236 They were paid less than men: Strebe 2009, 53.

236 But at last American women: ibid., 8–9.

236 WASP pilots had to cope with: Merry, 70; Strebe 2009, 38–39.

237 There was even nasty and deliberate: Merry 99, 102.

237 A 1944 Hollywood movie: Strebe 2009, 43.

237 "I was never so embarrassed in my life": Caro Bayley Bosca quoted in Strebe 2009, 43.

237 But perhaps best of all was that, in June 1943: Curtis, 200; Merry, 48, 99.

CHAPTER 31: LOSS AND HONOR FOR THE DIVE-BOMBERS

238 in the summer of 1943 their crews: Pennington 2001, 99.

238 Early in July, the German army: Beevor & Vinogradova in Grossman 2006, xvi; Hook, 123.

238 The tanks were defended: Vinogradova 2015, 284; Wetterhahn, 56–61.

238 By the end of August, the Red Army: Hook, 122.

239 One hot, hazy, dusty day: Valentina Kravchenko in Cottam 1997, 80.

239 That's what happened to pilot Sasha: Valentina Kravchenko in Cottam 1997, 83; Nina Karaseva in Cottam 1997, 86–87.

240 "For the third time . . . starboard wing were burning": Nina Karaseva in Cottam 1997, 88.

240 Sasha ordered Nina and Aleksandr: Valentina Kravchenko in Cottam 1997, 84; Nina Karaseva in Cottam 1997, 88.

240 Sasha, the pilot, hit the ground hard: Valentina Kravchenko in Cottam 1997, 83–85.

241 Behind enemy lines, Sasha's navigator Nina: Nina Karaseva in Cottam 1997, 88.

241 "Their eyes were wild-looking and their faces distorted": ibid.

241 "Don't touch!": ibid.

241 It all happened so quickly: ibid.

241 Nina and Aleksandr had been taken: Valentina Kravchenko in Cottam 1997, 85.

241 "Don't mention it to anyone. We don't shoot at women": Artur Gartner quoting his commanding officer in *Wasps and Witches*, 38:00 ff.

242 Nina had to endure something far: Nina Karaseva in Cottam 1997, 89–91.

242 It would be years before the pilot: Valentina Kravchenko in Cottam 1997, 85.

242 Yet another Pe-2 crew came to grief: Galina Dzhunkovskaya in Cottam 1997, 120–23; Cottam 1998, 142; Markova 1983, 71, 72; Pennington 2001, 100.

243 Antonina Bondareva—the pilot: Antonina Grigoryevna Bondareva in Alexievich 2017, 28; Antonina Bondareva-Spitsina in Noggle, 106–7 (the same woman, interviewed and quoted by different people under both her maiden name and her married name).

243 "Don't come back, you may not come back, I won't let you in!": Antonina Bondareva-Spitsina quoting her father, Grigoriy Bondarev, in Noggle, 107.

243 But her mother let her go: Antonina Bondareva-Spitsina in Noggle, 107.

243 Also—she had a toddler: Antonina Grigoryevna Bondareva in Alexievich 2017, 29.

243 By 1943 her husband had been killed: Antonina Grigoryevna Bondareva in Alexievich 2017, 29; Antonina Bondareva-Spitsina in Noggle, 107.

244 Yekaterina Chujkova joined the 587th: Yekaterina Chujkova in Noggle, 142.

244 In January 1943, Soviet soldiers: Hook, 108.

244 Yekaterina's sister worked at a factory: Yekaterina Chujkova in Noggle, 142–43.

244 Each aircrew usually flew three: Yevgeniya Zapolnova in Cottam 1997, 110.

244 "I'm sorry, but I'm going to shoot; excuse me, I'm going to shoot!": Yekaterina Chujkova in Noggle, 143.

245 One night, a figure appeared: ibid.

245 They were rewarded for it: Merry, 110, 152–53; Pennington 2001, 90, 100.

246 "When we are awarded orders . . . instead of the crystal": Yekaterina Chujkova in Noggle, 142.

246 September 1943 also marked a significant: Hook, 127.

246 But the nations of Europe: ibid., 123–24.

246 It was a slow but steady process: Pennington 2001, 73.

246 On October 14 they lost three: Valentina Kravchenko in Cottam 1997, 79; Pennington 2001, 100.

247 "little yellow flames, in the rays of the setting sun": Valentina Kravchenko in Cottam 1997, 79.

247 O black raven!: Quoted by Valentina Kravchenko in Cottam 1997, 79. It is a traditional Russian folk song. The English translation is my own, based on several English versions.

CHAPTER 32: OVER THE BLACK SEA

248 They were now named the 46th Taman Guards: Pennington 2001, 85.

248 That same month, Marina Chechneva: Marina Chechneva in Cottam 1997, 169.

248 "Take the 'crown,' . . . before the war ends": Mariya Smirnova quoted by Marina Chechneva in Cottam 1997, 171.

249 The German army's blockade of the city: See Anderson, 2015, for a detailed account of the Leningrad blockade.

249 Some Soviet citizens, thinking positively: Beevor & Vinogradova in Grossman 2006, 266.

249 On March 8, 1944, International Women's Day: Pennington 2001, 74.

250 "We don't need any helpers, we're managing just fine on our own!": quoted in Pennington 2001, 74, from "Bomber at Night" by N. Chaika, Vol. 2, 152–53; see Pennington, 2001, 242, note 10, and 276.

250 "But . . . much better in the women's regiment": Olga Yerokhina-Averjanova in Noggle, 58.

250 They moved to a base in a resort area: Kaleriya Rylskaya-Tsiss in Cottam 1997, 184; Nadezhda Popova in Noggle, 82; Overy, 236; Pennington 2001, 73, 86.

250 Once, when the 46th Guards arrived: Mariya Smirnova in Noggle, 34.

251 "You must get up . . . your aircraft are burning!": Anonymous hostess quoted by Klavdiya Ilushina in Noggle, 51.

251 Klavdiya and her companions: Klavdiya Ilushina in Noggle, 51.

252 "A broads' regiment . . . Well, well": Black Sea Fleet pilots quoted by Serafima Amosova-Taranenko in Cottam 1997, 180.

252 "There were snow-white sheets . . . containers on tables": Serafima Amosova-Taranenko in Cottam 1997, 180.

252 The young women wondered: ibid.

252 Despite their lukewarm first impression: ibid., 182.

252 One of the jobs that the 46th Guards had: Marina Chechneva in Cottam 1997, 171.

253 "Take your 'presents,' brothers! . . . Women's Air Regiment!": Marina

Chechneva, quoting conversation with her navigator in Cottam 1997, 172.

253 "The whistling of the wind . . . hear the voices": Marina Chechneva in Cottam 1997, 172.

253 On April 9, 1944, Chief Navigator: Nadezhda Popova in Noggle, 84.

253 Pilot Kaleriya Rylskaya and navigator: Kaleriya Rylskaya-Tsiss in Cottam 1997, 184, 185.

253 They had trouble taking aim: Cottam 1998, 97.

254 "Who came back?": Ground crew quoted by Kaleriya Rylskaya-Tsiss in Cottam, 185.

254 *This is silly . . . best time of my life*: Zhenya Rudneva, diary entry for December 2, 1942, quoted in Cottam 1997, 220.

254 "I saw their aircraft . . . hold it in their lights": Nadezhda Popova in Noggle, 84.

254 Zhenya and Polina were both killed: Kaleriya Rylskaya-Tsiss in Cottam 1997, 185; Krylova 2010, 37, 286.

254 It had been Zhenya's 645th combat mission: Nadezhda Popova in Noggle, 84.

254 "Grief paralyzed me . . . regiment on the ground": Irina Rakobolskaya in Noggle, 30.

255 Zhenya Rudneva, astronomy student: Nadezhda Popova in Noggle, 84.

255 Larisa Rozanova took her place: Cottam 1998, 63.

255 "Below, quite near, the white crests . . . sprinkled with many stars": Serafima Amosova-Taranenko in Cottam 1997, 181.

CHAPTER 33: CROSSING THE LINE

256 In the personal histories: See Alexievich 2017 for the many different experiences of women who served in the Soviet military in roles other than aviation.

256 There certainly were problems: Markwick & Cardona 2012, 139, 140.

256–257 Olga Lisikova, who flew . . . early the next morning: The story and quotations are those of Olga Lisikova as told in Noggle, 242.

257 Yelena Karakorskaya . . . "the girls hung on his arm and prevented it": This story and the quotations are as told by Yelena Karakorskaya in Noggle, 214.

257 Instead of being shot: ibid., 215.

258 "Why aren't the pilots in their cockpits by now?": Yekaterina Fedotova quoting a visiting dignitary in Cottam 1997, 113.

258 Katya had to unfasten her straps: Yekaterina Fedotova in Cottam 1997, 114.

258 Tail gunner Tonya Khokhlova . . . "last drop of our blood. Thank you!": This story, and the quoted message, are told by Antonina Khokhlova-Dubkova in Noggle, 113.

258 returning the joke by dropping homemade wooden dolls: Markova 1983, 125.

CHAPTER 34: ALLIED FORCES

260 The 586th spent the fall of 1943 defending Kursk: Valentina Petrochenkova-Neminushaya in Noggle, 177; Pennington 2001, 122–23.

261 On June 5, 1944, 586th pilot Klavdiya: Klavdiya Pankratova in Cottam 1997, 283.

261 "We flew home wing tip . . . received a fatal wound": ibid., 284.

261 The "second front" had been a dream: Overy, 240.

261–262 The 46th Guards Night Bomber Aviation Regiment was part of the storm: ibid., 241.

262–263 Late in 1943, an unusual section of the French Air Force: Galina Brok-Beltsova in Cottam 1997, 131; Galina Turabelidze in Cottam, 143.

264 "Delighted, we watched . . . in very poor visibility": Léon Cuffaut, quoted by Galina Turabelidze in Cottam 1997, 143.

264 He and the other French pilots: Galina Turabelidze in Cottam 1997, 143–44.

264 "When there were friends . . . seemed less terrible": Galina Brok-Beltsova in Cottam 1997, 131.

264 Yevdokia Bershanskaya, the commander of the 46th: Krylova 2010, 287.

264 Tamara Pamyatnykh, the 586th Regiment's squadron: Tamara Pamyatnykh in Noggle, 162.

265 Several women of the 125th Guards ended up married: Mariya Dolina in Noggle, 122; Pennington 2001, 98.

265 Tonya Khokhlova, the tail gunner: Noggle, 118.

265 After the war, Valentin Markov himself married: Cottam 1998, 135.

265 "they didn't act in any way . . . carried Galya out of the plane": Antonina Lepilina in Noggle, 129.

265 There was, however, a bit of a double standard: Markwick & Cardona 2012, 103–4.

265 "She bombed the Germans while pregnant. What a hero!": K. A. Vershinin, quoted in Markwick & Cardona 2012, 104.

265 It wasn't a joke for the 46th Guards, though: Markwick & Cardona 2012, 103.

266 Brotherhood and sisterhood in wartime: ibid., 104.

Sidebar: *Taran*: Aerial ramming

262 The celebrated Russian aviator: Legge, April 12, 2016; Reichhardt, October 4, 2014; Von Hardesty & Grinberg, 31.

262 As you can imagine, this desperate measure: Vinogradova 2015, 123; Von Hardesty & Grinberg, 31.

263 Only one woman, the Soviet pilot: Cottam 1998, 33; Merry, 111.

CHAPTER 35: THE EDGE OF THE CLOUDS

267 In the spring of 1944, as poor weather: Markova 1983, 65–67.

268 "I don't like doing two things at the same time": Klavdiya Fomicheva as quoted by Galina Dzhunkovskaya in Markova 1983, 75.

268 And she noticed that Klava still carried: Markova 1983, 89.

268 On June 23, 1944, the 125th's commander: Yekaterina Fedotova in Cottam 1997, 53.

269 Only minutes before, Galya had been checking: Markova 1983, 97.

269 "Was he killed? . . . Was he really killed?": Galina Dzhunkovskaya in Markova 1983, 98.

269 soon the entire left wing was blazing: Mariya Dolina in Cottam 1997, 69; Markova 1983, 98.

269 "They were mentally saying goodbye to us": Galina Dzhunkovskaya in Markova 1983, 98.

269 But Klava and Galya didn't yet dare: Markova, 1983, 99.

270 "flew off instantly, like a piece of paper": Galina Dzhunkovskaya in Markova 1983, 99.

270 But when Klava tried to tip: Mariya Dolina in Cottam 1997, 70; Markova 1983, 99.

270 They fought and struggled to get free: Markova 1983, 99–100.

270 Klava's boots were dragged off: Mariya Dolina in Cottam 1997, 70; Markova 1983, 100.

270 Valentin Markov lifted Galya: Antonina Lepilina in Noggle, 129.

270 About a month later, the members of the 125th were honored: L. Yerusalimchik in Cottam 1997, 74; Mariya Dolina in Noggle, 123.

270 "flourish, continue peacetime jobs . . . our job at the front": Mariya Dolina in Noggle, 123.

271 "Around this time, all kinds . . . charged with explosives": Vera Tikhomirova in Cottam 1997, 353.

271 A group of young women: ibid.

271 Belorussia was still crawling with Nazi forces: Overy, 236.

271 That summer the young women of the 46th Taman Guards: Pennington 2001, 73, 86.

271 Decomposing bodies hung from lampposts: Saywell, 153.

271 Among the dead was the little boy: Markwick & Cardona 2012, 115; Litvinova 1977, 248–49.

272 The woodland of Belorussia: Antonina Vakhromeyeva in Cottam 1997, 190.

272 "led a 'gypsy' life . . . bedroom, and dining room": Kaleriya Rylskaya-Tsiss in Cottam, 186.

272 "Then she would bustle . . . disturb the sleeping crew": ibid.

273 "Please take revenge . . . nothing is left": Nadezhda Popova quoting anonymous woman, in Saywell, 154.

273 "For the next few weeks . . . faces of those children": Nadezhda Popova quoted in Saywell, 154.

273 For the rest of her life, pilot Yevgeniya: Yevgeniya Zhigulenko in Noggle, 57–58.

273 "a symbol of the great Russian tragedy . . . orphaned children": ibid., 58.

273 In August 1944 the 46th Guards moved: Pennington 2001, 73.

273 where they would eventually take part in the battle: Markwick & Cardona 2012, 116.

273 They spent the last part of that summer: Natalya Meklin-Kravtsova in Cottam 1997, 203.

273 While they were based here, Tanya: Natalya Meklin-Kravtsova in Cottam 1997, 203–4; Pennington 2001, 87.

276 On one of these missions Kaleriya: Kaleriya Rylskaya-Tsiss in Cottam 1997, 187.

277 Latvian port of Riga on the Baltic Sea: ibid., 186.

277 Klava Fomicheva and her navigator: Galina Dzhunkovskaya in Cottam 1997, 124.

277 "Now we can relax": ibid.

277 There, the sky was so dark with smoke: ibid., 124–25.

278 "I looked behind . . . their mission so well": ibid., 125.

278 "that the fighter attack . . . had never happened": Galina Dzhunkovskaya in Markova 1983, 108.

278 The 125th Guards paused in their bombing missions: Markova 1983, 109.

279 "Smiling shyly and snapping . . . laughing and exuded joy": Galina Dzhunkovskaya in Cottam 1997, 127.

Sidebar: "Russia Has Noted Women War Flyers"—and America Admires Them

274 When Marina Raskova began teaching: *Arizona Republic*, June 11, 1936, 18.

274 "buxom Amazon of the civil air force . . . the teen-age girl": *Chillicothe Constitution-Tribune*, January 20, 1939, 4.

274 The *New York Times* ran a story: *New York Times*, March 22, 1942, 11; February 14, 1943, 18.

274 American radio fans could hear: *Asbury Park Press*, February 3, 1943, 14.

274 Tamara Pamyatnykh and Raisa Surnachevskaya: *Wilmington Morning News*, April 5, 1943, 11.

274 In June 1943, an American ship: *Troy Record*, June 27, 1943, 13; *Amarillo Globe*, September 3, 1943, 9.

275 In December 1943, an Associated Press: *Gettysburg Times*, December 27, 1943, 6.

275 In an article called . . . "fight against race discrimination": Maurer, 109.

275 Quentin Reynolds, an American journalist: Reynolds, 119–32.

275 And in July 1944, *Aviation* magazine . . . "she is now a fighter pilot": Blitzstein, 117.

CHAPTER 36: FROM THE VOLGA TO BERLIN

280 It should be no surprise that now Josef Stalin: Overy, 255–57.

280 would finish the war in Lithuania: Pennington 2001, 92.

280 would end up in Budapest, Hungary: Yekaterina Polunina in Noggle, 164; Pennington 2001, 104–6.

280 The night bombers of the 46th Guards would fly: Pennington 2001, 72.

281 586th Regiment didn't see much enemy: ibid., 123.

281 They were stationed first in Romania: Cottam 1997, 252; Pennington 2001, 104, 105, 123.

281 Masha Batrokova, who'd already: Valentina Gvozdikova in Cottam 1997, 340.

281 Galina Burdina learned how close: Galina Burdina in Noggle, 208.

281 "So he gave me back my life": ibid.

281 now considered one of the best aircrews: Yekaterina Fedotova in Cottam 1997, 116.

281 The 125th Guards operated in the German region of Prussia: Cottam 1997, 30; Pennington 2001, 102.

282 Katya, Klara and Tonya were shot down: Antonina Khokhlova-Dubkova in Noggle, 115.

282 "Because there was no one . . . and buried them": ibid., 116.

282 For example, someone in a position: Galina Brok-Beltsova in Noggle, 133–34.

283 "We were next in line . . . a successful mission": ibid., 134.

283 "We felt it dragging us back to earth": ibid.

283 "It was a victory . . . over ourselves": ibid.

283 In February 1945, when they were in western: Pennington 2001, 73.

283 "I made the flight . . . It was snowing very hard": Zoya Parfyonova in Noggle, 71.

284 "German infantrymen began . . . wounded in the leg": ibid.

284 In a shaking, damaged aircraft: ibid., 72.

284 By March, the fields were so muddy: Alexandra Akimova in Noggle, 93.

284 "pilots' rations of vodka, biscuits, and milk": ibid.

284 As the hard frosts grew less reliable: Antonina Vakhromeyeva in Cottam 1997, 190; Irina Rakobolskaya in Noggle, 28.

284 Finally, the ground crew would lift: Antonina Vakhromeyeva in Cottam 1997, 190.

285 "Our regiment made 300 combat . . . those conditions": Irina Rakobolskaya in Noggle, 28.

285 When she'd been captured: Nina Karaseva in Cottam 1997, 89–90.

285 Nina saw firsthand the undiluted horror: ibid., 91.

285 Every last Soviet citizen liberated: Overy, 261.

285 That's exactly what happened to Tamara: Tamara Pamyatnykh in Noggle, 162.

286 The 46th Guards made their way steadily: Pennington 2001, 73.

286 stationed north of Berlin: Irina Rakobolskaya in Noggle, 28; Pennington 2001, 88.

286 "But why did . . . What did they want?": Vasily Grossman in Grossman, 342.

286 How could the people who owned: Grossman, 341; Irina Rakobolskaya, quoted in Markwick & Cardona 2012, 116.

286 "Everybody knew that the end . . . no one wanted to die": Polina Gelman in Noggle, 42.

286 But the commanders were eager: ibid.

287 "It could be on . . . anyone": ibid.

287 "Everything was ready . . . I burst out crying": ibid.

288 everyone was in bed and no one: Yekaterina Fedotova in Cottam 1997, 116.

288 "The war has ended!": Masha Kirillova quoted by Yekaterina Fedotova in Cottam 1997, 116.

288 "We just couldn't believe it . . . we cried": Galina Brok-Beltsova in Cottam 1997, 131.

288 But hugging and kissing weren't enough: Yekaterina Fedotova in Cottam 1997, 116.

288 The 586th Regiment lined up: Vera Tikhomirova in Cottam 1997, 354.

288 "To the Homeland . . . bravely and fell . . .": Regimental victory song of the 586th Regiment as quoted by Nina Potapova in Cottam, 348.

289 "I wanted to cry . . . 'Yes, I'll marry you'": Anonymous pilot quoted in Alexievich 2017, xvii.

CHAPTER 37: ONE THOUSAND NIGHTS IN COMBAT

293 "After the war we had . . . one thousand nights in combat": Serafima Amosova-Taranenko in Noggle, 47.

293 Mariya Smirnova, who flew 935: Mariya Smirnova in Noggle, 31.

293 In their three years on the front: Pennington 2001, 73.

293 In the winter's long darknesses: Olga Yerokhina-Averjanova in Noggle, 60.

293 Twenty-four of these women were given: Cottam 1997, 148; Merry, 107; Markwick & Cardona 2012, 97; Noggle, 20; Pennington 2001, 72, 265.

294 Quality, not quantity, shines in the 1,134: Cottam 1997, 29–30; Pennington 2001, 90.

294 Five women in the regiment were awarded: Noggle, 100; Pennington 2001, 90.

294 They made over nine thousand solo flights: Merry, 105; Noggle, 159; Yekaterina Polunina in Noggle, 164; Pennington 2001, 104, 125.

294 A frustrating epilogue to their story: Merry, 106; Pennington 2001, 122, 124.

295 Twenty-five years after Lilya Litvyak: Cottam 1998, 153.

295 A stone monument in her memory: Inna Pasportnikova in Noggle, 194.

295 Inna Pasportnikova, who'd been: Vinogradova 2015, 313.

296 "We found thirty aircraft but not hers": Inna Pasportnikova in Noggle, 199.

296 In 1979, Inna discovered: Cottam 1998, 154; Pennington 2001, 141.

296 On May 5, 1990, nearly fifty: Cottam 1998, 154; Inna Pasportnikova in Noggle, 200; Pennington 2001, 141.

296 Cautious estimates begin: Overy, xvi.

296 how many Soviet airwomen: Merry, 112.

297 Yevgeniya Zhigulenko, a 46th Guards pilot, said: ibid.

297 Reina Pennington, counting staff: Pennington 2001, 177–92; see also Merry, 112, and Noggle, 159.

CHAPTER 38: "DO NOT TALK ABOUT THE SERVICES YOU HAVE RENDERED"

298 "Women in the USSR . . . social and political life": Article 122 of the 1936 Constitution of the USSR.

298 "absolute equal opportunity with men": Klavdiya Ilushina in Noggle, 49.

298 "were frustrated . . . levels of the military": Harris 2008, 223.

298 Posters printed in the 1930s: ibid., 29.

299 "In this unusual war . . . with arms in hand": M. I. Kalinin, 455.

299 Kalinin pointed out right away: ibid., 459.

299 which it did: Markwick & Cardona 2012, 235.

299 "Do not give yourself . . . That will be better": M. I. Kalinin, 459–60.

299 they had to sign a pledge: Markwick & Cardona 2012, 233.

300 His opinion was that women were: Cottam 1998, xxi; *Wasps and Witches*, 48:28 ff.

300 The Red Army closed down: Merry, 122.

300 Many women who had flown: Mariya Smirnova in Noggle, 37.

300 "Life is life . . . especially for a woman": Ludmila Popova in Noggle, 147.

301 "You can't have . . . no woman's soul": Antonina Grigoryevna Bondareva quoting her (unnamed) sister-in-law in Alexievich 2017, 288.

301 "Many of us left . . . We stayed women": Antonina Grigoryevna Bondareva in Alexievich 2017, 289.

301 "The very nature . . . to help our people": Alexandra Akimova in Noggle, 94.

301 "I myself could not . . . all the women too": Alexandra Makunina in Noggle, 166.

301 Masha Dolina, the 125th Guards: L. Yerusalimchik in Cottam 1997, 74–75.

301 "I want you to underline . . . to fight—to kill": Mariya Dolina in Noggle, 119.

301 She kept the promise she'd made: Vinogradova 2015, 303.

302 female veterans of World War II began: Markwick & Cardona, 233.

302 over thirty more memoirs: Harris 2008, 217.

303 But the young women who played the roles: Yevgeniya Zhigulenko, in Dlugach, 15.

303 By 1941, nearly one-third of all: Gibson, 119; Merry, 105; Christine A. White in Noggle, 6–7, 14; Pennington 2001, 10; Strebe 2009, 22.

303 "physiologically unsuitable . . . civilian pilots": Cottam 1998, xxi.

303 Today, about 12 percent: Federal Aviation Administration, U.S. Civil Airmen Statistics 2015, Tables 1 & 2; Goyer 2010; Carsenat & Rossini, 2014.

303 American government decided: Merry, 115; Strebe 2009, 64.

303 Because they'd never been connected: Merry, 134.

303 The British ATA continued ferrying aircraft: Curtis, 284; Merry, 123.

304 British flying jobs went: Jackie Moggridge in *Wasps and Witches*, 47:50 ff.

304 Mariya Akilina, from the 46th: Mariya Akilina in Noggle, 98.

304 Alexandra Krivonogova, from the 125th: A. M. Bereznitskaya in Cottam 1997, 103–4.

304 Several pilots from the 586th also: Pennington 2001, 150.

304 Galina Burdina flew as a civilian: Glancey, December 15, 2001.

304 Tamara Pamyatnykh became an air: Agniya Polyantseva in Cottam 1997, 265.

304 The 125th Guards weren't officially: Pennington 2001, 103.

305 "I often have dreams . . . my favorite dream": Antonina Bondareva-Spitsina in Noggle, 109.

305 In Russia in 1998: Cottam 1998, 24; Merry, 130.

305 It took Svetlana Protasova: Babichev, 1997; Strebe 2009, 80–81; Warren, July 8, 1999.

305 by 2004 she was struggling: Chechneva, 2016.

305 Few Russian women who became: Marina Bouraia, quoted in Brock, 2016.

305 "Among pilots, there are . . . with the industry": Anastasia Dagaeva, in BBC News Europe, "The Ballerina Who Takes to the Skies," August 30, 2017.

305 The good news is that in October 2017: BBC News Europe, "Russia to Train Female Fighter Pilots," August 13, 2017; Egorov, October 4, 2017; Peck, 2017.

305 "I have more than . . . eighth of November": Zoya Malkova in Noggle, 219.

306 The members of Marina Raskova's regiments: Harris 2008, 230.

306 With no uniforms, they would dress: Krylova 2010, 3.

306 Later, as they ate and drank: Noggle, 317.

306-307 "The war made us not . . . I go to meet my sisters": Anna Kirilina in Noggle, 124.

BIBLIOGRAPHY

We are very lucky that so many of the Soviet women aviators who served during the Great Patriotic War kept diaries, wrote memoirs, and gave interviews. We have firsthand accounts of their incredible wartime experiences spent in the air and on the ground. Like anyone's memories, they are not always accurate; and they lose further accuracy in translation into English. But taken as a whole, they are *real*. They tell an emotional and historical truth that is worth celebrating.

I do not read Russian, which to my mind has sorely limited my ability to research this book. I have a rudimentary knowledge of the Cyrillic alphabet and can make sense of a text or title using Google Translate, so I have been able to browse some of my sources in rough translation. In this bibliography, I include several Russian publications either because they are important to this study (like Marina Raskova's autobiography, *Notes of a Navigator*) or because they have been referred to or quoted in English in my own sources.

MEMOIRS

Alexievich, Svetlana. *The Unwomanly Face of War*. Translated by Richard Pevear and Larissa Volokhonsky. London: Penguin Books, 2017. First published 1985.

Aronova, Raisa E. *Night Witches* (in Russian as *Nochnye ved'my*). Revised and expanded second edition. Moscow: Sovetskaya Rossiya, 1980. First published 1969.

Burgess, Helene. "Facing the Future Unafraid" [memoirs of Nadezhda Popova]. In *Our Lives, Our Dreams: Soviet Women Speak*. Moscow: Progress Publishers, 1988.

Cottam, Kazimiera Janina, editor and translator. *In the Sky above the Front: A Collection* of Memoirs of Soviet Airwomen Participants in the Great Patriotic War. Manhattan, KS: Kansas State University, 1984.

———. Soviet Airwomen in Combat in World War II. Manhattan, KS: Military Affairs/ Aerospace Historian, 1983.

———. Women in Air War: The Eastern Front of World War II. New York: Legas, 1997.

Dlugach, Alexander. "Those Magnificent Women in Their Flying Machines" [Interview with Yevgeniya Zhigulenko]. Soviet Life, May 1990, 12–13, 15.

Dokutovich, Galina. The Heart and the Wings: Diary of a Navigator of a Women's Aviation Regiment (in Belorussian as Sertsa I kryly. Dzennik shturmana zhanochaga aviyatsyinaga palka). Minsk: State Publishing House of the Belorussian SSR, 1957.

Dubova, Anna Akimovna. "Living Someone Else's Life." In A Revolution of Their Own: Voices of Women in Soviet History. Edited by Barbara Alpern Engel and Anastasia Posadskaya-Vanderbeck et al. and translated by Sona Hoisington, 17–37. Boulder, CO: Westview Press, 1998.

Durova, Nadezhda. The Cavalry Maiden: Journals of a Female Russian Officer in the Napoleonic Wars. Translated by Mary Fleming Zirin. London: Paladin, 1990.

Grossman, Vasily. A Writer at War: Vasily Grossman with the Red Army 1941–1945. Edited and translated by Antony Beevor and L[y]uba Vinogradova. London: Pimlico, 2006.

Kazarinova, M. A., and A. A. Polyantseva, editors. In the Sky above the Front: A Collection of Memoirs of Soviet Pilots Participating in the Great Patriotic War (in Russian as V nebe frontovom: sbornik vospominanii sovetskikh letchits-uchastnits Velikoi Otechestvennoi voiny). 2nd ed. Moscow: Molodaya Gvardiya, 1971. First published 1962.

Keyssar, Helene G., and Vladimir Willem Pozner. Remembering War: A U.S.-Soviet Dialogue. New York: Oxford University Press, 1990.

Levin, I. S. The Terrible Years (in Russian as Groznye Gody). Saratov: Privolzhskoe, 1984. http://militera.lib.ru/memo/russian/levin_is/pre.html.

Litvinova, Larisa. "Women's Regiment of Night Bombers." In The Road of Battle and Glory. Edited by I. Danishevsky and translated by David Skvirsky. Moscow: Foreign Languages Publishing House, n.d. [1977].

Markova, Galina Ivanovna. Youth Under Fire: The Story of Klavdiya Fomicheva, A Woman Dive Bomber Pilot. Edited and translated by Kazimiera Janina Cottam. In Soviet Airwomen in Combat in World War II, 65–131. Manhattan, KS: Military Affairs/ Aerospace Historian, 1983.

Newman, Dina. "Soviet Woman Bomber Pilot." Interview with Yelena Malyutina and Lyuba Vinogradova. Witness, BBC World Service, December 6, 2016.

www.bbc.co.uk/programmes/p04j9sk3.

Noggle, Anna. *A Dance with Death: Soviet Airwomen in World War II*. College Station: Texas A&M University Press, 2007. First published 1994.

Polunina, Yekaterina. *Girls, Girlfriends, Pilots* (in Russian as *Devchonki, podruzhki, letchitsy*). Moscow: Vestnik Vozdushnogo Flota, 2004.

Raskova, Marina. *Notes of a Navigator* (in Russian as *Zapiski Shturmana*). Moscow: Central Committee of the Komsomol "Young Guard," 1939.

Rudneva, Yevgeniya (Zhenya). *For as Long as My Heart Is Beating: Diaries and Letters of Hero of the Soviet Union Yevgeniya Rudneva* (in Russian as *Poka stuchit serdtse: Dnevniki i pisma Geroya Sovetskovo Soyuza Evgenii Rudnevoi*). Edited by I. V. Rakobolskaya. 3rd ed. Moscow: Izdatelstvo Moskovskogo Universiteta, 1995. First published 1955 by Molodaya Gvardiya (Moscow).

Saywell, Shelley. *Women in War: First-Hand Accounts from World War II to El Salvador*. Tunbridge Wells, UK: Costello, 1987.

Timofeyeva-Yegorova, Anna. *Red Sky, Black Death: A Soviet Woman Pilot's Memoir of the Eastern Front*. Translated by Margarita Ponomaryova and Kim Green. Bloomington, IN: Slavica, 2009.

Zhigulenko, Yevgeniya Andreyevna. Oral history in *Remembering War: A U.S.-Soviet Dialogue*, by Helene G. Keyssar and Vladimir Willem Pozner, 37–45. New York: Oxford University Press, 1990.

NEWSPAPER & MAGAZINE ARTICLES, 1936–1944

Amarillo (TX) Globe. "Ship Will Be Named for Soviet Woman." September 3, 1943, 9.

Arizona Republic (Phoenix, AZ). "Woman Becomes Soviet Air Ace." June 11, 1936, 18.

Asbury Park (NJ) Press. "Radio Programs for 24 Hours: Wednesday's Highlights." February 3, 1943, 14.

Blitzstein, Madelin. "How Women Flyers Fight Russia's Air War." *Aviation*, July 19, 1944, 115–117, 255, 257.

Chicago Tribune. "Aid Dropped by Parachute to 3 Soviet Women Fliers." October 5, 1938, 23.

Chillicothe (MO) Constitution-Tribune. "Establishes New Status for Women." Women's Pages. January 20, 1939, 4.

Daily Chronicle (De Kalb, IL). "Find Airplane Lost for Week." October 4, 1938, 7.

Gettysburg (PA) Times. "Russia Has Noted Women War Flyers." December 27, 1943, 6.

Los Angeles Times. "City Hunting for Source of 'Gas Attack.'" July 27, 1943, 1.

Maurer, Rose. "Those Russian Women." *Survey Graphic*, February 1944, 109, 152, 155, 157.

Moats, Alice Leone. "Russian Women at War." *Collier's Weekly*, October 18, 1941, 18, 49–51.

Parker, Ralph. "Moscow Hails Tanya." *New York Times Magazine*, March 22, 1942, 11. www.nytimes.com/1942/03/22/archives/moscow-hails-tanya.html.

———. "Women Workers of the Russian Miracle." *New York Times Magazine*, February 14, 1943, 18. www.nytimes.com/1943/02/14/archives/women-workers-of-the-russian-miracle-mobilized-for-war-like-the-men.html.

Pittsburgh Press. "Famed Soviet Woman Flier, Bomber Commander, Killed." January 9, 1943, 1.

Skariatina, Irina. "The Fearless Women of Russia." *Collier's Weekly*, November 7, 1942, 15, 46, 48–49.

Stewart, Charles P. "Washington at a Glance." *Washington C.H. (OH) Record-Herald*, September 20, 1941, 4.

Troy (NY) Record. "Ship Named after Russian Girl Pilot Launched Today." June 22, 1943, 13.

Wilmington (DE) Morning News. "Women Fliers Mentioned." April 5, 1943, 11.

OTHER PRIMARY SOURCES

1936 Constitution of the USSR. Bucknell University, Russian Studies Department Website. Adopted December 1936. www.departments.bucknell.edu/russian/const/36cons01.html.

Aeronautical Chamber of Commerce of America. *The Aircraft Yearbook for 1935.* Vol. 17. New York: Aeronautical Chamber of Commerce of America, 1935.

———. *The Aircraft Yearbook for 1938.* Vol. 20. New York: Aeronautical Chamber of Commerce of America, 1938.

Federal Aviation Administration. *U.S. Civil Airmen Statistics 2015.* Oklahoma City: Federal Aviation Administration Aeronautical Center, 2015. www.faa.gov/data_research/aviation_data_statistics/civil_airmen_statistics/media/2015-civil-airmen-stats.xlsx.

Gruliow, Leo, and Sidonie K. Lederer. *Russia Fights Famine: A Russian War Relief Report.* New York: Russian War Relief, n.d. [Summer 1943]. https://babel.hathitrust.org/cgi/pt?id=coo.31924013759117;view=1up;seq=3.

Kalinin, M. I. "Glorious Daughters of the Soviet People." In *On Communist Education:*

Selected Speeches and Articles, 455–60. Moscow: Foreign Languages Publishing House, 1950.

Krupskaya, Nadezhda. *The Woman Worker*. Translated by Mick Costello. Nottingham, UK: Manifesto Press, 2017. First published 1900 by Iskra (Saint Petersburg).

Lenin, V. I. *The April Theses: The Tasks of the Proletariat in the Present Revolution* (levellerreprints 002). London: Leveller Reprints, 2011. First published April 7, 1917 in *Pravda*, 26.

———. *Women and Society* (Little Lenin Library 23). New York: International Publishers, 1938.

Stalin, Josef. *On the Great Patriotic War of the Soviet Union* [November 6, 1941– September 3, 1945]. Moscow: Foreign Languages Publishing House, 1946. Prepared for the Internet by David J. Romagnolo, 2003. www.archive.org /stream/OnTheGreatPatrioticWarOfTheSovietUnion/GPW_djvu.txt.

———. *On the Great Patriotic War of the Soviet Union: Speeches, Orders of the Day, and Answers to Foreign Press Correspondents* [July 3, 1941–September 25, 1943]. London: Hutchinson, n.d. [1944?].

Trotsky, Leon. *The History of the Russian Revolution*. Translated by Max Eastman. 3 vols. New York: Simon and Schuster, 1932. www.marxists.org/archive/trotsky/1930/hrr/index.htm.

SOURCES ON THE SOVIET AIRWOMEN

Atkins, Violet, and William Bacher. *Diary of a Red Army Woman*. In *Faulkner: A Comprehensive Guide to the Brodsky Collection*. Vol. 4, *Battle Cry, A Screenplay by William Faulkner*, edited by Louis Daniel Brodsky and Robert W. Hamblin, 19–57. Jackson: University Press of Mississippi, 1985.

Belyakov, Vladimir. "Russia's Women Top Guns." *Aviation History*, March 2002, 34–40.

Bhuvasorakul, Jessica Leigh. "Unit Cohesion among the Three Soviet Women's Air Regiments during World War II." Master's thesis, Florida State University, 2004. Florida State University Libraries: Electronic Theses, Treatises and Dissertations of the Graduate School, 2004.

Brontman, Lazar, and Lev Borisovich Khvat. *The Heroic Flight of the Rodina*. Moscow: Foreign Languages Publishing House, 1938.

Campbell, D'Ann. "Women in Combat: The World War II Experience in the United States, Great Britain, Germany, and the Soviet Union." *Journal of*

Military History 57:2 (April 1993): 301–23.

Chaika, N. "Night Bomber" (in Russian as "Na nochnom bombardirovshchike"). In Heroines: Essays on Women Heroes of the Soviet Union (in Russian as Geroini: ocherki o zhenshchinakh—Geroiakh Sovetskogo Soiuza). 2 Vols. Edited by L. F. Toropov. Moscow: Politizdat, 1969.

Cottam, Kazimiera Janina. "Lidya (Lily) Vladimirovna Litvyak (b. 1921)," Red Army Online, 2006. www.redarmyonline.org/FI_Article_by_KJ_Cottam.html.

———. "Marina Mikhailovna Raskova." In Vol. 3 of World War II: The Definitive Encyclopedia and Document Collection. Edited by Spencer C. Tucker, 1389–90. Santa Barbara, CA: ABC-Clio, 2016.

———. "Soviet Women in Combat in World War II: The Ground/Air Defense Forces." In Women in Eastern Europe and the Soviet Union, edited by Tova Yedlin, 115–27. New York: Praeger, 1980.

———. "Soviet Women Soldiers in World War II: Three Biographical Sketches." Minerva 18:3–4 (December 31, 2000): 16–36.

———. Women in War and Resistance: Selected Biographies of Soviet Women Soldiers. Nepean, ON, Canada: New Military Publishing, 1998.

Dowswell, Paul. Usborne True Stories: The Second World War. Illustrated by Jeremy Gower and Kuo Kang Chen. London: Usborne Publishing, 2007.

Erickson, John. "Soviet Women at War." In World War 2 and the Soviet People: Selected Papers from the Fourth World Congress for Soviet and East European Studies, Harrogate, 1990. Edited by John Garrard and Carol Garrard, 50–76. London: St. Martin's Press, 1993.

Flerovsky, Alexei. "Women Flyers of Fighter Planes." Soviet Life, May 1975, 28.

"Galina Gavrilovna Korchuganova." Biography in Women in Aviation International. www.wai.org/pioneers/2006/galina-gavrilovna-korchuganova.

Garber, Megan. "Night Witches: The Female Fighter Pilots of World War II." Atlantic, July 15, 2013. www.theatlantic.com/technology/archive/2013/07/night -witches-the-female-fighter-pilots-of-world-war-ii/277779.

Gibson, Karen Bush. Women Aviators: 26 Stories of Pioneer Flights, Daring Missions, and Record-Setting Journeys. Chicago: Chicago Review Press, 2013.

Glancey, Jonathan. "The Very Few." Guardian, December 15, 2001. www.theguardian.com/lifeandstyle/2001/dec/15/weekend.jonathanglancey.

Guardian. "The White Rose of Stalingrad," Notes and Queries. www.theguardian.com/notesandqueries/query/0,5753,-18520,00.html.

Harris, Adrienne. "The Myth of the Woman Warrior and World War II in Soviet

Culture." PhD thesis, University of Kansas, 2008. KU ScholarWorks. https://kuscholarworks.ku.edu/bitstream/handle/1808/4136/umi-ku-2564_1 .pdf?sequence=1&isAllowed=y.

———. "Yulia Drunina: The 'Blond-Braided Soldier' On the Poetic Front." *Slavic and East European Journal* 54:4 (Winter 2010): 643–65.

Krylova, Anna. *Soviet Women in Combat: A History of Violence on the Eastern Front*. New York: Cambridge University Press, 2010.

———. "Stalinist Identity from the Viewpoint of Gender: Rearing a Generation of Professionally Violent Women-Fighters in 1930s Stalinist Russia." *Gender & History* 16:3 (November 2004): 626–53.

Lambert, Bruce. "Valentina S. Grizodubova, 83, A Pioneer Aviator for the Soviets." Obituary in *New York Times*, May 1, 1993. www.nytimes.com/1993/05/01 /obituaries/valentina-s-grizodubova-83-a-pioneer-aviator-for-the-soviets.html.

Lilya Litvyak website, maintained by Reina Pennington. www.lilylitviak.org.

Markova, Galina Ivanovna. *Take-Off: The Story of the Hero of the Soviet Union, M. M. Raskova* (in Russian as *Vzlet: O Geroe Sovetskogo Soyuza M. M. Raskovoi*). Moscow: Politizdat, 1986. https://translate.google.co.uk/translate?hl=en&sl=ru&u=http://militera.lib.ru /bio/markova_gi/index.html&prev=searcha.

Markwick, Roger. "Irina Rakobolskaya." Obituary in *Guardian*, October 16, 2016. www.theguardian.com/world/2016/oct/16/irina-rakobolskaya-obituary.

——— and Euridice Charon Cardona. *Soviet Women on the Front Line in the Second World War*. New York: Palgrave Macmillan, 2012.

Meos., E. "Russian Women Fighter Pilots." *Flight International*, December 27, 1962, 1019–20.

Merry, Lois K. *Women Military Pilots of World War II: A History with Biographies of American, British, Russian and German Aviators*. Jefferson, NC: McFarland, 2011.

Milanetti, Gian Piero. *Soviet Airwomen of the Great Patriotic War: A Pictorial History*. Rome: Istituto Bibliografico Napoleone, 2013.

Myers, Beth Ann. "Soviet and American Airwomen during World War II: A Comparison of Their Formation, Treatment and Dismissal." Master's thesis, Defense Technical Information Center, 2003. www.dtic.mil/dtic/tr/fulltext/u2/a416572.pdf.

Myles, Bruce. *Night Witches: The Untold Story of Soviet Women in Combat*. Chicago, IL: Academy Chicago, 1990.

Pennington, Reina. "'Do Not Speak of the Services You Rendered': Women Veterans of Aviation in the Soviet Union." In *A Soldier and a Woman: Sexual Integration in the Military*, edited by Gerard de Groot and Corinna Peniston-Bird, 153–71. Harlow, UK: Longman, 2000.

———. *Wings, Women & War: Soviet Airwomen in World War II Combat*. Foreword by John Erickson. Lawrence: University Press of Kansas, 2001.

———, editor. *Amazons to Fighter Pilots: A Biographical Dictionary of Military Women*, Vol. 1, A–Q. Westport, CT: Greenwood Press, 2003.

———. *Amazons to Fighter Pilots: A Biographical Dictionary of Military Women*, Vol. 2, R–Z. Westport, CT: Greenwood Press, 2003.

Reynolds, Quentin. "Three Russian Women." In *The Curtain Rises*, 119–32. New York: Random House, 1944.

Sakaida, Henry. *Heroines of the Soviet Union 1941–45*. Oxford: Osprey, 2003.

Sandbrook, Dominic. "Cockpit Heroines: The Female Soviet Fighter Pilots Were the First Women Ever Thrown into the Front-Line Battle." *Sunday Times* (of London), April 12, 2015. www.thetimes.co.uk/article/cockpit-heroines-26vfg6vcmv9.

Strebe, Amy Goodpaster. *Flying for Her Country: The American and Soviet Women Military Pilots of World War II*. Washington, DC: Potomac Books, 2009.

———. "Marina Raskova & the Soviet Women Aviators of World War II." *Russian Life* 46:1 (January–February 2003): 42–47.

Vinogradova, Lyuba. *Defending the Motherland: The Soviet Women Who Fought Hitler's Aces*. Translated from the Russian by Arch Tait. London: MacLehose Press, Quercus, 2015.

White, Christine A. Introduction to *A Dance with Death: Soviet Airwomen in World War II*, by Anna Noggle, 3–14. College Station: Texas A&M University Press, 2007. First published in 1994.

OTHER SOURCES ON AIRWOMEN

Babichev, Sergei. "A Woman's Affair (Russian Pilot Svetlana Protasova)." *Russian Life* 40:3 (March 1997): 9–12.

BBC News, Europe. "The Ballerina Who Takes to the Skies." August 30, 2017. www.bbc.co.uk/news/av/world-europe-41091263/the-ballerina-who-takes-to -the-skies.

———. "Russia to Train Female Fighter Pilots." August 13, 2017. www.bbc.co.uk/news/world-europe-40917550.

Brock, Elizabeth, editor. "Moscow Russia–Aviatrisa 2004 Newsletter." *Woman Pilot*,
November 27, 2016. www.womanpilot.com/?p=423.

Carsenat, Elian, and Elena Rossini. "Airline Pilots." GenderGapGrader.com, 2014.
www.gendergapgrader.com/studies/airline-pilots.

Curtis, Lettice. *The Forgotten Pilots: A Story of the Air Transport Auxiliary 1939–45*. Olney,
UK: Nelson and Saunders, 1971.

Egorov, Boris. "Queens of the Sky: The Girls Taking Russia's Air Force by Storm."
Russia Beyond: Science & Tech, October 4, 2017.
www.rbth.com/science-and-tech/326321-queens-of-sky-girls.

Goyer, Mireille. "Five Decades of Female Pilots Statistics in the United States. How
Did We Do?" *Women of Aviation Week*. Institute for Women of Aviation Worldwide,
2010. www.womenofaviationweek.org/five-decades-of-women-pilots-in
-the-united-states-how-did-we-do.

Maksel, Rebecca. "Why Are There So Few Female Pilots? Identifying the Barriers
That Stop Women from Flying." *Air & Space*, February 6, 2015.
www.airspacemag.com/daily-planet/why-are-there-so-few-female
-pilots-180954115.

Peck, Michael. "Russia Is Now Letting Women Become Fighter Pilots." *National
Interest*, August 20, 2017. www.nationalinterest.org/blog/the-buzz/russia-now
-letting-women-become-fighter-pilots-21968.

Warren, Marcus. "MiG Pilot Flies in Face of Russian Male Prejudice." *Daily Telegraph*,
July 8, 1999.

Zegenhagen, Evelyn. "'The Holy Desire to Serve the Poor and Tortured Fatherland':
German Women Motor Pilots of the Inter-War Era and Their Political Mission."
German Studies Review 30:3 (October 2007): 579–96.

GENERAL SOURCES

Abraham, Richard. "Mariia L. Bochkareva and the Russian Amazons of 1917." In
Women and Society in Russia and the Soviet Union, edited by Linda Edmondson, 124–
44. Cambridge: Cambridge University Press, 1992.

Anderson, M. T. *Symphony for the City of the Dead: Dmitri Shostakovich and the Siege of
Leningrad*. Somerville, MA: Candlewick Press, 2015.

Bailes, K. E. "Technology and Legitimacy: Soviet Aviation and Stalinism in the
1930s." *Technology and Culture* 17:1 (January 1976): 55–81.

Beevor, Antony, and L[y]uba Vinogradova. Editor's gloss to *A Writer at War: Vasily*

Grossman with the Red Army 1941–1945. Edited and translated by Antony Beevor and L[y]uba Vinogradova. London: Pimlico, 2006.

Boyd, Alexander. *The Soviet Air Force since 1918*. London: MacDonald and Jane's, 1977.

Clarke, John D. *French Eagles, Soviet Heroes: The 'Normandie-Niemen' Squadrons on the Eastern Front*. Thrupp, UK: Sutton Publishing, 2005.

Drabkin, Artem. *Barbarossa & the Retreat to Moscow: Recollections of Fighter Pilots on the Eastern Front*. Barnsley, UK: Pen & Sword Military, 2007.

Drury, Ian. "Stand at Ease! New Army Boots Will Be Issued for Women Soldiers." *Daily Mail*, August 30, 2012. www.dailymail.co.uk/news/article-2195560/New -Army-boots-issued-women-soldiers.html.

Edmondson, Linda. "Women's Rights, Civil Rights and the Debate over Citizenship in the 1905 Revolution." In *Women and Society in Russia and the Soviet Union*, edited by Linda Edmondson, 77–100. Cambridge: Cambridge University Press, 1992.

Engel, Barbara Alpern, Anastasia Posadskaya-Vanderbeck, and Sona Hoisington. *A Revolution of Their Own: Voices of Women in Soviet History*. Boulder, CO: Westview Press, 1998.

Everitt, Chris, and Martin Middlebrook. *The Bomber Command War Diaries: An Operational Reference Book*. Barnsley, UK: Pen and Sword, 2014.

Faulkner, William. *Faulkner: A Comprehensive Guide to the Brodsky Collection*. Vol. 4, *Battle Cry, A Screenplay by William Faulkner*, edited by Louis Daniel Brodsky and Robert W. Hamblin. Jackson: University Press of Mississippi, 1985.

Figes, Orlando. "The Women's Protest That Sparked the Russian Revolution." *Guardian*, March 8, 2017. www.theguardian.com/world/2017/mar/08 /womens-protest-sparked-russian-revolution-international-womens-day.

Fleming, Candace. *The Family Romanov: Murder, Rebellion & the Fall of Imperial Russia*. New York: Schwartz & Wade Books, 2014.

Gunston, Bill. *The Osprey Encyclopedia of Russian Aircraft 1875–1995*. London: Osprey Aerospace, 1995.

Hamblin, Robert W., and Louis Daniel Brodsky. Introduction to *Battle Cry, A Screenplay by William Faulkner*, xv–xliii. Vol. 4 of *Faulkner: A Comprehensive Guide to the Brodsky Collection*, edited by Louis Daniel Brodsky and Robert W. Hamblin. Jackson: University Press of Mississippi, 1985.

Hardesty, Von, and Ilya Grinberg. *Red Phoenix Rising: The Soviet Air Force in World War II*. Lawrence: University Press of Kansas, 2012.

Hook, Alex. *World War II Day by Day*. Rochester, UK: Grange Books, 2004.

LaFeber, Walter, and Richard Polenberg. *The American Century: A History of the United States Since the 1890s*. New York: John Wiley & Sons. 1979.

Legge, Charles. "Aces Who Fired First." *Scottish Daily Mail*, April 12, 2016.

Lejenäs, Harald. "The Severe Winter in Europe 1941–1942: The Large-Scale Circulation, Cut-off Lows, and Blocking." *Bulletin of the American Meteorological Society* 70:3 (March 1989): 271–81.

McNeal, Robert H. "The Early Decrees of Zhenotdel." In *Women in Eastern Europe and the Soviet Union*, edited by Tova Yedlin, 75–86. New York: Praeger, 1980.

Montefiore, Simon Sebag. *Stalin: The Court of the Red Tsar*. London: Weidenfeld & Nicolson, 2003.

Overy, Richard. *Russia's War*. London: Penguin Books 1999.

Petrone, Karen. *Life Has Become More Joyous, Comrades: Celebrations in the Time of Stalin*. Bloomington: Indiana University Press, 2000.

Reichhardt, Tony. "The First Aerial Combat Victory: Airplane vs. Airplane over France in 1914." *Air & Space*, October 4, 2014. www.airspacemag.com/daily-planet /first-aerial-combat-victory-180952933.

Rury, John. "Vocationalism for Home and Work: Women's Education in the United States, 1880–1930." *History of Education Quarterly* 24:1 (Spring 1984): 21–44.

Scarborough, Rowan. "U.S. Military Pressed to Design Special Line of Combat Boots Just for Women." *Washington Times*, May 14, 2015. www.washingtontimes.com /news/2015/may/14/military-pressed-to-design-line-of-women-friendly-.

Schneider, Steven P. "Lost Generation." In *A William Faulkner Encyclopedia*, edited by Robert W. Hamblin and Charles A. Peek, 234–37. Westport, CT: Greenwood Press, 1999.

Stites, Richard. *The Women's Liberation Movement in Russia: Feminism, Nihilism, and Bolshevism, 1860–1930*. Princeton, NJ: Princeton University Press, 1978.

Stolfi, Russel H. S. "Chance in History: The Russian Winter of 1941–1942." *History* 65:214 (1980): 214–28.

Wetterhahn, Ralph. "Kursk: The Greatest Tank Battle in History Might Have Ended Differently Had It Not Been for the Action in the Air." *Air & Space*, April/May 2015.

Wilde, Meta Carpenter, and Orin Borsten. "Faulkner: Hollywood: 1943." In *Battle Cry, A Screenplay by William Faulkner*, ix–xiv. Vol. 4 of *Faulkner: A Comprehensive Guide to the Brodsky Collection*, edited by Louis Daniel Brodsky and Robert W. Hamblin. Jackson: University Press of Mississippi, 1985.

FILMS

The Night Witches: Soviet Air Women in World War II. Documentary film, produced and directed by Sissi Hüetlin and Elizabeth McKay. London: Move a Mountain Productions, 1994.

"Night Witches" in the Sky (in Russian as *V nebe "Nochnye bed'my"*). Produced and directed by Yevgeniya Andreyevna Zhigulenko. Moscow: Kinstudiia im. M. Gorkogo, 1981.

Wasps & Witches: Women Pilots of World War II. Documentary film, produced and directed by Jamie Doran. New York: Films Media Group, 2012.

AUTHOR'S NOTE: A FEW EXCUSES AND A LOT OF GRATITUDE

I made up stories before I went to school. I'd written two "novels" before I got my high school diploma. So you could say I was a fiction writer first.

But I spent seven years working on a PhD in Folklore and Folklife, and so my actual training is as an academic. The need to quote my sources has stuck, as anyone who's read the back matter to my novels will tell you. Indeed, my own children will tell you this—from grade school onward I have insisted they give full source credit for every piece of research they produce. As they've both found, if you're planning to do a research project ever, it's actually a very useful habit to practice from an early age.

But the reason I like writing fiction has nothing to do with avoiding citations. I like fiction because you can bend things. You can speculate. You can claim connections that haven't been proven or don't even have any basis in fact. As a credible historian, you have to base your story on what you know. (My most recent piece of published fiction suggests that the Grand Duchess Anastasia Romanova became a fighter pilot—not an idea I could have entertained as a historian.)

My biggest stumbling block to writing *A Thousand Sisters* is that I don't read Russian. There are primary sources in Russian to which I have not had access, and of which I would have been able to make only limited use if I had. Pulling together a thorough history of Marina Raskova's regiments is an impossible task for a non–Russian speaker who is utterly reliant on translators. I am very lucky that there are excellent source materials already translated, as well as some excellent original studies in English by scholars who *do* read Russian—Anna Krylova and Reina Pennington in particular.

Ultimately, *A Thousand Sisters* isn't academic research. It's an accessible (I hope) introduction to a fascinating topic, and it's aimed at young readers who mostly won't have any more Russian than I do. There is always room for a more complete treatment of Raskova's regiments. But I am proud of what I've done here, and I do hope my work can be considered a contribution to the existing literature.

One problem I ran into during my research is that some of my key sources, notably those by Kazimiera J. Cottam and Anna Noggle, don't have indexes. Before I wrote a word of *A Thousand Sisters*, I had to create a sort of rudimentary master index listing each woman aviator and her appearance in a number of different books. It wasn't the most complete or accurate system, but I would have been utterly lost without it. I hope that readers using *A Thousand Sisters* for their own research will find my source notes to be a useful cross-reference.

Russian is a complicated language. My editors and I have mostly used the BGN (United States Board on Geographic Names) system to transliterate Russian names and words, but sometimes we've deviated from this system for the sake of simplicity or clarity. Occasionally I've used an English variation on a Russian name because it's already in common use in English (for example, "Maria" rather than "Mariya" Bochkareva). Bearing in mind that the majority of my readers will find individual Russian names unfamiliar and possibly difficult, I've tried to simplify matters by mostly using first names and unmarried family names in the text (few of the young women in these pages were already married during their wartime aviation exploits, so didn't have married names until after the war). I've also chosen to use nicknames for many of the women mentioned in the text—partly because they used these names themselves in fondness and familiarity, partly because they add a friendly level of informality for the reader, and partly because they reduce the difficulty of unfamiliar Russian names.

Likewise, I've decided not to include military rank titles throughout the text, in an attempt to keep a complex story as uncluttered as possible. I feel obliged to point this out. The absence of these formal ranks is in no way intended to reduce their importance, and readers should remember that the women of Raskova's regiments all served as soldiers, not as civilians.

Enough excuses. The gratitude is more important to me. To everyone who made *A Thousand Sisters* come together: *spasibo*, as they say in Russia— *thank you*.

Though I'm the one with my name on the cover of this book and have been given the responsibility for researching and writing it, its true creator is my editor Kristin Rens. It was her idea in the first place. I'm the artisan who willingly joined forces with her to bring it to life. My agent, Ginger Clark—to whom this book is dedicated, I should point out!—was the matchmaker who brought us together. I don't think any one of us had any inkling of what an enormous undertaking it would turn out to be. Backed by an amazing team at HarperCollins, Kristin has been patient, tolerant, wildly enthusiastic, and focused, guiding this project with a light touch on the control column as I navigated it hither and thither against the wind.

I'm awed by the amount of background reading the whole editorial team had to do just to keep pace with the manuscript. (Shout-out to Kelsey Murphy, Renée Cafiero, and Megan Gendell, among others!) I am so very, very grateful to Kristin and her coworkers for their support and unflagging interest in this project.

There are a number of other people who encouraged and assisted me, none more so than fellow young adult author Amber Lough. A former US Air Force intelligence officer and a veteran of Iraq, Amber wanted to go to Russia in 2016 to research her own project about Russian women in combat—she was writing a novel, *Summer of War*, about the Women's Death Battalion and the Russian Revolution (see Chapter 1, "The Early Life and Times of Marina Raskova, Navigator and Pilot"). We cooked up a very sudden plan to become traveling companions, which is how I ended up going to Russia with someone I met on the internet. No lie—Amber and I met In Real Life for the first time in a hotel in Saint Petersburg. We became fast friends and had an amazing and whirlwind couple of weeks knee-deep in snow in temperatures well below freezing, visiting museums and historic sites, meeting people, and discussing literature.

I'm also grateful to Kim Green, who helped translate Anna Timofeyeva-Yegorova's autobiography *Red Sky, Black Death* into English, and who encouraged my Russian adventure and introduced me to pilots Irina Bubynina and Inna Frolova. Inna is a board member of the Russian women pilots' organization Aviatrisa. Like me, both she and Irina are members of the Ninety-Nines, the International Organization of Women Pilots—a wonderful icebreaker we weren't aware of until we'd already met. Inna is the governor of the Russian Section of the Ninety-Nines. She and Irina were both generous and patient as tour guides, ensuring that Amber and I participated in a moving memorial ceremony in Red Square to commemorate the breakthrough at the battle of Stalingrad in 1943. Irina joined us in a visit to Marina Raskova's grave in the Kremlin wall. It would be my great pleasure to be able to return their hospitality someday should our paths cross again.

Thanks are also due to Alexander from Angel Tours. He too spent an entire day with us as guide and translator, working in conjunction with retired Russian Air Force officer Colonel Vladimir Ivanovich, who was acting as a docent at the Central Air Force Museum in Monino in the Moscow Oblast. We were the first foreign women touring the museum who weren't traveling with a male companion, and our visit inspired Alexander to add a segment about women aviators on his future tours.

Reina Pennington's exhaustive scholarly work on Raskova's regiments is one of the backbones for my own work. I am honored that she agreed to read and critique *A Thousand Sisters* in manuscript form. And no doubt the entire staff of HarperCollins is eternally grateful to Anatoly Plyac, the son of Raisa Aronova, a navigator and pilot with the 588th. Anatoly graciously and generously provided many of the photographs reproduced in this book.

I was lucky enough to spend a couple of informal afternoons with Steve Sheinkin during the creation of *A Thousand Sisters*, and in addition to being wholly encouraging, he was most patient in responding to my naive and endless questions about source notes, photographs, citations, and permissions. And although they may not know it, M. T. Anderson and Candace Fleming have served as inspirations—partly because they've both written excellent young adult nonfiction (notably—and respectively—*Symphony for the City of the Dead* and *The Family Romanov*), which actually provided me with very relevant background information for *A Thousand Sisters*, but also because their books are so well organized that they gave me excellent templates for this one.

Of course the people close to me are the ones who had to cope with this project on a daily basis—thanks are due to my aunts Susan Whitaker and Kate Adams for accepting mail for me at US addresses when I couldn't get books shipped directly to the UK; my husband, Tim Gatland, who supported every step of this endeavor, including my disappearance to Russia for two weeks at short notice; and my children, Mark and Sara, who willingly shared their references as they worked on their own, not unrelated, essays about Shostakovich and the Romanovs.

And finally, I am grateful to William Faulkner. I am grateful to him for writing *Battle Cry*. I am grateful to him for being a pilot, and for his role in attempting to bring a version of this story to the silver screen. Apparently he considered *Battle Cry* his war work, his contribution to the war effort; I cannot imagine how frustrated and heartbroken he must have been when he learned it would never be filmed.

But if it had been, maybe we would already know about Raskova's regiments and there would be no need for this book. If *Battle Cry* was William Faulkner's war work, this is mine. It is an honor and a privilege to have been able to write *A Thousand Sisters*.

Elizabeth Wein
Salisbury, England, May 2018

INDEX

NOTE TO READER: Soviet women involved in aerial combat included pilots, navigators, tail gunners, and various types of ground crews. The term "airwomen" is used here to refer to all these women collectively.

Photographs are indicated by *italicized* page numbers.

and the battle at Krasnodar, 200–203
crash landing, 203–4
at the Dnipropetrovsk Flying School,
61–62
flight crew, 199
on learning of Raskova's death, 172
reassignment to the 587th, 168–69
thank-you flight over Borisov, 270
on women in combat, 301
Don Front, 168–69
Dospanova, Khivaz, 97
Drobovich, Galina (chief aircraft mechanic),
105, 164
Dubkova, Klara (navigator)
and the battle at Krasnodar, 203
crash landing, 206
flying skills, 281
partnered with Fedotova and Khokhlova,
205
shooting down of, 282
"Dugout, The" (song), 91–92
Dzhunkovskaya, Galina "Galya" (navigator)
awards and honors, 294
bailing from disabled Pe-2, 269–70
battle over Riga, 277–78
crash landing, 203–4
life after war, 302
Markov's tenderness toward, 265, 270
marriage, 265, 302
as part of Dolina's crew, 199
as part of Fomicheva's crew, 267–68

Eastern Front. See also World War II
German retreat from, 280
participation of Allied troops, 262–63
Red Army attacks on, 60
size of, 60
emergency flight procedures, 235
Engels Flying School. See also 122nd Composite
Air Group
arrival of trainees at, 78
funerals, 109
training at, 82, 95
trip to from Moscow, 76–77
Erofeev, Nikolai (tail gunner), 169, 171
Experimental Aviation Institute, 31

famines, 18, 25, 28, 113, 151–52
fascism, defined, 47
Faulkner, William, 2, 4, 7, 221
Favorskaya, Irina (armorer), 95

Fedotova, Yekaterina "Katya" (pilot)
assignment with friends, 92
battle at Krasnodar, 202, 203
care shown by Markov for, 179
crash landing, 206
description of Khokhlova by, 205
on initial reactions to Markov, 178
on mourning for Raskova, 176
partnered with Dubkova and Khokhlova,
205
on piloting the Pe-2, 127
renown of, for flying skills, 281
shooting down in Prussia, 282
female pilots. See airwomen, Soviet; pilots,
female
Finland, Soviet invasion of, 54
flowers, 158–59
fog, flying and landing in, 133. See also blind
flying
Fomicheva, Klavdiya "Klava" (pilot), 268
awards and honors, 294
bailing out of a Pe-2, 269–70
battle at Krasnodar, 201–2
battle over Riga, 277–78
burns, 243
continuing career in aviation, 304
crash landing, 242–43
flying disabled plane while wounded,
269
New Year's dance, 278–79
personality, leadership style, 268
food
American canned treats, 152
disparities based on rank, 152
and famines, 18, 25, 28, 152
fruit, fresh, 148, 206, 248–49
pilots' field rations, 284
For as Long as My Heart Is Beating (Rudneva), 302
France
declaration of war on Germany, 53
Normandie-Niemen Regiment, 263–64
The Future War (Tukhachevsky), 20

Gartner, Artur (pilot), 103, 241
Gasheva, Rufina (pilot), 223
Gdansk, Poland, pursuit of retreating Germans
at, 276
Gelman, Polina (navigator)
awards and honors, 294
on blinding by searchlights, 181
daughter, Galya, 301
efforts to join Red Army, 64

Munich Agreement, 44
mustard gas, 271

Nachthexen ("night witches"), 232–33
navigators
    aboard the Pe-2, 128
    piloting skills, 181
navigators. See also specific airwomen and battles
    assistance with takeoffs, 127
    blind flying, 19, 107–108, 180-81
    first flights, 90
    numbers needed, 82
    training, 82
Nazi Germany. See also Hitler, Adolf; the
    Luftwaffe
    annexation of Czechoslovakia, 44
    and Axis powers, 54–55
    building up of air force, 23–24
    continued fighting into 1945, 281
    declaration of war on US, 85
    defeat at Stalingrad, 175
    as fascist country, 47, 271
    initiation of the holocaust, 113
    invasion of Europe, 54
    invasion of Soviet Union, 55–56, 60
    meaning of word "Nazi," 47n9
    merger with Austria, 36
    wealth in during war, 286
Nesterov, Pyotr (pilot), 262
New York Times, article about Soviet women's
    wartime jobs, 274
Nicholas II, Czar, 15–16
night flying/bombings, 107–8, 180–81. See also
    blind flying; Po-2 biplanes
Night Witches (Aronova), 302
Nikitin, Nikolai (navigator), 177, 198, 268
Nikulina, Dina (pilot), 83, 181, 306
NKVD (People's Commissariat for Internal
    Affairs), 29, 32–33
Normandie-Niemen Regiment (French
    aviators), 262–64
Nosal, Yevdokia "Dusya" (pilot), 208–209, 209,
    224
Notes of a Navigator (Raskova), 50

Ogonyok (magazine), article about Litvyak and
    Budanova, 213
okhotnik ("free hunter") fighter pilot status, 212
Olkhovskaya, Lyuba (pilot), 121

Operation Barbarossa, 56, 59–60, 84
Operation Blue, 114
Operation Citadel, 175
Operation Star, 189
Order 0099 (female aviation group), 69
Order 227 (no-retreat order), 131–32, 136, 171
Order 270 (no-capture order), 64, 130
Osipenko. Polina (pilot), 37
    aboard the Rodina, 36
    death and burial, 46–47
    honors received by, 44–45
    record-breaking flights, 33
    rescue, 43
Osipova, Sofya (mechanic), 165, 189–91
Osoaviakhim clubs, 21–22, 30
Ozerkova, Sonya (chief engineer), 130–31,
    183–84

Pamyatnykh, Tamara (pilot, squadron
    commander)
    articles about, 274
    battle near Kastornaya railroad, 192–93
    escape from damaged plane, 195–96
    honors and awards, 196–97
    marriage, 264–65
    night flight to Stalingrad, 135
    pairing with Burdina, 112
    postwar aviation career, 304
Pankratova, Klavdiya (pilot), 150, 261
Parfyonova, Zoya (pilot), 283–84
Parker, Ralph, 274
Pashkovskaya (Krasnodar), Nosal's burial at,
    208, 209
Pasportnikova, Inna (mechanic), 83, 212,
    295–96
Pe-2 dive-bombers, 126. See also 586th Fighter
    Aviation Regiment
    armorers, 129
    attacks on, 199
    awards for, 101
    courage needed to fly, 239
    decorations on, 281
    as embroidery motif, 160
    guns and armament on, 128–29, 282–83
    tail gunners, 128, 205
    three-person crew, 128
    training needed to fly, 126–27, 168
Pearl Harbor, Japanese attack on, 85
People's Commissariat for Internal Affairs
    (NKVD). See NKVD (People's Commissariat